MANY THINGS IN PARABLES

*To the Memory of
my Mother and Father*

MANY THINGS IN PARABLES

Expository Studies

RONALD S. WALLACE
M.A., B.Sc.

Wipf & Stock
PUBLISHERS
Eugene, Oregon

Wipf and Stock Publishers
199 West 8th Avenue, Suite 3
Eugene, Oregon 97401

Many Things In Parables
Expository Studies
By Wallace, Ronald S.
Copyright©1955 by Wallace, Ronald S.
ISBN: 1-57910-060-0
Publication date 10/17/1997
Previously published by Oliver and Boyd, 1955

CONTENTS

THE MYSTERY OF THE KINGDOM

The Sower	3
The Seed Growing Secretly	10
The Mustard Seed, and the Leaven	18
The Tares and the Wheat, and the Drag Net	26

THE OFFER AND COST OF CITIZENSHIP

The Hidden Treasure, and the Pearl of Great Price	41
The Lost Sheep, and the Lost Coin	48
The Prodigal Son	55
The Great Supper	63
The Unjust Steward	71

THE MARKS OF THE TRUE CITIZEN

The Selfish Neighbour, and the Importunate Widow	81
The Two Debtors	91
The Pharisee and the Publican	99
The Good Samaritan	105
The Unprofitable Servant	112
The Labourers in the Vineyard	119
The Talents	127
The Pounds	135

THE TRAGEDY OF THOSE WITHOUT

The Rich Fool	145
Dives and Lazarus	151
The Wicked Husbandmen, and the Barren Fig Tree	158

WARNINGS TO ALL

The Unforgiving Debtor	169
The Wise and Foolish Virgins	178
The Sheep and the Goats	185
The Royal Wedding Feast	193

APPENDIX

The Parable and the Preacher	203

FOREWORD

Most of the expositions in this book have been preached in a different form on Sunday evenings as a series of sermons. They are offered in print in the belief that there is always a need in the Church for the publication of current Biblical exposition.

In preparing these studies I constantly consulted the standard works on the Parables, and read many sermons by others. I remember being indebted especially to the sermons on the Parables that are found scattered through several volumes by Karl Heim, and also a little book by Emil Brunner entitled *Saat und Frucht*. It is hoped that this book in its turn will be of service to ministers and teachers who are using the Parables, and that for the ordinary reader it will focus and reflect in a simple way some of the new and vital insights into the meaning of the Gospel which have come to the Church in recent theological discussion and research. An article outlining the principles by which the Parables have been interpreted is given at the end of the work. It is placed there so that no one need imagine that it must be mastered before reading the book with understanding.

I would like to thank my wife for her painstaking work on the MS. and proofs, and her constant wise advice; and the Rev. Prof. J. S. Stewart, D.D., New College, Edinburgh, for reading the book through in an early stage and giving encouragement and helpful comment; also Mr and Mrs Laurence Cameron, Lanark, for typing much of the final draft and going over the proofs. I am greatly indebted to the publishers for their courtesy and help, and for correcting and greatly improving the MS. in many details when it was in their hands.

RONALD S. WALLACE

St Kentigern's Manse
    Lanark

THE MYSTERY OF THE
KINGDOM

THE SOWER

Behold, a sower went forth to sow; and when he sowed, some seeds fell by the way side, and the fowls came and devoured them up: some fell upon stony places, where they had not much earth: and forthwith they sprung up, because they had no deepness of earth: and when the sun was up, they were scorched; and because they had no root, they withered away. And some fell among thorns; and the thorns sprung up, and choked them: but other fell into good ground, and brought forth fruit, some an hundredfold, some sixtyfold, some thirtyfold. Who hath ears to hear, let him hear.

Hear ye therefore the parable of the sower. When any one heareth the word of the kingdom, and understandeth it not, then cometh the wicked one, and catcheth away that which was sown in his heart. This is he which received seed by the way side. But he that received the seed into stony places, the same is he that heareth the word, and anon with joy receiveth it; yet hath he not root in himself, but dureth for a while: for when tribulation or persecution ariseth because of the word, by and by he is offended. He also that received seed among the thorns is he that heareth the word; and the care of this world, and the deceitfulness of riches, choke the word, and he becometh unfruitful. But he that received seed into the good ground is he that heareth the word, and understandeth it; which also beareth fruit, and bringeth forth, some an hundredfold, some sixty, some thirty. MATTHEW 13.3-9, 18-23

The Word of the Kingdom

No one can read the New Testament without being struck by the way in which words are made by God to become the vehicles of His power and grace. One remarkable feature of the ministry of Jesus Christ on earth was the way He used words, and the power which seemed to reside in the words which He uttered. 'His word was with power.'[1] His words seemed to make comfort and health and courage and peace spring up wherever He uttered them. The spoken word was the main instrument He used to work His miracles. 'He cast out the spirits with his word.'[2] 'Peace, be still,'[3] He said to the waves, and there was a great calm. 'Be thou clean,'[4] He said

[1] Luke 4.32 [2] Matt. 8.16 [3] Mark 4.39 [4] Mark 1.41

to the leper, and His Word was immediately fulfilled. It was by speaking the Word that He raised the dead and made the lame walk. It was as if 'He spake, and it was done'.[1] When Jesus Himself was hanging helpless upon the Cross, one word from Him was enough to assure the dying thief of the forgiveness of his sin and of his entrance into Paradise.[2]

In the same way the Apostles whom Jesus sent forth in His name to continue His work found as they spoke and preached in the name of Christ that their word had power as the Word of Jesus had. Sometimes their word had the power to heal diseases and to raise the dead, often it had power to cast out devils, but always it was powerful to cleanse the soul and to forgive sins, to restore dead souls to life, to open the eyes of blinded minds to the reality of God.

In the parable of the sower Jesus explains why it is that His own words and the words of His disciples have such power. He tells us that the words He himself speaks and the words spoken in His name are the seed of the Kingdom of God. Wherever these words are sown in the hearts of men there the Kingdom of God is sown in the life of this earth. Through the words that Jesus speaks and gives the rule of God is restored to this world.

This is something that is quite beyond our understanding—that mere words should be the instrument God uses to bring in His Kingdom! When we think of the state of affairs in this world in which it pleases God to have the Word sown, it seems impossible that such a frail instrument should ever be of use against such huge and established forces of evil. For God seems to have been dethroned and excluded from the seat of authority and power in the world which He made to be His Kingdom. God's will is not done among men. This earth is the centre of a stubborn resistance movement against its true Lord and Master. Man is a rebel who hates even the idea of God's rule, and all over the earth he lives in defiance of His Maker. Instead of being a Kingdom of God, the earth has become a kingdom of sin and of the devil, and yet God's promise is: 'My word . . . shall not return unto me void, but it . . . shall prosper in the thing whereto I sent it.'[3] The parable tells us that wherever the seed is sown and given a chance, God's Kingdom comes. A seed seems a frail little

[1] Ps. 33.9   [2] Luke 23.39-43   [3] Isa. 55.11

thing as it lies upon the face of the soil, but let it get in underneath, in ground that will give it a chance, and mighty things will happen. It will take root and claim and possess the ground, and it will grow and increase with irresistible power, and bring forth fruit, '*some an hundredfold, some sixty, some thirty*'. In the same way the Word of God will affect the lives and hearts of men. The Word which God speaks through His servants will dispossess the powers of evil of their present rule, and reclaim for God's Kingdom that which has long remained alien to Him.

The Power of the Word in the Heart of Man

The Word of God can accomplish this purpose because it can penetrate into the heart. The seat of the resistance to God in our human life, and the source of the disorder and sin that spoil men and society, are in the heart of man. 'Out of the heart,' said Jesus, 'proceed evil thoughts, murders, adulteries, fornications, thefts, false witness, blasphemies.'[1] If order, cleanliness and love are to be restored, God must begin at the source of such evil things. Where other methods would fail, the Word of God can sink right into a man's heart and work in those depths so closed to light and life and God. Even our human words, as our speech acknowledges, can 'penetrate' and 'cut' and 'sink in' and 'rankle' deep in the hearts of others. Much more penetrating is the Word of God. 'The word of God is quick, and powerful, and sharper than any twoedged sword, piercing even to the dividing asunder of soul and spirit, and of the joints and marrow, and is a discerner of the thoughts and intents of the heart.'[2]

The Word of God when it penetrates and takes root is mighty and powerful in its workings. The history of the Church can furnish us with countless illustrations of how a text (a mere seed!) coming direct from the Bible, and taking root in a hearer's heart, has had the effect of changing the form and fashion of this world. It was by such a frail word that St. Augustine was converted. He was in the garden, sick at heart, sick in sin, and he seemed to hear a voice urging him, 'Take and read!' He took up the book that was at his side. It was St. Paul's letter to the Romans. He read the verses, 'Not in

[1] Matt. 15.19   [2] Heb. 4.12

rioting and drunkenness, not in chambering and wantonness, not in strife and envying. But put ye on the Lord Jesus Christ, and make not provision for the flesh, to fulfil the lusts thereof.'[1] He read no further; there was no need. With these words the light and grace and power of God burst into his soul —and few will deny that that event has decisively influenced the course of European history. At all times of revival in the life of the Church it has been in the Word that men have found the source of new life.

We know that mere human words have great power and force when they are received by emotionally receptive and attentive hearers, but such parallels cannot give any adequate explanation of the power that the Word of the Bible seems at times to take for the mysterious work of restoring the Kingdom of God in the hearts of men. We can only say that here we have a work of God's living Spirit, a work of the living Christ. It pleases God, through the frail words of Scripture going home to the human soul, to convey to the hearts of men all the blessings which Jesus Christ died on the Cross to win for them— new life and the forgiveness of sins. It pleases God through words to inspire, guide, comfort, convert and edify, and to feed His Church with the life of Christ.

This means that today as always the first task of the Church is that of speaking in the name of Christ and of sowing His Word of power in the hearts and lives of men and nations so that His Kingdom may advance. This is why we give the preaching of the Word such prominence in all our activity. Of course there are other things that we have to do for Jesus Christ besides speaking. As Jesus prayed for men and cared for their bodily welfare and laid down His whole life on the Cross in sacrifice for mankind, so the Church must also pray, and take upon its mind and heart the social problems of its day, and lay down its life in loving service. Nevertheless we must remember that all that Jesus did was made effectual in the lives of men through the Word which He spoke, and that Jesus today can cause the words which He sows through His servants on earth to become as potent seeds of the Kingdom as were His own words when He fulfilled His own ministry in the flesh.

[1] Rom. 13.13-14

THE WORD REJECTED

The Word of God must be received by man with gladness and faith if it is to penetrate into the depths of man's heart and work with power there. It is not always received thus, nor is it always given freedom to do its true work. Man is free to make a perverse response to the Word of God and can hinder or reject it. The Word of God thus divides men. When Jesus spoke some received His Word wholeheartedly, and they received, with the Word, salvation. But often in the Gospels we read such sentences as 'They were offended at him',[1] 'Many . . . went back, and walked no more with him'.[2] When Paul went to Athens and preached the Word 'some mocked: and others said We will hear thee again . . . certain men clave unto him, and believed'.[3] The same Word produces varied response. God seeks to redeem man as a free man, therefore He uses a Word which calls for a free response. Thus the Word is often rejected.

There are some who reject the Word of God because 'it has so little to show'. After all, it is merely a word, and man is by nature prepared to be impressed more by seeing things done, and that on a large scale, than by hearing things spoken. The Word of God speaks of a Kingdom of God, but it does not prove it. It does not show us this Kingdom as a great manifest reality. The message of this Kingdom centres on a man who was insignificant in many ways, and very unlike a king. The cry of men is for something more noble and artistic and idealistic than this Word offers. They '*hear the word of the kingdom and understand it not*'. They judge it by its frail and poor outward appearance and leave the seed to lie there as a thing of no value. They are offended by the apparent insignificance of the Word of God. But the Devil knows its value and significance and he soon obliterates all remembrance of the Word from their minds.

And there are others who are offended by the unpopularity they are involved in through this Word. A man may receive the Word with gladness, not realising at first what is involved in taking this Word as the inspiration of life and allowing it room to work. But he discovers that the Word of God is not popular. He discovers that if the Word is allowed to work within, then the heart must open and the soil must yield to the

[1] Mark 6.3   [2] John 6.66   [3] Acts 17.32-34

seed; for the power of God through the Word seeks to break up our naturally hard core of self-centredness. Through His Word God seeks to open our hearts to Himself, thus opening them also to our fellow men. This means a life of self-sacrifice. The Word of God working in the heart seeks to disturb our inner selfishness and to create love within us. But men do not like this demand and this inner process of transformation. *'When tribulation or persecution ariseth because of the word, by and by he is offended.'* Men are offended by the practical implications of the Word.

There are others who are offended by the totalitarian claim that the Word of God makes on the whole heart. The Word of God, when it interferes with life, demands possession of all our heart and soul and mind and strength. But—so men argue —is religion not after all simply one department of human life? Religion is valuable, certainly, but a thing to be kept in its place. 'Moderation in all things!' men cry. 'Give Christ a place, likewise give everything else a like place—business, culture, pleasure, religion—a four-square life!' The Word of God cannot flourish when men take this attitude, for the Word of God always claims priority. Christ through the Word claims to be the One in whom are hid all treasures of wisdom and knowledge. If He is not given a supreme place, then He is indeed rejected and His Word is of no effect within us. The Word cannot flourish on an equal footing with every other pursuit of life. These other things mentioned, being more at home in the heart, *'choke the word and he becometh unfruitful'*.

This parable reminds us that the Word of God claims not only the whole life of those who hear it but also the whole life of those who sow it. No man and no church can truly preach this Word of the Kingdom without at the same time *suffering*. The manifold rejection and contempt which humanity metes out to the Word which is the whole treasure, and the only weapon of the Church, will also be meted out to those who give their lives to the spreading of the Word. When Jesus Christ sowed the seed of the Kingdom of God by means of His Word, He suffered in His own body the antagonism of men. He was despised and rejected by men. The Word is so closely bound up with the person of Christ that the bearer of the Word in every generation must share the reproach of Christ. As the whole life of Christ was laid down in witness to the truth of His Word, so must the servants of Christ lay down their lives in sowing in the hearts of men the Word of the Gospel.

The Church that remains ever faithful to the Word of God will not require to seek this suffering. The reproach of the world will be levelled against it unsought, as it strives in every generation to interpret to men the message of the Scripture, for that message is the Word of the Cross, which is 'unto the Jews a stumblingblock, and unto the Greeks foolishness; But unto them which are called, both Jews and Greeks, Christ the power of God, and the wisdom of God'.[1]

[1] 1 Cor. 1.23-24

THE SEED GROWING SECRETLY

And he said, So is the kingdom of God, as if a man should cast seed into the ground; and should sleep, and rise night and day, and the seed should spring and grow up, he knoweth not how. For the earth bringeth forth fruit of herself; first the blade, then the ear, after that the full corn in the ear. But when the fruit is brought forth, immediately he putteth in the sickle, because the harvest is come.
MARK 4.26-29

THE KINGDOM IS AT HAND

When the men of His time heard Jesus speaking of the Kingdom of God they were apt to think of it as an event or state of affairs in the distant future, too remote to be very challenging. They had been trained to think of the Kingdom as a state of affairs that would come suddenly in a great crisis at the end of time when God would invade this world with supernatural power in the reign of the promised Messiah. When the Kingdom came thus every one would know! The signs of its presence would be catastrophic and visible, involving even earthquakes, and strange seasons of darkness, and signs in the sun and moon and stars. Till all this began to happen, however, there could be no Kingdom of God. One could only go on praying and hoping wistfully for that age, as the Fathers had already done for centuries with no sign of fulfilment.

Jesus taught, on the contrary, that the Kingdom of God is here and now a present reality, a living force and an accomplished fact in the life of this world. In this parable of the seed growing secretly He teaches that the powers of the Kingdom have already invaded this present world and that the life of the Kingdom is powerfully astir, here and now. It is a seed which has been already cast into the soil and whose powers of life are already stirring under the surface of the ground. '*So is the kingdom of God, as if a man should cast seed into the ground.*'

Jesus looked on the miracles which He worked as being due to the mighty powers of the Kingdom which were at the disposal of His Word and will. After He cast out a devil from a possessed man and healed his mind, Jesus called on His hearers to see in this miracle a sign that the powers of the Kingdom of God were here at work to cure men's woes, to destroy the rule of Satan and usher in the rule of God. 'If I with the finger of God cast out devils, no doubt the kingdom of God is come upon you.'[1] He was always anxious to impress upon His disciples that the powers of the Kingdom of God have already invaded this present world, and that these very powers can be experienced in the life of men. There are several parables which teach this same lesson—particularly those of the hidden treasure, the pearl of great price, the leaven, and the great supper.

Among the many forces and powers and movements in this world, therefore, there are at work the powers of a new deathless world. This means that we who live today can experience and contact the powers and blessings of two different worlds. This present world, which is corrupted by death and decay and transitoriness, has been invaded by another realm whose borders are already so near and accessible to us that we can travel across them. Thus, even while we live as citizens of this earth, we can also become citizens of the Kingdom of Heaven.

It is all a great mystery; but can we not expect to be confronted with facts that pass our comprehension and our ability to piece them together when we try to take into our minds the facts proclaimed in the Gospel of Christ? At the heart of the Gospel there is an astounding mystery. The Gospel affirms that in the life and death of Jesus God became a man and dwelt amongst us in a hidden manner, 'in the likeness of sinful flesh'.[2] Here, surely, is a very mysterious invasion into this world of space and time! The more we seek to probe this, and the more we understand its meaning, the greater does the mystery become and the more do we realise that it passes our knowledge. It is no less of a mystery that here and now, in this present age, the powers of a new age ushered in by Jesus are now at work; that here and now as we walk in the midst of our present sphere of earthly life with all its claims and delights we can at the same time also find ourselves living in the midst of a new divine realm.

[1] Luke 11.20   [2] Rom. 8.3

THE KINGDOM IS GROWING TOWARDS CRISIS

Jesus further teaches in this parable that the Kingdom of God is not only present in this world but is also present as a growing and developing force in the history of this earth's life. He teaches that the hidden and secret growth of the Kingdom of God at the heart of this world will find its climax in the glorious future consummation of a final harvest in which will be reaped all the fruits of the process of growth. The Kingdom of God, therefore, as time passes is spreading abroad its influence in this earth, is gathering strength and force, and is consolidating its position against all opposition.

There are passages in the teaching of Jesus where undoubtedly He speaks of the Kingdom as of something that will break suddenly from beyond into this world in all its completeness and glory in a great visible crisis. The Kingdom, He teaches, will break upon this world 'as the lightning that lighteneth out of the one part under heaven, shineth unto the other'.[1] There is no hint here of its beginning at one place and spreading and growing. There is no hint here of its coming as a gradual process. The picture is of a Kingdom of God being thrown down from heaven into a hitherto God-forsaken world. The whole comes, complete, in one great crisis which will take place at the same time as His own second coming in power and manifest glory. Can we square all these other sayings of Jesus with the teaching brought out in this parable—or is there a real contradiction here?

There are analogies from life that might help us to solve the contradiction in our own thinking. When a landslide or an avalanche takes place, that is a crisis, a sudden, mighty outburst, but for years before it happens a gradual and largely hidden process has been going on, working towards that crisis. Water or soil or stones have been gathering in one great mass to prepare for this visible outburst. So it is, we can imagine, with the Kingdom of God. It spreads and increases in a process of secret and gradual growth, but this process will find its culmination in one great crisis when the glory and gathering power of that Kingdom will suddenly break forth.

But all this is merely an attempt to explain what cannot be explained. We simply cannot square the teaching of Jesus on

[1] Luke 17.24

the subject of the Kingdom of God. If Jesus had been teaching mathematics we might hope to square His teaching. Even if He had been teaching philosophy or morals we might manage to find a certain logical consistency in what He said. But Jesus, in speaking of the Kingdom of God, is speaking of a 'mystery' —a living supernatural, personal realm, an event which can be paralleled only by the Incarnation of God in the man Jesus. The Kingdom is a new creation of God. We must not be offended, therefore, if we cannot master in our thought this great subject of the Kingdom; we are bound to be baffled when we bring our limited powers of thought to measure and analyse the Kingdom of God. At one time we can see only one of its aspects, at another moment only another isolated one, and, seeing, can only wonder and believe. There is no viewpoint above it on which we can take our stand in order to master nicely its unity and its neat proportions.

But however impotent we are to understand the full nature of this Kingdom, let us accept the challenge and encouragement that the teaching of Jesus is meant to bring us. He assures us that the Kingdom is here and now. It is like a subtle spreading influence that has been at work in this world for centuries. The kingdoms of men and the kingdom of Satan are not the only kingdoms on this earth; God has been at work amongst men in a sovereign way all through past centuries, ruling in the hearts of His people. There are hidden spheres where God's will is done; there is an invisible network spread through the nations, growing and entwining itself in this world like a hidden mass of underground roots. We have heard much during the past years of underground movements, invisible organisations that work below the surface to undermine prevailing circumstances. They are deeply secret but they are powerful for the overthrow of existing governments. The Kingdom of God is in the midst of this world working like an underground movement of cosmic significance towards a glorious future climax. We must ask ourselves if we are within this movement. The writer of the Epistle to the Hebrews speaks of Christians as those who 'have tasted . . . the powers of the world to come'.[1] The powers of the Kingdom of God are seeking to invade our hearts in Jesus Christ, who stands at the door and knocks. He

[1] Heb. 6.5

is seeking to conscript us now into the service of this movement, and to introduce into our lives the privileges and power it can bestow.

THE GROWTH OF THE KINGDOM IS INEVITABLE AND SPONTANEOUS

If seed is planted in good soil where it can take root it grows spontaneously and inevitably; the farmer need do little more for it than plant it. So it is with the Kingdom of God. Once the divine seed of the Kingdom, which is the Word of God, has taken root in the hearts of men, then a spontaneous and irresistible process of growth will go on. Let those who are called to sow the seed of this Kingdom by proclaiming the Word of God take heart! Once they have planted the seed and know that it has taken a firm hold on prepared ground, they can be at ease. They can rest their souls in quiet confidence. '*So is the kingdom of God, as if a man should cast seed into the ground; and should sleep, and rise night and day, and the seed should spring and grow up, he knoweth not how. For the earth bringeth forth fruit of herself.*' Those who have sown the seed of the Word of God can have serene faith that through their work the Kingdom is inevitably advancing. They need not have the least anxiety about 'results'. No matter what they see in the effect of their scattering abroad of the divine seed, they can sleep and rise and go about other business night and day. There is spontaneous life in the seed; there is an alliance between the earth and the seed that will inevitably bring forth a glorious fruition.

This parable was spoken not to make the workers of the Kingdom lazy, but to encourage them to greater efforts in realising that their work must lead to inevitable success. They have to receive the seed into their own lives and let it produce its own effects there without hindrance. They must also go forth and plant the seed of the Word all over the earth. 'Go ye therefore, and teach all nations, baptising them in the name of the Father, and of the Son, and of the Holy Ghost: teaching them to observe all things whatsoever I have commanded you.'[1] If they do this, God will look after the results, and these will be glorious. Whether there has been apparent failure or apparent success they can sleep and rest, for meanwhile the life of the seed they have planted will go on with irresistible power.

[1] Matt. 28.19-20

Jesus Himself showed this serene confidence in the spontaneous growth and the ultimate triumph of His work on this earth. When He was about to go to His death He spoke calmly to His disciples about the glorious future of His reign. In His prayer to His Father He said, 'I have finished the work which thou gavest me to do.'[1] On the Cross He cried, 'It is finished,'[2] and then He said, 'Father, into thy hands I commend my spirit.'[3] These are the words and attitude of One who knows that He has done enough to ensure the full completion and glorious fulfilment of His life's purpose. What had Jesus done during these three years of His ministry on earth? He had planted this powerful divine seed, the seed of the Kingdom of God, at the heart of this present world, for He had planted it in a few prepared human hearts. He knew that there where He had planted it the Kingdom would grow, and that nothing could hinder it from spreading its influence throughout the whole world. It is significant that the occasion on which Jesus prophesied most definitely about the future greatness and stability of His Church was just that moment when He discovered that Simon Peter had believed in Him. Jesus had been teaching the disciples about Himself, and afterwards He tested whether the Word He had spoken about Himself had taken effect. Simon gave Him the proof He sought, for he said, 'Thou art the Christ, the Son of the living God.' Jesus was deeply content with this reply and went on to speak with great elation of His Church as a firmly established fact in this earth. 'Blessed art thou, Simon Bar-jona: for flesh and blood hath not revealed it unto thee, but my Father which is in heaven. And I say also unto thee, That thou art Peter, and upon this rock I will build my church; and the gates of hell shall not prevail against it.'[4] His Church was safe because a human heart had received His Word and believed in Him; Simon had received the seed of the Kingdom. There was no need to fear for the future of His cause. This Word He had sown in the heart of Simon Peter was a divine seed full of mighty power to alter human destiny and fill this earth with its growth. He Himself, having sown the seed of the Word of His Kingdom, knew with quiet confidence that now its growth would be spontaneous and inevitable.

We are meant to follow His example and believe in the

[1] John 17.4 [2] John 19.30 [3] Luke 23.46 [4] Matt. 16.17-18

power of the Word of the Kingdom which He has given us. We are meant to go forth and sow this Word, laying down our very lives indeed in the sowing, but nevertheless having no anxious care about results. A seed thrown into the earth will grow. The farmer who has sown it does not need to stir it up, nurse it, fuss over it, or go out to look each day at its progress. He himself no longer matters, for the seed and the earth will do their work without him. He can sleep and rise, night and day, and meanwhile the seed will grow 'of itself'. There is a mystery in the seed. The Kingdom of God is there! The man who believes in the power of the Word of God will not spend his life in anxiety over results. He has sown a mighty seed that does not need after-care. Perhaps he will see results, perhaps not. He can go on with a quiet and confident mind, for the Kingdom of God will grow. Nor will he be over-zealous in his interference with the young plants. The life in the seed will find its own form of outward expression. The wise sower will not try to force developments according to his own plans and schemes but will let the life of the Word produce its own organisation.

To Wait for the Kingdom requires Patience

The growth of the Kingdom will take time: *'First the blade, then the ear, after that the full corn in the ear.'* A field that has been sown one day does not look different on the next. Similarly, the signs of the presence of the Kingdom are largely below the surface of the world. Those who have opened their hearts to the influence of the Kingdom of God know of its presence, and can discern here and there the signs of the working of this mystery. But these signs are very 'insignificant'. The workers in the Kingdom must have patience. At first there may appear only a tiny blade, then an ear. This is not quite what our enthusiasm at first expected, but we must not expect immediate and fully mature results.

We must be patient too if the first signs of life from the seed we have sought to sow in the hearts of men are crude and disappointing. Those in whose hearts we trusted that the seed of the Word of God was bringing life are sometimes impetuous, intolerant and unchristian, but we need not doubt that these things may be the sign of that life, for it is *'first the blade'*.

Maturity of Christian life often comes after crude beginnings. We must not be discouraged if after years of patient toil the results still evade us. Dr Morison laboured for seven years in China before one man was converted, and at his death there were only seven converts as fruit for his life's work.

In the work of the Kingdom great things often have small beginnings. No one can tell where a great movement in the Kingdom of God begins. It starts with a tiny seed falling into a heart. Sometimes no man can tell when that happens, for it seemed so insignificant an event that no one took note of it. The very man who received the seed does not always know when, and how, and through whose agency, this great influence came into his life. He only knows that now it is there, working powerfully, changing his whole life and outlook, urging and impelling him on, and that even if he wanted to resist, he could not undo the effects of this tiny seed that somehow one day found its way into his heart and began to grow of itself.

Jesus Christ has left us with seed to sow for His Kingdom. We must do that work, proclaiming and witnessing to this Gospel with all our heart and mind and life. Some of our efforts may be in vain, for there is ground in which the seed is not received, but where the seed is received it will grow, and we need not fear for results. These are not our concern but God's. Our only care should be the fulfilment of our commissioned task, which lies in proclaiming with all our powers and resources the Word of God.

THE MUSTARD SEED, AND THE LEAVEN

Another parable put he forth unto them, saying, The kingdom of heaven is like to a grain of mustard seed, which a man took, and sowed in his field: which indeed is the least of all seeds: but when it is grown, it is the greatest among herbs, and becometh a tree, so that the birds of the air come and lodge in the branches thereof.

Another parable spake he unto them; The kingdom of heaven is like unto leaven, which a woman took, and hid in three measures of meal, till the whole was leavened.   MATTHEW 13.31-33

In the parables of the sower and of the seed growing secretly Jesus taught that wherever the Word of God is truly sown and wholeheartedly received in faith there the Kingdom of God grows and spreads with spontaneous and irresistible power. This growth is largely a secret one. The Kingdom of God, though present and active here and now in the world, is present and active in a hidden manner. It is not a thing whose power and influence we can see directly before us, as, for instance, we can see the power and influence of a great nation. The Kingdom of God is something we believe in rather than behold.

In the two parables of the mustard tree and the leaven, however, Jesus teaches that, obscure and concealed though it is, the spread of the Kingdom of God in the midst of this present world will have a visible effect on the life of society. It will give the historian something extra to write about; it will give rise to movements and institutions which man will have to reckon with. The pressure of the Kingdom of God on the spheres of the life of this world will actually produce, on a large scale, outward symptoms and signs that here a power not of this world is at work. These two parables are designed by Jesus to illustrate the effect of the presence and the pressure of the Kingdom of God on the life of earthly society.

THE GROWTH OF THE CHURCH

'The kingdom of heaven is like to a grain of mustard seed, which a man took, and sowed in his field: which indeed is the least of all seeds:

but when it is grown, it is the greatest among herbs, and becometh a tree, so that the birds of the air come and lodge in the branches thereof.'

In this parable Jesus is speaking about the Church which He knew would one day grow wherever His Kingdom was allowed to manifest itself. On several occasions He spoke of His Church and prophesied about its appearance. He spoke of it as being founded on the Word that proclaimed Him as the Christ, and He said that, so founded, the gates of Hell would not prevail against it.[1] Another very clear prophecy about the future rise of the Church is given in the parable of the wicked husbandmen, where, after foretelling the rejection of the Jewish nation as the appointed stewards of His vineyard, He tells the Jewish leaders that the vineyard will be taken away from them, and given to a 'nation' which will yield up to God more readily the fruits of righteousness which He sought.[2] Here again it is obvious that Jesus is thinking of His Church, and thinking of it as a definite and organised body of people on the stage of human history. In this parable of the mustard seed He is again speaking on the same theme. In the book of Ezekiel[3] the very symbol which He uses here, that of a tree sheltering birds, is used as standing for a visible earthly kingdom with a great political organisation, many far-reaching branches and functions, and a complicated internal structure. Jesus takes this figure and says, 'That is what will appear on the earth where the Word of My Kingdom takes root and spreads.' A new 'nation' will arise, an organised body of people who claim allegiance to the Kingdom of God.

The effect, then, of the planting of the seed of the Kingdom will not be entirely underground and hidden. Something will appear and spring up before the very eyes of men on earth, drawing attention as a tree draws the eyes of men, proclaiming constantly that a seed was once cast here, and invisible work was done, to produce this visible monument. There will appear on earth a Church with buildings and congregations and officials.

It is a fairly modest prophecy that is made here about the Church. When a grain of mustard seed reaches its full stature it becomes a bush so big that it has a right to be called a tree. It is able to take its place alongside the other trees of the earth

[1] Matt. 16.18 [2] Matt. 21.43 [3] Ezek. 17.23

without appearing dwarfed or ridiculous. Jesus is suggesting to the minds of His disciples that the Church will not of necessity be the largest and most imposing organisation of men that has ever appeared on the face of the earth. They might be tempted to imagine that because the Kingdom of God is a new creation of such wonder and glory, its headquarters on earth are likely to be of a magnificence surpassing anything man has ever seen, manifesting a greater outward show of grandeur than any earthly empire. They are warned here against expecting this. The Church that will arise out of the Word will certainly be a great organisation of which men will be forced to take notice, and about which they will have to make decisions. Historians will have to mention it, and it may even become a political force, but the Church will not as an organised movement dominate the whole life of the earth. It will grow till it becomes a great force to be reckoned with, standing in the midst of the life of the nations beside the trade unions, the great business concerns, the political parties, and all the various unions of clubs and movements which form the life of society.

We can recognise the Church of today in this parable, for there is today a World Church of which its members are proud to speak, and in partaking of the varied activity of this Church men feel that they are in the midst of something that is indeed great and important in the life of mankind. It is true that, to our sorrow, some of the branches of this great tree are dying or dead. There is visible decay here and there, but there is also vigorous new life. No one who understands these things can read of how today the World Church is putting forth its great new living branches in the mission fields without being thrilled to realise that the Kingdom of God is perhaps more mightily at work today than at any other time in the history of the earth.

'*When it is grown, it is the greatest among herbs, and becometh a tree, so that the birds of the air come and lodge in the branches thereof.*' What does Jesus mean here by '*the birds of the air*' which come and find friendly hospitality amongst the branches of the Church? Most commentators think that Jesus has in mind the poor outcasts of every nation who will find a home in the Church, and a protection under its care that none other can offer. But the Church has given hospitality within its friendly branches to much more than the poor and outcast individuals of the earth. Such a picture as Jesus here paints reminds us that the Church has been a friendly organisation towards the outside life of the world, and has given shelter and hospitality and nourishment within her branches to much that brought blessing to mankind. There was a time when medical science, education and even the arts found that the Church was able to lodge them securely and comfortably when the world outside offered them little foothold and encouragement. We need not mourn too much that these birds which once found that their best place of abode was within the sphere of the Church have now taken wing and asserted their independence. The Church can never attempt to dominate the whole life of mankind. Nothing could surely have a worse effect on the spiritual health of the Church than that it should find itself universally acknowledged as leader of the life of mankind. But it is good that the Church should always keep itself open to give hospitality and inspiration and shelter to those outside independent spheres; and if these birds of the air are wise, they will realise that within the sphere of the Church they can find an inspiration and a stability that can come to them from no other source. It is good to see a multiplicity of secular organisations still acknowledging that it is worth while, even for a moment, once a year, to rest symbolically in the branches of the Church by maintaining annual parades and occasional official Church services. Perhaps in all these things, and in this strange picture of the birds in the parable, we are meant to see a faint foreshadowing of the day when all the glory of the Gentiles shall be brought into the Temple of God and when the kingdoms of this world shall become the Kingdoms of Our Lord.

In view of this parable and its teaching, let us not be suspicious of the Church because it seems too big and great to be Christian; for there are those who feel that if anything is to be consistent with the religion of Jesus Christ it must of necessity be small and despicable in the eyes of men. They do not like anything in connexion with the Church that has a show of greatness. Let us remember that it was Christ's foreknowledge and will that there should appear on the earth, as a result of the hidden spread and growth of His Kingdom, such a visible organisation as the Church. Our Lord knew the weakness of our human nature and it was His will that our faith should be strengthened and that we should be encouraged in our Christian witness by finding ourselves in the midst of a great family of God, as members of a great visible institution. It is His will that our souls should find help and inspiration through belonging to some branch of the great historic Church. There are dangers, of course, which arise from the very fact that the Church has become an institution owning property and endowments, and offering social status and even power to its representatives. The history of the Church should teach us these dangers only too well.

We must beware of thinking of the Church as the Kingdom of God. There are those who assert that the Church is the Kingdom of God on earth, but the Church is, rather, the sphere where the Kingdom of God most forcibly impinges and presses in upon our human life. The Kingdom of God is the hidden new realm behind the Church, but the Church, as an organisation, is very much part of this world, sharing all the frailties and temptations and much of the worldliness that beset any corporate body of men banded together for whatever purpose.

THE LEAVENING OF SOCIETY

'*The kingdom of heaven is like unto leaven, which a woman took, and hid in three measures of meal, till the whole was leavened.*'

Jesus here teaches that the gradual and hidden spread and growth of the Kingdom of God will not only produce a visible Church but will also have a most powerful effect on the life of society around the Church. It will affect the business life, the social customs, the morals, the political life, the art, music and poetry of this world. In every sphere of that society where the Gospel is preached and received there will be changes and modifications. The presence of the Kingdom of God in this world will, in fact, produce a new type of society—a society leavened by the Gospel. This prophecy of Jesus has been fulfilled no less certainly than that in the parable of the mustard seed, for wherever the Gospel has been vigorously propagated, not only has a Church been produced, but also profound and disturbing social effects have resulted. The Kingdom of God has acted as leaven in the mass of society.

When leaven is introduced into dough there may at first be

little effect, but soon there is upheaval and disturbance, a violent fermentation spreading through the whole mass of the dough. The influence of the leaven penetrates every particle and nothing is left unchanged. Nothing can prevent the leaven, once introduced, from modifying every part of the whole mass. That is Jesus' prophecy of how His Gospel will act on human society. It will produce disturbance, reaction and conflict wherever it is sown, right through the whole range of human life. 'I am come to send fire on the earth; and what will I, if it be already kindled?... Suppose ye that I am come to give peace on earth? I tell you, Nay; but rather division: For from henceforth there shall be five in one house divided, three against two, and two against three.'[1]

We do not need to read far in the New Testament to find early examples of the disturbing social effects of the Gospel, which foreshadow the effects it was later to produce on an imperial scale. When Jesus went to the country of the Gadarenes and cast out the devils from the possessed demoniacs, the devils went into the herd of swine, which ran violently down the hillside and drowned themselves with tremendous noise and disturbance in the sea.[2] It was not only a physical disturbance, the loss of these swine, but also a social one that was bound to have far-reaching effects in the district, for many people had a financial interest in the herd. The people of the district besought Jesus to depart. They did not wish the evil powers in their kingdom to be disturbed by such violent and expensive reactions to the Kingdom of God. They would rather have the devils undisturbed. When Paul went to Ephesus[3] and preached the Word, the economic effects of the Gospel on the trade of the makers of images were soon so marked that they stirred up a great riot with the purpose of making things too hot for Paul. It was not without reason that Paul and his companions were called 'these that have turned the world upside down'.[4]

These incidents from the New Testament may seem trivial; nevertheless they were the small beginnings of a process that was to go on and on, to result in the leavening of the whole life of this world by the Gospel. When Mary Slessor went to Africa and after years of toil and prayer succeeded in taming the

[1] Luke 12.49-52 [2] Mark 5.12 [3] Acts 19 [4] Acts 17.6

savage customs of the wild tribes she worked among, it was simply a continuation of the process which had its beginnings here in the New Testament. The Gospel at first produced fierce and devilish reactions in the Roman world where it was sown, as the persecutions and martyrdoms of the early Christians bear witness. Then, after the first fierce reaction had died down, the Gospel was found to produce great and humane modifications in the customs and laws of the Empire. It made society to a certain extent more kindly. Gladiatorial shows, for instance were stopped, and the treatment of women was mercifully modified. Slavery was not abolished, it is true, but it became less terrible in practice than it had been. Even though the large majority of Roman citizens did not acknowledge the Lordship of Christ, they nevertheless, in spite of what they might otherwise have wished, became outwardly 'christianised'. Wherever the Gospel is freely preached and freely received, not only does a Church rise up, but also a profound and modifying effect on the whole of society takes place.

It is with good reason that Dr T. R. Glover, in discussing this matter, reminds us of the story of the two little girls quarrelling about the last book of the Bible. 'No, Barbara,' replied the elder, 'the Bible does not end in Timothy. It ends in Revolutions.' The Word of God may seem a frail and weak instrument but it has been the potent cause of many a widespread social revolution. Perhaps those who call Christianity 'dope' owe more of their revolutionary spirit than they know to the very Gospel they despise. Let us never underestimate the influence of the Gospel on the history of our society. The Word of God can get into the statute book, and liberate slaves, and control those who exploit their fellows. How small the leaven looks in face of the dull, dead mass into which it is thrust! Yet it spreads through all and alters everything. A tiny seed lodged in the cranny of a great boulder will, in the course of time, send out its rootlets deep into the fissure and grow into a sapling and eventually a tree, and the stone is rent in two by what once seemed such an insignificant trifle.

It is the duty of the Church therefore to apply the Word of God to all the social problems of the time, for it is the Word of the Gospel alone that can assure the constant revolution in society necessary to keep it in good health. The leaven of the

Gospel must be continually and freshly introduced into this world. Wild cats can be tamed, but if they are allowed back, even after a few generations, to their natural surroundings, they will very soon lose all trace of their civilised existence. So even a society that has been leavened by the Gospel will go back to nature, and will become crude and cruel, even under an apparently Christian system, if continually the fresh leaven of the preaching of the Word of God is not introduced to keep alive that health-giving ferment.

Leavened society is not the Kingdom of God. There is an idea in the minds of many people that as time passes, and more and more the influence of the Gospel is felt on the social life of man, society may become better and better till indeed it actually is found to have become a real Kingdom of God on earth. Leavened society is, however, simply leavened society. Leaven does not change the flour into something else. It remains flour, no matter how violent the process it has gone through. This world, likewise, remains very much this world, no matter how much it has been brought under the influence of the Gospel.

THE TARES AND THE WHEAT, AND THE DRAG NET

Another parable put he forth unto them, saying, The kingdom of heaven is likened unto a man which sowed good seed in his field: but while men slept, his enemy came and sowed tares among the wheat, and went his way. But when the blade was sprung up, and brought forth fruit, then appeared the tares also. So the servants of the householder came and said unto him, Sir, didst not thou sow good seed in thy field? from whence then hath it tares? He said unto them, An enemy hath done this. The servants said unto him, Wilt thou then that we go and gather them up? But he said, Nay; lest while ye gather up the tares, ye root up also the wheat with them. Let both grow together until the harvest: and in the time of harvest I will say to the reapers, Gather ye together first the tares, and bind them in bundles to burn them: but gather the wheat into my barn.
MATTHEW 13.24-30

Then Jesus sent the multitude away, and went into the house: and his disciples came unto him, saying, Declare unto us the parable of the tares of the field. He answered and said unto them, He that soweth the good seed is the Son of man; the field is the world; the good seed are the children of the kingdom; but the tares are the children of the wicked one; the enemy that sowed them is the devil; the harvest is the end of the world; and the reapers are the angels. As therefore the tares are gathered and burned in the fire; so shall it be in the end of this world. The Son of man shall send forth his angels, and they shall gather out of his kingdom all things that offend, and them which do iniquity; and shall cast them into a furnace of fire: there shall be wailing and gnashing of teeth. Then shall the righteous shine forth as the sun in the kingdom of their Father.
MATTHEW 13.36-43

Again, the kingdom of heaven is like unto a net, that was cast into the sea, and gathered of every kind: which, when it was full, they drew to shore, and sat down, and gathered the good into vessels, but cast the bad away. So shall it be at the end of the world: the angels shall come forth, and sever the wicked from among the just, and shall cast them into the furnace of fire: there shall be wailing and gnashing of teeth.
MATTHEW 13.47-50

'*The kingdom of heaven is likened unto a man which sowed good seed in his field.*' As in the other parables of seed and growth which we have been considering, Jesus here reminds us that the purpose of His coming is to re-establish the rule of God over the hearts of men and the affairs of mankind. Through His life and death and resurrection that Kingdom has been founded, and through the Word that proclaims these events and conveys their power and virtue God is sowing in men's hearts the seeds that are meant to take root and bring them new life and conversion, and cause the growth and spread of His rule. He is sowing these seeds through the agency of those called to proclaim His Word in this world.

Jesus, in speaking of all this, calls it in one place 'the mystery of the kingdom of God'.[1] In this present parable of the tares and the wheat His purpose is to speak of another great mystery which Paul later refers to as 'the mystery of iniquity'.[2]

THE MYSTERY OF INIQUITY

'*The kingdom of heaven is likened unto a man which sowed good seed in his field: but while he slept, his enemy came and sowed tares among the wheat.*'

There is, then, an enemy of God at work who seeks dominion over the hearts of men and the affairs of this earth, and who hates to see God's Kingdom advancing. The disciples of Jesus are not the only people who have seed to sow or a Gospel to propagate. There is an anti-Christ who also has seed to sow, and a plan to execute that seeks to displace the true Lord and Creator from His throne. Jesus in His explanation of the parable declares quite bluntly that '*the enemy . . . is the Devil*'.

No one can deny that to Jesus the enemy was a most concrete and sinister personal reality. Jesus Christ did not speak of Himself as one who was fighting against fate, or against man, or against bad social conditions, or against wrong ideas, but as one who was fighting against a single personal will which had defied God in a sphere far greater than this earth, and whose widespread activity has seriously called in question the sovereignty of God. He called this one 'Satan'. When Jesus healed men, He looked on His healing ministry as destroying the works of the Devil. After He had cured the woman who had

[1] Mark 4.11   [2] 2 Thess. 2.7

been bound with a spirit of infirmity for eighteen years, He turned and said, 'Ought not this woman, being a daughter of Abraham, whom Satan hath bound, lo, these eighteen years, be loosed from this bond on the sabbath day?'[1] John summed up the whole purpose of His ministry when he said, 'For this purpose the Son of God was manifested, that He might destroy the works of the devil.'[2] When His ministry was a success Jesus rejoiced, because He saw in the success the foretaste of final victory over Satan. On the occasion when the disciples came back and told Him how well the work of the Kingdom was going, He rejoiced and said, 'I beheld Satan as lightning fall from heaven.'[3] When men joined in plotting against Him, He spoke as if they were allying themselves with the Devil in his reaction against the Kingdom of God. 'Ye are of your father the devil,'[4] He said to the Pharisees. He had come into this world to redeem men, not merely from an unfortunate state of chaos caused by the clashing wills of men at varied purposes, not merely from delusive ideas about God and life, not merely from godlessness, but from bondage to this evil one who had men in his hands and could use them as his slaves. 'Simon, Simon, behold, Satan hath desired to have you, that he may sift you as wheat: But I have prayed for thee, that thy faith fail not.'[5]

Moreover, when Jesus was faced by the Cross, He looked upon His approaching agony and death as the hour when He would enter into the decisive conflict with the powers of evil. He spoke of the hour of the Cross as being His hour. 'Mine hour is not yet come.'[6] He spoke of it also as the hour of the powers of evil. 'This is your hour, and the power of darkness.'[7] All through His life on earth He had been challenging these powers to this conflict. In the miracles in which He had released the demon-possessed He had thrown out a preliminary challenge and had shown that He had come to disturb their rule, but these incidents were only skirmishes on the frontier of evil. He knew that the works that He had done would produce a great planned decisive reaction in which Satan, knowing that his rule was threatened, would rally all his forces and throw them into one desperate battle. That battle took place on the

[1] Luke 13.16 [2] 1 John 3.8 [3] Luke 10.18 [4] John 8.44
[5] Luke 22.31-32 [6] John 2.4 [7] Luke 22.53

Cross, where it was not simply human enmity that was unleashed against Jesus but all the Satanic hatred which had been stored up from the beginning against the rule of God. Jesus cried upon the Cross, 'It is finished,'[1] and we can read into those words the announcement that the conflict with the powers of darkness was now over, that the victory was won, and the power of Satan broken. The Resurrection is the manifestation of His triumph and victory over the Devil and all his works.

The assertion is frequently made that all these references to Satan in the teaching of Jesus are merely a 'way of speaking'. Jesus, it is asserted, knew that Satan was not a reality, and in speaking of Satan He was using the language of the people of His time, the only language He could use. It seems impossible seriously to press this type of argument. It would mean that while involved in that glorious act of redeeming love upon the Cross, Jesus indulged in one of the cleverest pieces of theatrical display that have ever been seen on the grim stage of life. To Jesus, the power of evil was directed by one evil will, one great mind, having at its disposal hosts of agents and legions of emissaries, all moving according to a strategy planned to thwart the purpose of God. The headquarters of this evil power are beyond this earth, but he has made this earth his battleground on which he throws out his challenge to God. Paul was merely summing up the teaching of Jesus when he wrote to the Ephesians, 'We wrestle not against flesh and blood, but against principalities, against powers, against the rulers of the darkness of this world, against spiritual wickedness in high places.'[2]

This is all indeed a great mystery. When we try to think it out our minds are baffled. Where does the enemy come from? We can answer in reply to this question only that he is a creature of God. 'The Devil is God's Devil,' said Luther. Evil is not eternal. In the beginning was God, not 'Good and Evil'. But immediately we say this we are up against a fresh mystery. How does it come about that a mere creature can raise a rebellion against God of such sinister proportions? The facts are that the presence and the rise of this evil power in the midst of this universe have been the cause of such misery and woe throughout creation, and of such widespread revolt against the laws of God, as to have seriously raised the question of whether

[1] John 19.30   [2] Eph. 6.12

God rules at all on this earth. Moreover, this evil power has acquired such a hold over the hearts and destiny of mankind as to require the coming of God Himself in Person to put things right, for He alone had the power to loose this hold, and that not without becoming involved in the bitter conflict revealed in the Cross. The very fact that there has been such revolt against God in this world suggests of itself that these are huge and organised powers that have had the boldness to turn against Him who is Lord of all.

'I would certainly conclude,' writes Dora Greenwell, 'that in the great struggle between good and evil there is more equality between the combatants than ordinary theology admits of. It is not without cause that an athlete puts forth his full strength. Neither, in considering this subject do I forget Count de Maistre's significant saying to the effect that "we do not see the Duchy of Lucca invade France, nor Genoa declare war on England". The struggle between God and evil has been long and protracted and deadly; it has demanded on the part of God the costliest sacrifices.'

Notice that Jesus does not in this parable seek to explain this mystery. '*An enemy hath done this*' is all that the owner of the field says to the baffled workers who come for an explanation of the presence of the tares. He does not say where the enemy came from. Jesus' answer to the mystery of iniquity is not to explain it but to banish it, and to call on man to face it as a dread reality which must be resisted to the utmost or all will be lost.

In this story the enemy came and sowed tares among the wheat. Precisely where God has been most energetically at work and where the Kingdom is most likely to advance, there the Devil deliberately comes and concentrates his forces to prevent the spread of God's realm. This is one of the main reasons why so many evil things have marred the history of the Church of Christ. It is precisely in the sphere of the Church, where the good seed of the Gospel is most thickly strewn, that we can expect the Devil to be at work most subtly and powerfully, to prevent men from coming under the rule of God and His Word. The Devil desires to bring shame upon the name of Christ, therefore he concentrates on the Church. The history of the Church illustrates this only too well. Even from the

THE TARES AND THE WHEAT 31

start of the Church the tares began to appear where the Word was sown. The Apostles themselves continually had to battle against false doctrines and false enthusiasms, and against teachers who would turn the Gospel into a new law and thereby destroy it. It is a most significant fact that the most subtle anti-Christian doctrines have arisen not in heathen countries but in the midst of societies where the Gospel has been preached. There is truth in the assertion that Nazism and materialistic Communism could not have been conceived except in reaction to the Gospel of Jesus Christ.

The pollution of God's field is often most subtly accomplished. In the parable the enemy comes by night and sows his seed secretly. At first when the seed sprouts it is difficult to distinguish the tares from the wheat. When the tiny shoots come up each looks alike. It is only after evil has developed that it is noticed, but by that time its roots have gained a firm and widespread hold amongst the wheat. How skilfully the Devil goes forth to his work! It is not always as a 'roaring lion'[1] that he seeks to do his work on earth. He comes in subtle and shining and respectable forms as an 'angel of light'.[2] He disguises himself as a sower of the good seed. There is often no appearance of anything gross or sensual or second-rate about the Devil when he comes to win men to his service, and those whom he persuades to follow him can imagine that they are following the very highest for which a man can give his life.

PRACTICAL ADVICE

When the servants saw the tares in the field they were bewildered and angry. They felt that they must immediately start uprooting all traces of this evil intrusion. They went to the owner of the field to tell him so but they received astonishing advice. '*Let both grow together until the harvest.*' They must not imagine that by sheer blind zeal they could solve the problem of the presence of evil in the midst of the sphere of the Kingdom of God. They must patiently endure seeing evil grow mixed up with the good until the time of harvest.

Christ here counsels His disciples to have patience in the face of all the havoc that evil seems to be allowed to create in the midst of the sphere of God's working. He warns His disciples

[1] 1 Pet. 5.8   [2] 2 Cor. 11.14

that after having done all that is in their power, they will have to reconcile themselves to watching evil grow in a way against which they will be powerless to do anything except wait for God to act. To wait is often the only wise policy. When we see evil and hypocrisy flaunting themselves manifestly in the Church, we may decide that it must be ruthlessly cleaned up. But how difficult it is to 'clean up' the Church! In our zeal to have a holy Church we sometimes only make it easier for self-righteousness to flourish amongst the holiness. We may decide that we must be strict in uprooting from the sphere of the Church all the sins that cause public scandal, but we may find, after we have done so, that we have left the more room for, and given the more encouragement to, the subtler sins of the spirit. There is no quick and definite solution to this problem of evil, either in theory or in practice, till the last day.

It is possible that in this parable Jesus had the immediate purpose of addressing a special word of advice to John the Baptist and his followers. John was a man with a great passion for righteousness, who had taught that the Messiah would come and deal in a spectacular way with the social evils of his time. He would baptise 'with the Holy Ghost and with fire: whose fan is in his hand, and he will throughly purge his floor, and will gather the wheat into his garner; but the chaff he will burn with fire unquenchable'.[1] John was disappointed when, having acknowledged Jesus as the Messiah, he did not see Him set to work immediately in this extreme way. When he was in prison he sent messengers to Jesus, saying, 'Art thou he that should come, or do we look for another?'[2] It was partly the righteous indignation they had inherited from John the Baptist which made James and John ask, concerning the Samaritan village which had refused lodging to our Lord, 'Wilt thou that we command fire to come down from heaven, and consume them, even as Elias did?'[3] Jesus, in this parable, is speaking to such zealous followers of John and advising patience and tolerance. We must not be too ready to judge what is tares and what is wheat amongst the ripening crop in God's field. 'Judge nothing before the time,' writes Paul, 'until the Lord come, who both will bring to light the hidden things of darkness, and will make manifest the counsels of the hearts.'[4] Therefore we must re-

[1] Luke 3.16-17   [2] Matt. 11.3   [3] Luke 9.54   [4] 1 Cor. 4.5

THE TARES AND THE WHEAT

concile ourselves to the presence of evil within the sphere of the Church. 'Nowhere else,' writes Karl Adam, 'does evil become so visible because nowhere else is it so keenly fought.'

This does not mean that we are not to battle against evil when we see it manifest, and that discipline within the Church should be allowed to become slack and careless. Jesus Himself said that if a man was unforgiving and unrepentant in his unloving spirit he was to be excluded from the fellowship of the Church.[1] Nevertheless in all our zeal for cleansing the Church Jesus urges us to proceed with extreme caution. The result of our zealous action might not be what we expect. In uprooting tares we might find that we had uprooted wheat also and had deprived the work of God of vigorous support. We must resign ourselves to seeing within the Church in the world, no matter how great our efforts, a perplexing mixture everywhere of good and evil until the end. We must believe that God is ever concerned with the separation of the righteous from the unjust, and that He will cleanse His creation in His good time.

A Word of Comfort and Reassurance

Let us, at this point, take notice of a great truth which is not explicitly mentioned here in the parable but is implied throughout. Since the Kingdom of God has come into this world, evil has lost all initiative. Evil works now only in reaction to the Kingdom of God. It was Jesus Himself who took the initiative against the powers of evil in entering the world and challenging them to decisive conflict. The attempt of evil, in the Cross, to thwart the work of Christ was a mere reaction to His first move towards the decisive battle. Jesus Christ chose the scene and the time of the conflict. It was all planned, and it was planned by God. Evil is here wholly under the command of God. When Judas went out to do his Satanic work and betray Jesus into the hands of His enemies it was Jesus who ordered him to this task. 'That thou doest, do quickly.'[2] In the sixth chapter of Revelation, when the Apocalyptic riders come forth (those four strange horsemen who represent and do the work of the principalities and powers of darkness), they come to their work in obedience to the command of Him who sits on the throne. 'Come' is the command from the throne of God, and they come

[1] Matt. 18.17 [2] John 13.27

forth one after another. Since the Kingdom of God has entered this world the powers of evil can work against that Kingdom only in response to the challenge and command of Him who is Lord. We can take comfort and encouragement from this fact in these days of world-wide crisis. The whole of world history, even in its most violent and devilish phases, is under the control of Jesus Christ, who is King and Lord, and no great movement of evil that may appear on the earth can be anything other than a reaction to the Kingdom of God which has been introduced into this world by Jesus Christ.

Moreover, evil can only obscure the growing Kingdom of God but cannot hinder it. Jesus finishes the parable with reassuring words from the owner implying the safety of the wheat crop: *'Let both grow together until the harvest: and in the time of harvest I will say to the reapers, Gather ye together first the tares, and bind them in bundles to burn them: but gather the wheat into my barn.'* In His interpretation He gave the sense of this passage thus: *'The Son of man shall send forth his angels, and they shall gather out of his kingdom all things that offend, and them which do iniquity; and shall cast them into a furnace of fire. . . . Then shall the righteous shine forth as the sun in the kingdom of their Father.'* No matter how vigorously evil seems to grow and flourish, the good cannot be damaged but only obscured. Even though the tares obscure the wheat, they cannot damage the good crop. Even though evil fills the Church and obscures the glory of the harvest which is ripening for God there, it can only obscure that harvest for a time. In the time of reaping, and in the time of judgment and separation, the good crop will all be there, and after the separation, then shall the just shine forth as the sun. 'Your labour is not in vain in the Lord,'[1] says Paul. It may seem to be in vain, the results may be obscured, but 'charity never faileth'.[2] One day the harvest will be seen, and it will be seen in a completeness and glory that will prove that evil has no power to hinder the development of that which is good.

A further heartening truth is taught by Jesus: if evil is growing and developing, it is merely in order to ripen for its own destruction. God in dealing with evil allows it to ripen so that it may destroy itself. He allows it to develop until it has revealed itself in all its hideous and ghastly proportions and in

[1] 1 Cor. 15.58   [2] 1 Cor. 13.8

THE TARES AND THE WHEAT 35

all its monstrous ugliness. In the seventy-third Psalm the writer tells us that he was pained at heart when he saw the prosperity of the wicked. He could not understand why God allowed evil such free rein and such full scope upon this earth, and he had no clue to the solution of the problem till, in the sanctuary of God, he realised that if God allows evil to grow and spread and to attain such huge proportions, it is merely in order to cast it down suddenly to destruction. Evil must be allowed a certain degree of success, for only so can it reveal itself. In its hideous development it judges and finally dooms itself. To this development God has set decisive limits which must not be passed. It seems therefore as if God has to wait till evil has developed to a certain pitch before He will destroy it. He waited till the sin of the Amorites was ripe before He sent Joshua into the promised land to destroy them.[1] He has often allowed great, proud, wicked empires to grow and wax strong and to assume mighty proportions before, suddenly, they were destroyed. 'When the fulness of the time was come,' says Paul, 'God sent forth his Son.'[2] Jesus Christ came into this earth exactly at the time when the evil of the whole world had developed to such an extent as to be dealt with conclusively and decisively.

We must take these matters into account in determining our view of the course which we may expect world events to take in the future of this earth. Jesus Christ never taught that the movement of earth's history would take the form of a slow but steady development of the good upon this earth accompanied by the gradual elimination of its evil. He taught rather that the more good developed, the more evil might also develop to ripen with the good. He seemed to visualise a state of affairs in which evil will have developed to such an extent that what is good on the earth may also be completely obscured. Jesus prophesied that just before the very day of His approaching final triumph, when His Kingdom had grown to its consummation and was ready to burst forth and fill this earth with its glory—at that very moment, evil might be at its height upon the earth in such force and display that it would be difficult to find faith among men. 'When the Son of man cometh, shall He find faith on the earth?'[3] That is why Jesus taught us,

[1] Gen. 15.16   [2] Gal. 4.4   [3] Luke 18.8

when we hear of wars and rumours of wars, to lift up our hearts because our redemption draweth nigh. It is because God's Kingdom is coming that evil is so violent in its rage upon the earth. A strong man in his house is at peace until one comes and seeks to cast him out, and then there is war and fighting.[1]

A CHALLENGE

The closing verses of the parable of the tares are very similar to the closing verses of the parable of the drag net, and it is in this context that we can best understand the message of this latter parable. '*The kingdom of heaven is like unto a net, that was cast into the sea, and gathered of every kind: which, when it was full, they drew to shore, and sat down, and gathered the good into vessels, but cast the bad away. So shall it be at the end of the world: the angels shall come forth, and sever the wicked from among the just, and shall cast them into the furnace of fire: there shall be wailing and gnashing of teeth.*'

This parable repeats lessons that have already been taught. It shows that a large admixture of hypocrites within the Church is inevitable, and it encourages us to cast the net of the Gospel over a wide area to draw in disciples, even though we know that we are thereby also enclosing those who are making a false profession. We cannot in the process of evangelism be entirely sure of separating the good from the bad. God will ultimately do the separation.

But this little additional parable has a message of its own which it is specially designed to enforce. Each one of us must make sure that we ourselves, in the day of separation, will be numbered among the elect. It is easy to delude ourselves in this matter. Let us not imagine that just because we seem to be caught in the net of the Church and because we rub shoulders daily with those who believe in Christ, we ourselves necessarily have the Divine Life stirring within our own hearts. The Kingdom of God is like a net widely cast, and membership of the Church does not guarantee that we will be numbered in the end amongst the just. Christ warns us in this parable, says Calvin, that 'it is not enough to be gathered into the fold unless we are His true and chosen sheep'. Professor Laidlaw points out that this series of parables in the thirteenth chapter of St

[1] Luke 11.21-2

Matthew's Gospel begins with a parable about the acceptance or rejection of the Word of God by the souls of men; it ends with a parable about the acceptance or rejection of the souls of men by God. There is only one test, and only one thing can make us certain to be numbered amongst the people of God. We must receive the Word into our hearts with true faith and full response; then that Word will indeed cause us to be born again into the new life of the Children of God.

THE OFFER AND COST OF CITIZENSHIP

THE HIDDEN TREASURE, AND THE PEARL OF GREAT PRICE

Again, the kingdom of heaven is like unto treasure hid in a field; the which when a man hath found, he hideth, and for joy thereof goeth and selleth all that he hath, and buyeth that field.
Again, the kingdom of heaven is like unto a merchant man, seeking goodly pearls: who, when he had found one pearl of great price, went and sold all that he had, and bought it.

MATTHEW 13.44-46

John Bright once eloquently stated the principle that the true worth of any kingdom or government is to be judged by the benefits it can impart to the humble individual who participates in it. 'I do not care for military greatness or military renown,' he said in a speech. 'I care for the condition of the people among whom I live. There is no man in England who is less likely to speak irreverently of the Crown and the Monarch of England than I am; but crowns, coronets, mitres, military display, the pomp of war and a huge empire are, in my view, trifles light as air and not worth considering unless with them you have a fair share of comfort and happiness among the great body of the people.' You can have much outward glory on the surface of society, and yet at the same time much misery at the hearts of its members. The age of Solomon was a glorious age in Israel, but so dissatisfied were the common people with their conditions of life under the rule of Solomon that at his death they sought to throw off the hateful yoke and to dissever themselves from his kingdom.

To enter the Kingdom of God, however, is not like taking part in the rest of human history, where all may be glory viewed from the outside, yet a most miserable and oppressive affair for its humble participants. The Kingdom of God is as glorious from the point of view of the least citizen therein as it is from its outward aspect. It was to give this assurance that Jesus, in the midst of all these other parables in this chapter which tell of the cosmic significance of the Kingdom of God, inserted these two short parables which teach that the Kingdom, though hidden from the sight of men, can be experienced in a vivid manner by the individuals who take part in it.

'*The kingdom of heaven is like unto treasure hid in a field; the which, when a man hath found, he hideth, and for joy thereof goeth and selleth all that he hath, and buyeth that field. Again, the kingdom of heaven is like unto a merchant man, seeking goodly pearls: who, when he had found one pearl of great price, went and sold all that he had, and bought it.*'

WHAT THE KINGDOM OF GOD OFFERS

Here Jesus tells of two men, each of whom discovers something that he would never have dreamed could be his till he saw it, and then realised it was within his grasp if he would have it. A farmer, ploughing a field according to his usual routine, finds a treasure of surpassing value. A pearl seeker finds one pearl of incomparable worth. Of such worth is it that, though he has been a pearl collector all his days, this pearl far outshines any other he has ever seen. In both cases the discoverer immediately makes a reckoning, and each says within himself, 'I can possess this thing if I can pay the price. And I can afford to pay the price!' Translated into the terms of our own life and experience, of which they are meant to speak, these parables tell us that the Kingdom of God offers us as humble insignificant individuals the possibility of an exalted and thrilling experience far surpassing all that we can ever have imagined as within our range.

Moreover, in the light of the glory and value of what is offered to us in the Kingdom of God, the value of everything else we have hitherto prized comes crashing down. When the farmer sees the treasure, he sells all that he has in order to buy the field. He parts with everything he has valued hitherto as if it were of no value to him any more in the light of what he has seen in that field. When the pearl collector sees the pearl of great price, and realises that its possession is within his reach, he goes and sells all his coveted collection of what to him, only the day before, were most magnificent pearls. He sells them now without a pang because they have been eclipsed in splendour by the pearl of great price. They are no longer in his eyes the pearls they were.

These two parables thus agree that the Kingdom of Heaven is like something which, when we catch a glimpse of it and realise that it can become ours, makes everything that has been most precious to us hitherto appear now as poor in comparison. 'Let us beseech you,' cried one of the covenanting preachers, 'draw aside the lap of time's curtain and look through the window to the great and endless eternity, and consider if a worldly price—suppose this whole round globe of clay were all your own—can be given for one smile of Christ's God-like countenance.' The Apostle Paul found this pearl of great price and stumbled across the treasure hid in a field when he met Jesus Christ on the Damascus road. Years later, writing to the Philippians, he described the change that the finding of this treasure made in his outlook. Once he had gloried in his ancestry, his education, his connexions as a Pharisee, his personal character, his zeal for God's law, but now, 'what things were gain to me, those I counted loss for Christ. Yea doubtless, and I count all things but loss for the excellency of the knowledge of Christ Jesus my Lord: for whom I have suffered the loss of all things, and do count them but dung, that I may win Christ.'[1]

WHAT THE KINGDOM OF GOD COSTS

Jesus informs us here that to enter the Kingdom of God costs everything. Before the farmer could have the treasure, he had to sell everything. Before the collector could possess the pearl, he too had to sell all that he had. In order to enter the Kingdom of God, we must let go of everything we have; this is the one condition. God receives men into His Kingdom only if they have rid themselves first of everything. If we are going to grasp Christ, we must grasp Him with empty hands. A rich young ruler came to Jesus and said, 'Good Master, what shall I do to inherit eternal life?'[2] He had seen a great possibility before him, and he called it 'eternal life'. We call it here 'the Kingdom of God'; it is all one and the same thing. He asked what it would cost. Jesus' reply was that it costs everything. 'Sell all that thou hast ... and thou shalt have treasure in heaven.' It was necessary that he should loosen his hold of these great possessions to which he was clinging too eagerly if

[1] Phil. 3.7-8 [2] Luke 18.18 ff

he was to be able to receive eternal life. We envy Abraham when we read his story, for he possessed the faith that can bear its owner through anything. But what did it all cost Abraham? 'Get thee out of thy country, and from thy kindred, and from thy father's house, unto a land that I will shew thee: and I will make of thee a great nation,' said the voice of God.[1]

It costs everything to enter the Kingdom, but it costs no more than simply that. Reading between the lines in these parables, we can observe that the farmer was not such a rich man as the pearl collector. Indeed he was probably quite poor. But the price was not beyond the reach of either the farmer or the rich merchant. The cost was, in both cases, the letting go of all possessions. The Kingdom can be gained by any man, no matter what he possesses, if only he will let go. There is no fixed price. A man may imagine that he has not so much to give in qualities of mind and heart and character as other men seem to have, but that does not mean that he has not enough. The only condition for partaking of the glory the Kingdom has to offer is to be wholeheartedly eager for it.

The cost is great, but the parables remind us that the cost is nothing compared with the glory of that which is offered— Jesus Christ. If we find difficulty in facing up to the cost, let us think again of these two men. They did not find it difficult to give up everything. They were, indeed, glad to sell all. The value of the new thing that was to be theirs was much greater than anything they were giving up. They kept their eyes and minds on the fact that a glorious prize was to be theirs. We must learn this lesson, and if we find difficulty in facing up to what Christ demands of us, we must look at what He offers us in Himself. Catherine Marsh was once seeking to persuade a brilliant young man of this world to decide for Jesus Christ. 'You want me to give up everything,' he complained. 'No, indeed,' she replied. 'I am asking you to accept everything in Jesus Christ.' Jesus suggests in these parables that once a man has seen what the Kingdom of God is worth, he will find it easy to part with his earthly treasures. It will be a decision not to give up everything, but to receive everything. Once a man has experienced how joyful a thing it is to sacrifice all for Christ, he never looks back with regret on what he has given up, for he

[1] Gen. 12.1-2

has found a thousandfold in return. 'And every one that hath forsaken houses, or brethren, or sisters, or father, or mother, or wife, or children, or lands, for my name's sake, shall receive an hundredfold, and shall inherit everlasting life.'[1]

Two Different Ways in Which Man May Discover the Kingdom of God

If we have been impressed by what Jesus says here about the glory of the individual experience in the Kingdom of God and have decided that we are prepared to face the cost of entrance into it, the question nevertheless remains: 'How can I find it?' How does it happen that we, living in the midst of this present world, come across this treasure and this pearl of great price? How do we make the discovery of the Kingdom for ourselves?

The parable of the hidden treasure suggests that we shall find the treasure of the Kingdom under most unlikely circumstances. A field under the plough is not a likely place to find treasure. Read in its context amongst the other parables in this thirteenth chapter of Matthew, this parable teaches us that it is within the Church when the Word of God is preached that men come up against the treasure of the Kingdom, the pearl of great price. The Church is both a field where the Word is sown and a field where men stumble against the hidden treasure, and the glorious possibilities of becoming citizens of the Kingdom of God are opened before them. There are those who do not understand this. The Church is to them simply a barren field with little in it. Dr Alexander Whyte once met a woman in his congregation who said to him, 'I did not like your sermon on Sunday.' But the same week her son had written to Dr Whyte and had told him, 'That sermon led me to Christ.' To one man the Church is no more than a most unlikely field in which to find anything of surpassing value. The preaching of the Word is to him no more than a purely human affair—a man giving his views about life, and they may be unacceptable views. But to another man the Church is the place where the true treasure is to be found, and the preaching of the Word can become the gate of Heaven itself.

We must ask ourselves if we, in our reading and hearing of the Scripture and sermon, in the midst of the Church, have

[1] Matt. 19.29

stumbled across this treasure and seen this hidden pearl, the living Jesus Christ. When Jesus met the woman of Samaria[1] at the well she thought at first that He was simply a tired, wandering, begging Jew. She approached Him in a superior manner and was almost condescending in her bearing. Then when he began to talk to her she concluded that He was at least a teacher with whom one could argue and she turned the conversation to the subject of worship in order to start discussion. But she had not gone far before she made the wonderful discovery that this man could give her 'living water', could solve the deepest problem of her life, and was none other than the Son of God. Thus we have to make the discovery that behind the outward form of the Church, the place where the Bible is opened and the Sacrament administered (and it often seems to be a poor and comparatively uninteresting outward form!), there can spring up for us a well of living water that can give us eternal life and solve all the problems of our guilt and sin. When Jacob went in his loneliness and exile from home to Bethel, he chose a stone for a pillow and lay down. He was weary and sick of life and utterly lonely, but there came to him that glorious vision of a ladder stretched between earth and Heaven, and a promise that was to sustain him through many a weary day, and he awoke saying, 'Surely the Lord is in this place; and I knew it not.'[2] God was there seeking him in a most unlikely place. So it is in the Church of Christ when men find the treasure hidden at its heart.

The man who found the pearl of great price was a seeker. The wonderful pearl was far more than what he was seeking and yet he seemed to find it as a result of his search. There are those who, when they come to believe in Christ, feel in this way that Christ is what they were seeking through all their restless and unsatisfied quest for the best and highest pearls that human thought and art and culture and religion can produce. On the other hand, the man who found the treasure in the field was not seeking anything. He was out to plough his field and nothing more. There are those whom the encounter with Christ takes completely by surprise. It is always by the grace of God that we enter the Kingdom. When His light shines into our minds it shines into darkness. When His life is breathed /

[1] John 4 [2] Gen. 28.16

into our hearts it brings a new creation. In the experience of some this may have been a gradual process of whose beginnings they were hardly conscious. To others it may have happened all in one glorious day. What does it matter, as long as the outcome is the same and the Good Shepherd has found the sheep that was lost?

If we have not experienced what Jesus describes here as our inheritance in the Kingdom of God, let us believe that there is such treasure to be found in the field of God's grace, where the Word is proclaimed and the Sacrament administered. Let us not imagine that in our life's experience apart from Christ we have exhausted the limits of what God can do for us. It is saddening to observe how men refuse to open their lives to the experiences spoken of in the New Testament as conversion, rebirth, salvation, as if the things these words stand for had no reality, and those who spoke about them were simply well-meaning enthusiasts guilty of gross exaggeration! The wonder of true evangelical experience cannot be exaggerated. No words can describe it. It is like treasure hid in a field that puts all else in the shade. It is like a pearl which surpasses even imagination. To scoff is easy but it is sometimes foolish. The King of Siam once scoffed at a European ambassador when he said that in his own land during winter water became so hard that men could walk on it. Let us not be too sure that in our religious experience we have sounded all the depths there are. There is glory for the individual in Jesus Christ surpassing all else that the best of this life can offer. Let us not rest till we too are like the treasure finder and the exultant pearl seeker, and for joy thereof are ready to part with all that we have.

THE LOST SHEEP, AND THE LOST COIN

Then drew near unto him all the publicans and sinners for to hear him. And the Pharisees and scribes murmured, saying, This man receiveth sinners, and eateth with them.

And he spake this parable unto them, saying, What man of you, having an hundred sheep, if he lose one of them, doth not leave the ninety and nine in the wilderness, and go after that which is lost, until he find it? And when he hath found it, he layeth it on his shoulders, rejoicing. And when he cometh home, he calleth together his friends and neighbours, saying unto them, Rejoice with me; for I have found my sheep which was lost. I say unto you, that likewise joy shall be in heaven over one sinner that repenteth, more than over ninety and nine just persons, which need no repentance.

Either what woman having ten pieces of silver, if she lose one piece, doth not light a candle, and sweep the house, and seek diligently till she find it? And when she hath found it, she calleth her friends and her neighbours together, saying, Rejoice with me; for I have found the piece which I had lost. Likewise, I say unto you, there is joy in the presence of the angels of God over one sinner that repenteth.

LUKE 15.1-10

THE HUMAN SITUATION

Both these stories are about lost things. A sheep strayed from the flock to become lost in the wild and destroying wilderness, and a coin rolled into a dark corner of the house under some heavy furniture where it could not be seen or reached.

Such is Jesus' description of the human situation in this world. The world is lost and we are lost within this world. Something has happened that has led us far from where we should be and that has separated us from the God who created us. A turning has been taken that has put us out of our true relation to His love and to our own surroundings.

We can understand how this applies to the life of the world. This world does not know where it is going or where it has come from. It does not know its creator or its owner, or even whether it has a creator or an owner. We can recognise a symptom of the lost state of this world even in the fact that we are so completely lost amongst our own scientific inventions, unable to control the very things we can invent. It is a present-day fact worthy of note that many who do not seem to be wholehearted in their agreement with the Christian message at least agree with this diagnosis of Jesus about the world. The man of the world, in spite of his natural unwillingness to face up to the reality of his situation, is nevertheless at times haunted by a dim consciousness that something is very far wrong with things as they are, and that this word 'lost' describes the situation better than any other.

When we think further of how it stands with us individually, we also feel that these two parables well sum up our situation. The sense of frustration that so many feel so keenly today goes to prove to the individual that he is lost. The world is full of individual men and women who feel that somehow they have strayed from the right path, and have missed the very best that life could have offered them had they kept to the way. They feel that they do not fit into their surroundings as they should. They are not at home in their home, or at their work, or among their friends. Some feel they have got lost like the coin. They have taken a wrong turning, chosen the wrong kind of friend, or the wrong career from the very start, and that one wrong turning years ago seems to have put their life completely out of line with what God meant for it. Some feel that they have gone astray like the lost sheep. The sheep goes astray by first of all becoming slightly separated from its fellows. Then it turns its head in the wrong direction and, catching sight of some tempting pasture which seems not too far away, it wanders slightly further on, and gradually it becomes lost. We cannot all point to one decisive moment, as in the case of the prodigal son, when we were conscious of turning deliberately from the path of right, but many of us have simply allowed ourselves to run on like straying sheep, walking where the path is easiest and making our selfish desires our guides, not knowing where we are going, hardly meaning to go astray. That is how our hearts have strayed from God. We have simply yielded to this or that little inclination, and in the long run we are lost, just as decisively as if we had taken one definite plunge from the path of right into the darkness of sin.

Thus far we have not mentioned the most tragic aspect of the human situation thus described by Jesus in these parables. No one can study these parables without being forced to notice that it is the owner who suffers most, more than the lost sheep and the lost coin. We human beings are lost to God, and it is this separation from Him who is our Owner that makes our lost condition so sinister and tragic. We are lost to the Creator who made us for Himself so that we would feel at home and find our true place in life only in His presence. Of course, we may not be lost in the geographical sense of the term, for we are always in this world, and God always sees us and knows exactly our circumstances, but our love and fellowship are lost to God unless He has our hearts, our trust, our devotion. If not, we are as far from Him as a lost sheep is from the shepherd, as a lost son is from the father—as far as Absalom was from David when he sorrowed over him: 'O my son Absalom, my son, my son Absalom! would God I had died for thee, O Absalom, my son, my son!'[1] To God we are like prodigal sons living in a far country with hard hearts of enmity against our fatherly Creator, 'without God in the world'.[2]

THE SEEKING LOVE OF GOD

We can best appreciate what God has done in this tragic human situation if we first think of what He might have done. He might have acted like the stern old father in stories where the name of the wayward son is scored out of the family list and deliberately put out of mind. No vacant bed is left, nor room, nor place, and life goes on as if the lost one had never existed. That would have been justice, for we have forfeited all right to existence. Or God might have decided to keep the name on the family list and to keep the old place vacant, in the hope that the son on his own initiative would come back. That would have been kindness. But Jesus informs us that God goes much farther than either justice or kindness would ever think of going. Jesus pictures God as saying, 'I will go Myself, and I will seek till I find, and bring the lost one back.' Having lost one of them does he not *'leave the ninety and nine in the wilderness, and go after that which is lost, until he find it?'* *'If she lose one piece, doth she not light a candle, and sweep the house, and seek diligently till she find it?'* This is what God does in this tragic human situation.

Here we are at the heart of the message of the Bible. Here

[1] 2 Sam. 18.33   [2] Eph. 2.12

we are reminded of Christmas and Good Friday. The first parable about the shepherd surely sums up all that is behind the coming of God into this world in the birth in the manger, and the Cross of Calvary. The shepherd left the ninety and nine sheep and, unable to rest content with them, went out into the desert, into the danger and the storm, to seek that poor one which was lost. The Son of God, though He was in equality with God, and possessed untold riches in Heaven, nevertheless emptied Himself and came from the infinitude of the heavens down to this little planet which seems but a speck of dust in the universe. 'Our Lord Jesus Christ . . . though he was rich, yet for your sakes He became poor.'[1]

> Lord, Thou hast here Thy ninety and nine;
> Are they not enough for Thee?
> But the Shepherd made answer, 'This of Mine
> Has wandered away from Me;
> And although the road be rough and steep,
> I go to the desert to find My sheep.'

He need not have come. He did not come because He was desolate and empty without us. In order to find us He chose out of His boundless mercy to make Himself a desolate, empty, seeking, suffering man, a man of sorrows yearning for fellowship, a man hanging on a cross crying, 'I thirst.'[2] The message of the Gospel is that there was no sacrifice too great for God to make to bring us back, no pain too hard to be borne, if only the Father might be able at the end of the day to say, 'This, my son, was lost, and is found.'

The search involves the Cross, the deep humiliation, the bitter agony, the bloody sweat, the abandonment in which the Seeking One reaches deeper than we can know in shame and dereliction to save us, and cries, 'My God, my God, why hast thou forsaken me?'[3] These parables, especially the parable of the lost sheep, challenge us to think of the cost of the search, and what it involved, not simply in heavenly sacrifice, but also in bodily pain and in mental agony for the One who came to seek and to save.

God goes all the way and He seeks till He finds. '*What man of you, having an hundred sheep,*' says Jesus, '*doth not leave the ninety and nine in the wilderness, and go after that which is lost,* until *he find*

[1] 2 Cor. 8.9   [2] John 19.28   [3] Matt. 27.46

it?' The search ends in the finding by God of the soul that has been lost. At the centre of the Christian faith there is the story of God's search and of God's finding of man. Christianity is different from other religions in this respect. In other religions it is really man's search for God that is the important thing; here we have God searching till He finds, and man is pictured as unable to do anything for himself. Has it not been so in our case? It is not because we were, and are, clever and persistent seekers for God that we find ourselves in the midst of a Church where God is known and worshipped; it is rather because God seeks till He finds. Christ comes to stand at the door and knock. That is the start of our religion. And behind all the missionary activity in the name of the Church over all the earth there is the same seeking love that brought Christ to the Cross. He, the Good Shepherd, is today completing His work, and seeking out every man and woman in this world.

THE JOY OF FINDING

What joy and gladness there is when the sheep is found and when the coin is found! The shepherd rejoices. The woman rejoices. The neighbours are called in and a feast is made. All are glad. Thus man should rejoice at the least sign of response to the Gospel of Christ that is seen in this world. Jesus rejoiced thus when He discovered that His Gospel was taking root in the earth and that men and women were responding. He was wearied one day and hungry, and He sent His disciples to a nearby village to buy food. They left Him sitting by a well, tired and famished, but a woman came and He spoke His Word to her and she believed and responded to His love.[1] When the disciples came back they found that all His weariness had vanished, that He had now no need of food but was refreshed in body and spirit because He had found a lost soul, and had seen the first fruits of His search for men. The angels also rejoice likewise. '*There is joy in the presence of the angels of God over one sinner that repenteth.*' Jesus in this parable is calling on men also to rejoice.

Why this joy in Heaven? Because the long and painful search is bringing forth fruit. There was once a precious section of cable lost at tremendous depth in mid-Atlantic. It

[1] John 4

seemed impossible that it could be retrieved but a great engineer decided to try. There was much careful calculation, and much thought, time and money were spent. A grappling apparatus was invented. A ship went out and from the deck they sought the lost cable till it was located and brought up. It was a feat of salvage quite unique and wonderful. We can imagine the thrill of gladness that went through the hearts of those concerned in that expedition, who knew just how great the feat was, and just how much care and ingenuity it had involved. How could they help but rejoice over the finding of the lost cable after such a search? So Jesus rejoices among these publicans and sinners who had responded to His love. So the angels rejoice over their return to Him, for they know and understand the cost of the search. And yet the Pharisees—and at their side do we not see ourselves?—fail to rejoice or to show enthusiasm about the finding. They are blind to the fact of *who* this Man is to whose presence among the sinners they are objecting. They do not see that in the least response on the part of sinners to this Man there is being reaped the fruit of infinite sacrifice. If they only understood, they would marvel!

Jesus' Self-defence

In these parables Jesus is defending Himself from the bitter attacks of the Pharisees and scribes. Jesus was criticised because He kept company with immoral people. '*This man receiveth sinners, and eateth with them,*' they said in scorn. These phrases suggest that to all outward appearance Jesus was in constant association with the moral outcasts of His day in a relationship of real friendship. The Pharisees were shocked and angry. It was not fitting, they argued, that a man of such profession should be so careless of His company. It seemed to them a matter of vital importance that the name of God should not be associated with any movement that was not of the highest moral character, and that no man of openly evil life or of doubtful reputation should be made to feel at ease about his position within a God-fearing society.

In His self-defence in these parables Jesus is saying in effect, 'These men and women whom you so despise are lost, and they cannot be expected, left to themselves, even to start out hopefully on their search for God. If they are to be found, the one who has lost them must go and seek them, and that is why I am here in the midst of them. I am the One who has lost them come to bring them back!'

How far were the Pharisees from any true understanding of Jesus Christ and His mission! Obviously they too were lost. They were as far from God and reality as the publicans whose fellowship with Jesus they were so severely criticising, but they did not know it. With all their religion they were in complete darkness. It was a religion without God, and they were all the more lost because they were unaware of how lost they were.

Unless we understand and feel and respond to something of this passion of Jesus Christ for the lost, we ourselves are in darkness. We ourselves reveal whether we have an understanding of His mind by our attitude towards those who are drawn into our midst, attracted by the grace and love of Christ, and of whom on first consideration we may be tempted to feel 'doubtful'. We also reveal the extent of our understanding of the mind of Christ by the measure of our support for that part of the work of the Church which finds Jesus particularly at work amongst those who seem to have been outcast from the more moral centres of human society.

Jesus told these two parables not simply for others but also for ourselves, and since He has so spoken, we must seek always to think of ourselves as those who were lost and are now found by Christ. Whenever we sit at a Communion service around the Lord's Table the same wonder of redeeming grace as was enacted before the eyes of the Pharisees is re-enacted before ours. Jesus Christ is receiving sinners and eating with them, and we are the sinners. Let us rejoice!

Let us not only rejoice, but let us also go out to seek that one which is still lost. Let us revise our attitude towards those whom we have been tempted to judge harshly and hastily, and towards the world. Let us think of the pathos of their situation, of the seeking love of God who yearns for them; let us think of the joy in Heaven when one sinner repents; and constrained by the love of the Good Shepherd let us live no longer unto ourselves but unto Him who died for us and rose again.

THE PRODIGAL SON

And he said, A certain man had two sons: and the younger of them said to his father, Father, give me the portion of goods that falleth to me. And he divided unto them his living. And not many days after the younger son gathered all together, and took his journey into a far country, and there wasted his substance with riotous living. And when he had spent all, there arose a mighty famine in that land; and he began to be in want. And he went and joined himself to a citizen of that country; and he sent him into his fields to feed swine. And he would fain have filled his belly with the husks that the swine did eat: and no man gave unto him. And when he came to himself, he said, How many hired servants of my father's have bread enough and to spare, and I perish with hunger! I will arise and go to my father, and will say unto him, Father, I have sinned against heaven, and before thee, and am no more worthy to be called thy son: make me as one of thy hired servants. And he arose, and came to his father. But when he was yet a great way off, his father saw him, and had compassion, and ran, and fell on his neck, and kissed him. And the son said unto him, Father, I have sinned against heaven, and in thy sight, and am no more worthy to be called thy son. But the father said to his servants, Bring forth the best robe, and put it on him; and put a ring on his hand, and shoes on his feet: and bring hither the fatted calf, and kill it; and let us eat, and be merry: for this my son was dead, and is alive again; he was lost, and is found. And they began to be merry.

Now his elder son was in the field: and as he came and drew nigh to the house, he heard musick and dancing. And he called one of the servants, and asked what these things meant. And he said unto him, Thy brother is come; and thy father hath killed the fatted calf, because he hath received him safe and sound. And he was angry, and would not go in: therefore came his father out and intreated him. And he answering said to his father, Lo, these many years do I serve thee, neither transgressed I at any time thy commandment: and yet thou never gavest me a kid, that I might make merry with my friends: but as soon as this thy son was come, which hath devoured thy living with harlots, thou hast killed for him the fatted calf. And he said unto him, Son, thou art ever with me, and all that I have is thine. It was meet that we should make merry, and be glad: for this thy brother was dead, and is alive again; and was lost, and is found.

LUKE 15.11-32

This parable was told on the occasion which called for the parables of the lost coin and the lost sheep. The Pharisees, angry at Jesus for speaking on easy terms to a company of publicans and sinners, showed their disgust and indignation. Jesus, in this story, draws for their own benefit a picture of the Pharisees that, could they have but understood it and taken its lesson in the right attitude, should have brought them back to God in deep penitence alongside the very publicans and sinners they were prone to despise.

A MAN CAN BE VERY NEAR TO GOD, AND YET VERY FAR AWAY

'*A certain man had two sons.*' Viewing the home described in the parable, we would imagine that nothing is lacking to create true happiness and to allow full and rich scope for every healthy desire on the part of those who dwell within it. The head of the home is a good father. He is wealthy and can indulge in plenty of honest fun. He can kill the fatted calf when occasion suggests, and can call on his people to eat, drink and be merry. Here is the best of homes, and in it there are two sons. They are near to everything that can give them true happiness, health and character, peace of mind, honour and wealth. They are dear to a father full of true love and goodness. 'How fortunate they are!' we say as we think of their happy circumstances. But when we watch these sons we see that there is something wrong with both of them. They are at home but they are not at home. They are living near to the father but their hearts in reality are far from home.

The younger lad is continually bitter in his thoughts as he goes about the duties of the farm. Something has spoiled the relationship between him and his father, and he has come to hate the place he lives in. Sick of the sight of the old familiar things, he feels that he will have a sense of frustration as long as he remains there. His thoughts about the old man are becoming more cynical from day to day. His heart is not at home, for he has heard of a far country where there are no such restrictions as seem to hold in this narrow existence at home. There, he imagines, there are thrilling excitements and a complete freedom and largeness of experience denied him by the very presence of his father. Thomas à Kempis once described the path to perdition in this way: 'At first there comes to the mind simply a thought, then strong imagination, then consent, and so by degrees the enemy gains full possession.' The beginnings of this process have taken place in the mind of this young man. An evil strain has been roused within him and it is being daily stimulated by a polluted imagination. He listens to every story he can hear of 'life' away from home. His appearing to live contentedly at home is becoming a mere sham. This process of estrangement from his father has been going on for some time—and the father has known it, for when one day the lad decides to force the issue and goes with his demand, '*Father, give me the portion of goods that falleth to me*,' the father expresses no surprise. He has expected this. Without any protest '*he divided unto them his living*'.

We know from the rest of the story that the elder brother would take his portion of goods with no less satisfaction than the younger, for he too had 'thoughts' about his father. He too in his mind and sympathy was as far from his father as his younger brother. He too, though living in his father's house, was not at home, because he was not at home with his father.

At home—yet not at home! Within God's house—yet far from God! How near one can be to God and at the same time how far away! We must allow the thought of this disturbing possibility to trouble us until we are sure that it is not the case with us. Most of us live very near to God. We are near to God as we move about the circles of Church life. Is not the Church His very house? We are near to God as we sit within the Church and listen to His Word read and preached to us. Is He Himself not there seeking us through His Word, as He sought through the Cross? We are near to God at the Lord's Table. And yet in reality we can be far from God even in the midst of these activities. 'This people draw near me with their mouth, and with their lips do honour me, but have removed their heart far from me.'[1] It was not only in the days of Isaiah that this sin was committed. If we are going through all the activities that take place in the normal life of the Church and at the same time our hearts are far away, then it is with us as it was with this elder son. If our wills are not wholly reconciled to the sphere where God wills that we should have fellowship with Himself in this world, if we are continuously fretting, discon-

[1] Isa. 29.13

tented, with a sense that the purpose of our life is being frustrated by limitations which we cannot break through, then it is with us as with the younger son. We can be near to God yet far away.

A Man can be Very Far from God, and yet Very Near

'*And he divided unto them his living. And not many days after the younger son gathered all together, and took his journey into a far country.*'

The father did nothing to keep the young lad at home. He handed over to him, without protest, the means he required to stray far and plunge his life into a course leading to destruction. When we read of this, the thought comes to mind, 'How easy God makes it for us to sin!' God gives us freely of the means which we can use to put us far from Himself. It almost seems as if He willingly puts into our hands the material for a whole career of flagrant sin, and having done so leaves us free to make our choice. He gives us minds that can think whatever thoughts we care to fill them with. He gives us bodies fearfully and wonderfully made, to control and to use exactly as we will. He gives us our wills, our emotional and instinctive natures and our talents, and He leaves us free to abuse them or use them as we decide. Such is the 'substance' He gives us. Through the possession of this rich endowment we can, if we will, go to fearful lengths in committing acts of sacrilege and wastefulness to reveal how far our hearts have strayed from God. We can fill our minds with blasphemy—we can use them even to prove that there is no God! We can sell our imagination to the devil. We can degrade our bodies, giving them no more significance than the dust. We can spend our emotions on vanity. God makes all this possible. The limits He sets to our evil are dreadful in the opportunities they leave to us. When we will to plunge into moral and spiritual and intellectual suicide we do not find our way barred.

The younger son took full advantage of his freedom. He strayed as far as he could and plunged recklessly into every form of debauchery. He '*took his journey into a far country and there wasted his substance with riotous living*'. He could not have gone further. He was possessed by that mood of abandonment in which a man will stop at nothing. He sought to explore every region of the realm of evil. How far he strayed from God! He broke every commandment, even the commandment 'Thou shalt not kill', for his whole life became a violent attempt to murder his father's love. Far from God!

Yet he was never really far from God. God makes it impossible for any man ever to stray far from Him. Notice that even in the far country at the height of his debauchery he was still closely tied to his father. The story reminds us that it was on his father's bounty that he lived even in his life of wastefulness. In spite of all the freedom which the young man had apparently achieved, he was nevertheless completely dependent upon his father's substance. He asked for it and received it from his father.

In a sense there is no man ever far from God or free from God. Even in Hell the Psalmist found that he was near to God: 'If I make my bed in hell, behold, thou art there.'[1] We can make the most desperate attempt, as this man did, to keep ourselves from God; nevertheless we live from day to day only through His mercy and goodness. Even the wicked live only because daily He sustains them in life and gives to them blessings out of His goodness. 'He maketh his sun to rise on the evil and on the good, and sendeth rain on the just and on the unjust.'[2] The most abandoned man on this earth, no matter how far he has plunged into wickedness, exists only because from hour to hour, by the mercy of God, he is upheld in life. The blasphemer may blaspheme and refuse entirely to acknowledge his Maker, but he can never escape the fact that he exists only because God is good. He is bound daily to contract more and more debt towards the One he hates.

One day the truth began to dawn on the prodigal that he was not so far from his father as he had imagined. He began to think, and in thinking, he found himself considering the possibility of going back home, for he had discovered the folly and vanity of the course he had taken. A thought came into his mind: '*How many hired servants of my father's have bread enough and to spare, and I perish with hunger!*' And from that moment it was all easy. Soon he was back. It was so easy to find himself reinstated; he did nothing except go home. He said, '*I will arise and go to my father, and I will say unto him, Father, I have sinned*

[1] Ps. 139.8   [2] Matt. 5.45

against heaven, and before thee, and am no more worthy to be called thy son: make me as one of thy hired servants.' But he found that the father had been waiting. Soon he was to find himself home and welcome! His father clothed him in the best robes, ordered a feast and called on everyone to rejoice because the son that was lost had been found. It had seemed so impossible in his mood of desperation in the far country that this could ever happen. He had seemed in those days, even to himself, to have strayed too far ever to return. In reality he had only to turn in his heart to God in order to be home and welcome. How far he was from God in that far country and yet how near!

There are those who say to themselves, 'I will let go of God. I will cease to care. I will cut myself off from Him for ever.' But God lets no man go. He remains still the Father. Men seek to escape from God sometimes, even to the extent of suicide, but a man cannot destroy himself. Only God can destroy. But God does not will to destroy. He wills to save. If God continues to feed us and clothe us, to keep our minds in sanity and to make His sun rise upon us from day to day, even in our rebellion against Him, it is because He wants us back. It is impossible to sever the bonds that bind a soul to God.

Even in our most godless state, if we will allow to come into our minds one thought of the possibility of returning to Him we will find that we are near to God. He is there waiting to manifest His love towards us. The father was waiting for the prodigal, for he knew he was coming. God is so near that He sees the least turn in the hearts of His children towards Him.

Dr John Paton tells of his brother, Walter. When Walter was a young lad he went to sea, and after a short time no more was heard of him. But his mother would never reconcile herself to the thought that she would never see her boy's face again. She resolved that if he ever came home, whatever the time, whatever his condition, he would be welcome. And so the last thing she did every night before she went to bed was to take the door off the latch and leave it open to admit the lost boy, should he ever come, even at midnight.

How far we can be from God, and yet at the same time how near! Jesus, when he told the story of the prodigal son, was in the company of publicans and sinners. They seemed to have strayed far, these people. They were not 'good people at heart yet misjudged by society'. They were bad in heart and life. Their past was indeed shameful. Yet they were near to God, for He, Jesus, was there in their midst. They needed only to yield to His influence to be back in their Heavenly Father's home and rejoicing in His love. There is never a time when it is not so with each one of us.

This Gospel is for Pharisees as well as Publicans

The elder brother has stayed at home all the time. Apparently he had never strayed far. But he has not changed; he is still at the same distance from his father. In spite of all the suffering they have undergone, these two are not yet reconciled. The alienation of the elder brother from the father in mind and heart is brought out when the younger brother comes back and is received with such gladness. The elder son is angry and will not go in to the house when he hears the sound of music and dancing within. His protest reveals the state of his mind. '*Lo, these many years do I serve thee, neither transgressed I at any time thy commandment: and yet thou never gavest me a kid, that I might make merry with my friends: but as soon as this thy son was come, which hath devoured thy living with harlots, thou hast killed for him the fatted calf.*'

Here is a strange fact. The prodigal, the one who had strayed farthest, was back reconciled to the father; yet the one who had apparently never strayed but had kept up such a fine appearance, showed such zeal in the business of the father, and kept all the commandments without transgressing any, was the one who in the end was the farther from the father's heart. It gives us matter for solemn consideration that Jesus addressed the parable of the prodigal son to the Pharisees as well as to the publicans and sinners. These Pharisees could have found themselves rejoicing in all the wealth of God's love if each had only said to himself, 'I too will arise and go to my Father. I too will enter into the joy of this movement whereby men and women are returning to God at the feet of Jesus Christ. God has opened His heart. I too will respond.' It was harder for the Pharisees to understand the message of Jesus than for the publicans and sinners, for the nearer we think we are to God by nature and privilege of birth, the harder it is for us to grasp the truth of the Gospel.

The father made an appeal specially to the elder son. '*Son, thou art ever with me, and all that I have is thine. It was meet that we should make merry, and be glad: for this thy brother was dead, and is alive again; and was lost, and is found.*' God has no preferences, but loves the Pharisees as much as He loves the more open sinners. The father was gentle in his reproach even towards this son whose heart was so hardened in his own self-righteousness. If he too had turned, there would have been another fatted calf, more music and dancing, and a miracle would have taken place as great as the return of the prodigal.

THE GREAT SUPPER

And when one of them that sat at meat with him heard these things, he said unto him, Blessed is he that shall eat bread in the kingdom of God. Then said he unto him, A certain man made a great supper, and bade many: and sent his servant at supper time to say to them that were bidden, Come; for all things are now ready. And they all with one consent began to make excuse. The first said unto him, I have bought a piece of ground, and I must needs go and see it: I pray thee have me excused. And another said, I have bought five yoke of oxen, and I go to prove them: I pray thee have me excused. And another said, I have married a wife, and therefore I cannot come. So that servant came, and shewed his lord these things. Then the master of the house being angry said to his servant, Go out quickly into the streets and lanes of the city, and bring in hither the poor, and the maimed, and the halt, and the blind. And the servant said, Lord, it is done as thou hast commanded, and yet there is room. And the lord said unto the servant, Go out into the highways and hedges, and compel them to come in, that my house may be filled. For I say unto you, That none of those men which were bidden shall taste of my supper.

LUKE 14.15-24

While He was speaking about the Kingdom one of the Pharisees exclaimed aloud, '*Blessed is he that shall eat bread in the kingdom of God.*' It is obvious that for this man the Kingdom of God was not much more than a pious hope to be talked about and prayed for. It was the goal of his life, certainly, to enter the Kingdom, and his aim was to ensure that one day he would find his inheritance within it, but when it was to come, he had no idea. To him the Kingdom was something future and utterly distant.

Such was not the nature of the Kingdom Jesus had come to introduce into this world and to proclaim. Therefore, to correct this wrong impression Jesus told this story in which it is clear that His teaching is in sharp contrast to the views held by the Pharisees, and indeed also to some of the views that find currency in our modern talk about the Kingdom of God.

WE CAN ENTER HERE AND NOW

'A certain man made a great supper, and bade many: and sent his servant at supper time to say to them that were bidden, Come: for all things are now ready.' Jesus' purpose is to affirm that the Kingdom of God is already here. *'Come: for all things are now ready.'* The Kingdom is a present, challenging reality. It is here and now right in the midst of this present world.

The Pharisees once asked Jesus when the Kingdom of God should come. They wanted Him to give some future date but He gave an astonishing reply: 'The Kingdom of God is among you.'[1] To Jesus, the Kingdom of God was already here in this world and His continual appeal to men is to enter this Kingdom and receive now of its blessings. 'The law and the prophets were until John,' He said on another occasion, 'since that time the kingdom of God is preached, and every man presseth into it.'[2] The Kingdom has come with His own coming, and the challenge of its immediate presence confronts men whenever the Gospel is preached. We do not need to wait to enter the Kingdom. We do not need to die before we can become citizens of the Kingdom of God.

Jesus spoke as if through His coming He had brought near to us the borders of an entirely new world, so much among us that men can enter into it now. Though this new world of the Kingdom of God is at hand, it is quite a different realm from this world of space and time, of pride and sin and disease and death, in which we are at present living. It is a world of glory and power and liberty, but it is invisible, and its presence does not radically alter this present world. Its presence cannot be seen, nevertheless it is here in all reality and power and it can be known and experienced by any believing man or woman. It does not come by a process of gradual reformation of earthly society to a state of perfection. It is therefore not something that will one day be fashioned out of this present world. It is already here as a seed cast into the midst of this present world, and through its own inherent life it is itself growing into fulness. Thus we can say that it is a new universe, a new creation, brought near through the coming of God into this world in Jesus. Yet at the same time we must say that in a way that is a

[1] Luke 17.20-21 (R.V. margin)
[2] Luke 16.16

mystery; it is connected so closely with this world as to grow out of it.

Jesus taught that there were two worlds in which men could live simultaneously. He once said, 'I am the door: by me if any man enter in, he shall be saved, and shall go in and out, and find pasture.'[1] Jesus is thinking of Himself as the door from this present world into this new divine, deathless world, the Kingdom of God, and His appeal to men is to enter through that door now. For the Kingdom of God is here and now. He taught a similar lesson when He spoke to Nicodemus and said, 'Except a man be born again, he cannot see the kingdom of God.'[2] The meaning is that a man must enter a new world if he is to see the Kingdom of God. Birth is the entrance into this world; new birth is the entrance into a new world. But this new birth is an event that can take place here and now. 'If you are born again, you will see it,' says Jesus.

In the person of Jesus Himself these two worlds have their meeting-place and their point of union. When Jesus moved among men, many people saw nothing in Him to justify the great claims He made. They saw nothing more in Him than could arise out of this world. He was to them merely human, a great teacher very much of this world—born of woman. The disciples, however, saw something else in Jesus. They saw something new, wonderful, wholly incorruptible. They saw His 'glory', as John expresses it in his Gospel. They caught a glimpse of a new world in Jesus Christ. They saw the light from another world about Him when He took them up into the mountain and was transfigured before them. There, as they knelt before Jesus, they seemed to be kneeling before the threshold of an eternal world. It was during the forty days between the Resurrection and the Ascension of Jesus that the disciples became most conscious of this new invisible world around them. Jesus came among them, then went from them as one who had two realms to move between. He was there in this world before them, yet He seemed to belong now to another realm. The sight of the risen Jesus in this world was to them like a beam of light shining into a dark shuttered room. It told them that outside, yet near at hand, there was a whole shining universe of glory. They felt that they were standing on the

[1] John 10.9   [2] John 3.3

threshold of a new, deathless age. They spoke of themselves as having entered that new world through Jesus. 'We know that we have passed from death unto life,'[1] they said. Paul speaks of Christians as those who have been 'delivered from the power of darkness and . . . translated into the kingdom of his dear Son'.[2] In a real sense for them the Kingdom of God had already come and, though citizens of this present world, they were also citizens of this new world.

'*Come: for all things are now ready.*' This is the message that the preachers of the Kingdom are commissioned to deliver. It does not mean that the Kingdom of God is not also a future Kingdom. Jesus taught that the Kingdom would come in its glory one day suddenly in the future. The veil that hides the glory of it from this present world will be torn away, and the Kingdom that has been growing and establishing itself here behind that veil will one day suddenly be revealed. But the Kingdom that will then come is the same Kingdom which we can enter now—the same Kingdom to which Jesus Christ is already the door through which He calls us.

This means that men can be assured of the eternal salvation of their souls now. It is not the fashion in these days to seek religious assurance with the anxiety with which it was pursued in previous generations. Many seem to resent the suggestion, and the claim on the part of others, that they can be assured of their eternal destiny. But the message of the New Testament is that a man can know that his eternal salvation is secure and that he is a member of the Kingdom of God, because the Kingdom of God is a realm we can enter now in a conscious act of response to the Word of Christ, after which assurance is born in the heart.

We can Enter without Preparation

'*All things are now ready.*' The Kingdom is not only here, but here in glorious wealth and completeness. Magnificent preparations have been made.

In saying this Jesus is refuting another delusion about the Kingdom of God. The Pharisee thought of the Kingdom of God as something that had to be prepared, and prepared for. He thought of it as something that required the efforts of good

[1] 1 John 3.14 [2] Col. 1.13

men like himself to complete. The Kingdom of God would come when all religious men like himself kept the law of God perfectly, but God must wait until then. That was why it was such a long way off. It needed the efforts of men to bring it in. We ourselves tend to think in the same way about the Kingdom of God. Jesus, we feel, has certainly founded it, but He has left us the task of somewhat laboriously building it up. We feel certain, of course, that it will one day come, but before that day mankind must expend labour and tears, must travail, struggle and rebel, in order to bring it in.

Is such a view of the Kingdom really in line with the teaching of Jesus on this matter? He likens the Kingdom to a glorious feast, completely ready, prepared by a munificent and hospitable man who would be offended if his guests tried to do anything to supplement the glory of the feast he has prepared. Jesus never spoke of the Kingdom in the terms we are fond of using today, as something which he has merely founded and which requires to be 'built up' or 'finished' by men. He did not speak of our building up the Kingdom, or even of our 'spreading' the Kingdom, but only of our receiving it and entering it. That is all a man can do. The final consummation of all things in this world, and the manifestation of the Kingdom in all its glory, await only God's word, God's decision, not our efforts. '*All things are now ready.*' If there is to be a process before this consummation, it is a process in which God rules over every detail. Is it not this truth that gives full significance to the words of Jesus Christ upon the Cross when He cried, 'It is finished'?[1] His work was complete and perfect. 'By one offering he hath perfected for ever them that are sanctified.'[2] Nothing more requires to be done to afford all men an entrance into this full glory. The Kingdom of God awaits us as something in which all the preparations needed have already been made.

This means that we need not prepare before we enter the full and glorious life of the Kingdom. Whatever our past has been like, however we have wasted ourselves, whatever we have lost, we need not hesitate. According to this parable, it is a very simple matter for anyone to enter this new world of God. The feast is prepared; the table is ready; the invitation goes

[1] John 19.30   [2] Heb. 10.14

out: '*Come: for all things are now ready*', and that means 'Come just as you are without delay, for God is expecting you, and he is expecting you just as you are.' He is ready for the beggars, the lame, the halt, the blind. He is prepared for those who have spent their lives in the highways and byways of life because they are not good enough or clever enough to move in the central currents. Yes, even for those we tend to call the scum of humanity the Gospel is an invitation that goes out as to all men. It tells us that we have nothing to do in order to be saved except come, accept the invitation. It tells us that we have nothing to do to build up the Kingdom of God except enter it. Nothing to do in order to be rich and privileged beyond measure except to open our lives to the wealth untold which God is ready to shower upon us. We must throw off altogether the idea that all we can do in this present life is start preparing to make ourselves worthy of entering the Kingdom of God. '*Come: for all things are now ready*,' says the message.

Of course we are bound to feel as the beggars in the highways felt: 'I am not ready for this feast.' We are bound to feel that it is a drawback that we have not wept over our past sufficiently, and that we are not ready with the repentance that God needs. But we must not allow such feelings to shut us out of the feast. Although we are not prepared, God is ready, and if we come and enter, we will soon find that God is able to make us truly repentant. No case is too difficult that it will take the lord of the feast aback. When the most desperate and wretched appear on the doorstep of the great guest chamber there will be no flurry or embarrassment within at the entrance of such a one. As Professor H. R. Mackintosh writes, 'The doors of the Father's house look out to all the winds of Heaven and they are shut neither day nor night. For the love of God is open and the heart of God is waiting. Like the entrance to a great city hospital they are never closed. However late the wanderer may arrive, however long after the rest he may stumble in broken and weary, he will find that he has been expected.'

Only the Desperate will Come

When we read the remainder of the parable we discover that many of the invited guests excused themselves, and it is obvious from their excuses that they did not want to come. They did not think it worth while entering. They simply went on with their business as usual.

But the poor and the maimed, and the halt and the blind from the streets and lanes of the city, and the beggars and tramps from the highways and byways came. They came gladly and there was plenty of room for all. The word went out '*Yet there is room*', and all the time the previously invited guests went on with their business, not knowing the glory of the feast they were despising nor realising that their desperate, outcast brethren were enjoying a feast that was life indeed. If they too had only been desperate for it, they too would have enjoyed the feast. The invitation came to them—even to those self-satisfied busy people—but they did not seem to realise its value.

One of the most acute problems for believing minds in this world was once expressed by Dr James Denney when he uttered his amazement that so many are perishing in a world where Christ died for all. Does this parable not give us a clue as to why there is so much blindness in this world to the fact that here and now, through faith in Christ, there is a great salvation to be enjoyed? Many receive the invitation; they may listen to it every Sunday in church. But business, and material things are of more importance. Moreover, they have to take so much of the Gospel on faith. The invited guests had to have faith in accepting the invitation. They could not see the great supper when the news of it reached them. It was just a message—a man came and told them about it. Likewise it is just a man that many see when they hear news of the Kingdom of God—a man in the pulpit, perhaps, telling them about a great feast prepared by the gracious Lord and Saviour, whose hospitality they can enjoy here and now. They cannot see the great feast, they can only see the man and hear his word, and they have to take too much on faith in this matter of the Kingdom of God. This world seems to offer them very much more in shapes and forms that they can handle and see and feel. Jesus teaches here that it is those who are beggars and the poor in this world, and who have the least expectations about what it can offer them, who are most likely to give heed to the message of the Kingdom.

Yet even these have to be compelled and pressed into the

Kingdom. So anxious is the lord of the feast that he is prepared to use every means to win the desperate, though he shuts out those who manifest no desire for his hospitality. '*Compel them to come in, that my house may be filled.*' There is a humility about this host which attracts the wayfarers, and at the same time a lordliness that resists the haughty. It is the empty who are filled and the full that are sent away empty.

'When I had been long vexed with this fear,' said John Bunyan, describing his terror lest he should lose Heaven, 'and was scarce able to take one step more, these words broke upon my mind—"Compel them to come in, that my house may be filled." These words, and especially them "and yet there is room" were sweet words to me; for truly I thought that by them I saw there was place enough in Heaven for me, and methought that when the Lord Jesus did speak these words He then did think of me; and that He, knowing that the time would come when I should be afflicted with fear that there was no place left in His bosom, did before speak this word and leave it upon record, that I might find help thereby against this vile temptation.'

THE UNJUST STEWARD

And he said also unto his disciples, There was a certain rich man, which had a steward; and the same was accused unto him that he had wasted his goods. And he called him, and said unto him, How is it that I hear this of thee? give an account of thy stewardship; for thou mayest be no longer steward. Then the steward said within himself, What shall I do? for my lord taketh away from me the stewardship: I cannot dig; to beg I am ashamed. I am resolved what to do, that, when I am put out of the stewardship, they may receive me into their houses. So he called every one of his lord's debtors unto him, and said unto the first, How much owest thou unto my lord? And he said, An hundred measures of oil. And he said unto him, Take thy bill, and sit down quickly, and write fifty. Then said he to another, And how much owest thou? And he said, An hundred measures of wheat. And he said unto him, Take thy bill, and write fourscore. And the lord commended the unjust steward, because he had done wisely: for the children of this world are in their generation wiser than the children of light. And I say unto you, Make to yourselves friends of the mammon of unrighteousness; that, when ye fail, they may receive you into everlasting habitations. He that is faithful in that which is least is faithful also in much: and he that is unjust in the least is unjust also in much. If therefore ye have not been faithful in the unrighteous mammon, who will commit to your trust the true riches? And if ye have not been faithful in that which is another man's, who shall give you that which is your own? No servant can serve two masters: for either he will hate the one, and love the other; or else he will hold to the one, and despise the other. Ye cannot serve God and mammon.

LUKE 16.1-13

This story of clever crime is exactly the kind of material that a popular newspaper editor would put on his front page under bold headlines. The details it furnishes of cool and clever embezzlement are the stuff the public wants. It is quite possible that it is a true story. The crime may have been well known in recent local history.

The criminal was a factor or estate overseer for an important local landlord. He was careless and his books got out of order. He did not keep check of either people or materials. He slipped into ways of conducting business that were easy for himself but ruinous for his master. Affairs developed till one day the fatal message came from the master that on a certain date the steward must appear before him with the estate books, to explain the situation and give an account of all the discrepancies and losses.

The steward, in reaction to this challenge, took a clever and very bold course of action. He changed his tactics. He said to himself, 'This game I have been enjoying is now up. I will have a last desperate fling on another line to make sure that when I am put out of a job and my house I will have plenty of good friends to help me and many hands ready to do me a good turn.' He called a meeting of all the people with whom he had throughout the years done business, and who owed his master accounts that were unpaid for years past, and huge in amount. No doubt there was great speculation among the debtors beforehand as to what the meeting could be about but it was not till the day arranged that the plan was revealed. The steward came into the meeting in a lordly manner. He began with a few words about the hardness of the times and went on to speak about the bad old days in the past when men were expected to pay their debts to the full. Now he was going to change all that. Why should not a new régime be started? Was it not time that people with wealth began to be a little more merciful and to share it out, releasing debts as the law of Moses commanded? Moreover, with whom should they share their wealth, if not with those who dealt with them in business?

'*So he called every one of his lord's debtors unto him, and said unto the first, How much owest thou unto my lord? And he said, An hundred measures of oil. And he said unto him, Take thy bill, and sit down quickly, and write fifty. Then said he to another, And how much owest thou? And he said, An hundred measures of wheat. And he said unto him, Take thy bill, and write fourscore.*'

He went round the company as if he were a benevolent millionaire with half a dozen fortunes to give away. With magnificent lordliness he altered his master's accounts so that the true state of affairs could never be discovered. He released one man from half his debt, another from a quarter of his debt, another from three quarters of it, giving all and each the impression that they were now very much in his own debt.

The reason for his action is clear. He was a desperate man

on the eve of a crash. He needed friends. He could not trust himself with money, for he could not keep money. He would not do menial work to earn his living and he was ashamed to beg. What he needed most was good friends who would support him in the hard days to come. He was going to make friends at the expense of his master, so that when the crash came he would not be left alone.

Here, in the example set us by the boldness and skill and desperate energy with which this wicked man acted, Jesus sets before us a pattern of the forethought and prudence He would like to see in the children of the Kingdom in the matter of seeking heavenly riches. '*The Lord commended the unjust steward.*' He held him up for an example to be copied, not, of course, in his dishonesty, but in his prudence, skill and energy.

OUR SITUATION IN LIFE IS ALWAYS CRITICAL

In the very fact that Jesus commended this man's example to us it is implied that our situation in life is very similar to his.

This man was faced by a crisis. His whole situation in life was going to be changed, and the question before him was how best to prepare for this change. His old ways of life would no longer fit the new situation with which he was to be faced. His present standards and habits, even his pleasures, would fail to meet the new circumstances. There would have to be a radical alteration in the things in which he trusted. He was, as it were, facing the prospect, whether he wished it or not, of having to adopt a new mode of life in which the currency which had stood him so well in his old world would not be accepted as valid. Such was his situation, and the steward faced up frankly and realistically to the approaching crisis. The implication is that we too are placed like this steward. We too are faced with a crisis, that is going to mean for us a change as complete and revolutionary. 'Look at him,' says Jesus, 'there is a man in your situation; copy him in realistic thinking.'

Jesus is not here saying anything that is not repeatedly said to us in the New Testament, where we are warned often that things as they are may be changed at any time, and that he alone is wise who will face this fact. The Kingdom of God is to come, and will inevitably come. In this Kingdom the whole mode of human existence will be quite different from that to which we are at present accustomed, and to which we cling as if it were our life itself. The currency that passes in this present world is of no use in this Kingdom of God which is at hand and which is pressing in upon this world. Here, in this present existence, it matters to be 'pushing'. Alas for the man who does not succeed in the struggle for position! But there, in the Kingdom of God, the first are last and the last first. Here the riches that perish with the using are the main currency. Money matters and money speaks. But there in the Kingdom of God is a new kind of treasure which Jesus calls '*true riches*', 'riches towards God', a kind of wealth that no man can heap up here, in either a spiritual or a material way. Here in this world 'the lust of the flesh, and the lust of the eyes, and the pride of life'[1] are the dominant motives in the choice of man's pleasure, but there, in the Kingdom of God, these things have all passed away and the Will of God is the ruling consideration in the hearts of its citizens. Here, blessed are those that are filled with abundance, but in the Kingdom of God 'blessed are they which do hunger and thirst'.[2] Here in this present existence there is room for concealment. Many men hide most of their lives from the eyes of their fellows. But there life is lived wholly in the light, and no secrets can be hidden.

In commending the unjust steward Our Lord is urging us to face these facts, and to be more frank than we are wont to be in admitting to ourselves the strangely uncertain nature of our hold on this present life. We stand in need of such a warning. These days we pride ourselves on our frankness in matters which to previous generations were taboo, especially in matters of sex; nevertheless we are not nearly so frank as our fathers were in facing up realistically to the transitory nature of this present world. One symptom of this lack of realism can be seen in the widespread, and in some cases regrettable, reluctance to reveal to those who are mortally ill the fact that they are going to die. It is wisdom, surely, that we should be prepared for every type of crisis in life, and above all that we should be prepared for the great and sudden change that our own death will bring upon us. Paul speaks of himself as prepared. 'We know,' he writes, 'that if our earthly house of this tabernacle were dissolved, we have a building of God, an house not

[1] 1 John 2.16   [2] Matt. 5.6

made with hands, eternal in the heavens.'[1] It is indeed in but a 'tabernacle' that we live here on earth. Our tenure of our goods, our homes, is most uncertain. At any moment the crisis, in which we will be ushered into a new form of life whose nature we cannot conceive, may come upon us. We shall all be changed, for we cannot escape, and we shall be changed either for our eternal gain or for our eternal loss. There is an old story of an elder who lay dying on a night when the wind was blowing furiously outside and laying the snow in deep drifts. His daughter started to read him a chapter from the Bible. 'Na, na, lassie!' he said. 'The storm's up noo. I thatched ma hoose in the calm weather.'

WE MUST ADAPT OURSELVES NOW TO THE APPROACHING CRISIS

The unjust steward not only faced up frankly to the coming crisis in his affairs, he also acted realistically. Another man in such circumstances, when he saw the danger signal in front of him warning him of the possible collapse of his whole way of life, might have abandoned himself completely to careless living. 'Let us eat and drink; for tomorrow we die.'[2] Since the crisis was inevitable, the steward might have decided to have his last few weeks of fun as undisturbed as possible by the thought of it. But he acted differently. He boldly prepared for the crisis with all his powers and resources. During the few days of his freedom that remained he became a man spurred to desperate action. Tirelessly he thought and planned. Day and night he was on the alert. All his powers and energies were concentrated on seizing the short-lived opportunity, and the imagination and shrewdness with which he acted are indeed remarkable. He had become a man alive with purpose and cleverness.

'*The lord commended the unjust steward, because he had done wisely.*' Jesus desired to find in the activity of His disciples in His service the same skill, boldness and energy as this man showed, and He lamented because too often He found it lacking. '*The children of this world are in their generation wiser than the children of light.*' There must be no fatalism or dreary resignation in the attitude of the Christian as he faces up to his critical life-situation and the demands which that situation makes upon

[1] 2 Cor. 5.1   [2] 1 Cor. 15.32

him. Jesus always urged men to vigorous action in the face of the inevitable coming of the Kingdom of God. 'Strive to enter in at the strait gate: for many, I say unto you, will seek to enter in, and shall not be able.'[1] While the door remains open and the least appearance of any opportunity lies before us, we must put every particle of energy and skill we have into ensuring for ourselves an entrance into the Kingdom. 'The kingdom of heaven suffereth violence, and the violent take it by force.'[2]

There is no more regrettable feature of our Church life than the listless attitude of our members towards the great issues Jesus Christ has raised in bringing nigh the Kingdom of God. The average Christian of today is not willing to put into the matter of his religion even a fraction of the perseverance, patience and intelligent concentration that the man who knows only this present world gives towards perfecting his technical knowledge for his business, or even towards his hobbies. Yet Jesus tells us that if we are to hope to secure true riches we must put even more energy into their pursuit than the world gives to its business. At the battle of Waterloo Nathan Meyer Rothschild was a spectator and is said to have watched the battle from a shot-proof tent. At sunset, when he saw the French beginning to give way, he sprang into the saddle and galloped all night, reaching the shore of the Channel at daybreak. He bribed a fisherman to take him across and reached London thirty-six hours before anyone else had heard the news of our victory. He used these hours in trading on the stock exchange to such advantage that he gained nearly two million pounds. Such is the action of a man of the world seeking earthly riches. If a man would pursue heavenly riches he must copy the man of the world who is so ruthless in his pursuit of the things of this world. He must bring to bear in his pursuit all the energy and desperate zeal that a man will give on earth who is faced with a desperate crisis that can be met only by desperate action. He must not be outdone by the *'children of this world'*.

For example, we can think of the unwillingness of the ordinary Christian to persevere and endure in prayer and in the cultivation of fellowship with God. Many give up trying to pray because they do not experience quick and visible results. Because their experiments seem to come to nothing, they soon

[1] Luke 13.24   [2] Matt. 11.12

lose heart. We can compare this attitude with that of men in the sphere of business or of science or art. When John Ruskin examined Turner's papers he found at least twenty thousand slips upon which the artist had sketched initial themes. Many a scientist has had no success until thousands of patient and detailed experiments have come to nothing. Jesus would urge us to take a lesson from the ways of this world.

The rogue in the parable was self-centred. We, however, must not make the message we read from it too self-centred. We must realise that it is as urgent that others should be pressed into the Kingdom of God as that we ourselves should enter therein, and in all our activity in seeking to win the outside world for Christ we must remember the example of this clever, desperate, energetic man. It is to our shame that in the matter of winning men for Christ we should find ourselves so outshone in zeal and skill by those whose cause is purely national or political. In the sphere of evangelism there is room for the exercise of all our wits and powers of invention. We must not be afraid to allow our sense of the desperate urgency of the problem to spur us on to every kind of bold action.

How to Obtain the True Riches

The plan of action decided upon by the unjust steward was very brilliant. He saw that in his situation it was of no use to amass money. He could not keep it. Even if he did manage to keep some till the crisis came, it might be taken from him if he were arrested and his goods confiscated. But one thing he could do between now and the day of his arrest was to make friends. His master might deprive him of his home and his property and his money, but he could not take away his friends. If he could put people in his debt between now and the day of his failure, it might mean everything to him in the new situation that would then arise. If he had good friends then, he could call on them in the days of hardship and they would be there to help him in his need. This was his policy. He resolved to make friends who would be there even if the worst happened. He would trade on their friendship and live on their bounty when every other resource had failed. It was for this reason that he was so ruthless in his final conspiracy and so generous towards his prospective 'friends'.

We would be wise to take the obvious hint that what matters in the midst of the great crisis that faces each one of us is friendship. There is One whose friendship can be made now. This friendship will never fail us, though everything else is likely to fail in the crisis. Certainly money will fail us in that hour; this vital personal relationship will stand. When we are faced, through the challenging words of Jesus, with the necessity of laying up for ourselves 'treasures in heaven',[1] we are apt to think that this is a very difficult thing to do, involving years of painful self-discipline and 'character training'. This is a false idea, for the essential thing in Christianity is making friends with Jesus Christ, and the true 'treasures in heaven' are simply this friendship with God in Christ. Jesus called men into this friendship. 'Henceforth I call you not servants . . . but friends.'[2] The *'true riches'* spoken of in this parable are nothing more than the friendship of God in Jesus Christ. The heavenly treasure does not lie in the moral character we form within our present personality through stern discipline of will and emotion or anything like that. Such 'righteousness' will be shown up as 'filthy rags' in the day of crisis. To lay up heavenly riches means to come now to Jesus Christ in personal trust and love. This friendship will abide for ever.

Jesus, in passing, urges that if a man is wise, he will put even his material resources into this matter of the service of God. *'Make to yourselves friends of the mammon of unrighteousness.'* All reliable commentators are agreed that Jesus in these words is calling for a wise stewardship of money in His service. That money is usually an evil thing is freely admitted here by Jesus. He calls it the *'mammon of unrighteousness'*. It is the source of trouble and strife on the earth. It causes wars, murders, hatreds, family quarrels. It is a tainted evil thing, and yet it can be made the instrument for forming those relationships that will last into the world beyond. The unjust steward made friends with his lord's money, using it to bind human hearts to himself. Filthy stolen money it was, but his action gives us a hint of what money can do in the service of God. Happy is the man who learns that by the grace of God, not only his brains and his energy and his imagination can be thrown into the service of God for an everlasting purpose, but also his money.

[1] Matt. 6.20   [2] John 15.15

THE MARKS OF THE TRUE CITIZEN

THE SELFISH NEIGHBOUR, AND THE IMPORTUNATE WIDOW

And he said unto them, Which of you shall have a friend, and shall go unto him at midnight, and say unto him, Friend, lend me three loaves; for a friend of mine in his journey is come to me, and I have nothing to set before him? And he from within shall answer and say, Trouble me not: the door is now shut, and my children are with me in bed; I cannot rise and give thee. I say unto you, Though he will not rise and give him, because he is his friend, yet because of his importunity he will arise and give him as many as he needeth. And I say unto you, Ask, and it shall be given you; seek, and ye shall find; knock, and it shall be opened unto you. For everyone that asketh receiveth; and he that seeketh findeth; and to him that knocketh it shall be opened. If a son shall ask bread of any of you that is a father, will he give him a stone? or if he ask a fish, will he for a fish give him a serpent? Or if he shall ask an egg, will he offer him a scorpion? If ye then, being evil, know how to give good gifts unto your children: how much more shall your heavenly Father give the Holy Spirit to them that ask him?

LUKE 11.5-13

And he spake a parable unto them to this end, that men ought always to pray, and not to faint; saying, There was in a city a judge, which feared not God, neither regarded man: and there was a widow in that city; and she came unto him, saying, Avenge me of mine adversary. And he would not for a while: but afterward he said within himself, Though I fear not God, nor regard man; yet because this widow troubleth me, I will avenge her, lest by her continual coming she weary me. And the Lord said, Hear what the unjust judge saith. And shall not God avenge his own elect, which cry day and night unto him, though he bear long with them? I tell you that he will avenge them speedily. Nevertheless when the Son of man cometh, shall he find faith on the earth? LUKE 18.1-8

In these two parables Jesus teaches the same lesson, that men are always to pray and not to give up. In each we are given a picture of someone in desperate need. In the one it is a woman who must remain in despair and wretchedness until justice is done to her. In the other it is a man who needs bread to set before a hungry traveller who has called upon him unexpectedly at midnight. Spurred on by their desperate sense of need, in both cases they are seeking by sheer force of will to disturb the peace of someone who alone can meet their need. The woman is day and night waylaying a judge, pestering him for justice. The man is seeking to rouse from his bed a selfish neighbour at midnight. In both cases there is a reluctance to be moved on the part of the one whom they are pestering, and the petitioners have to go on and on making a disturbance. The neighbour is unwilling to get out of his warm bed, surrounded as he is by his children all snugly tucked in. The judge is a hard man who fears neither God nor man, and very little can move him. But in both cases, for no other reason than that of a final desire to get rid of the petitioner whose persistent cries and knocks are becoming a thorough nuisance, the person who is besought gives way. The man in bed gets up and opens the door with an ill grace, and for the sake of peace he throws out the bread. The judge, for purely selfish reasons, yields to the woman's request.

Jesus tells these stories in order to urge us to be persistent in prayer. '*Ask, and it shall be given you; seek, and ye shall find; knock, and it shall be opened unto you,*' said Jesus after he told one of these stories. The tense of the verb in the Greek would justify the translation 'Keep on asking; keep on seeking; keep on knocking.'

It is obvious that these parables do not teach us everything about prayer that Jesus taught, but they are there to encourage us to persevere in prayer.

THE POSITION OF THE MAN WHO PRAYS

It is a fact of the utmost significance that when the disciples went to Jesus and asked Him to teach them to pray, in reply to their request Jesus told this story of a man who found himself one day at the end of his resources, faced with a claim that he could not meet unless he could successfully obtain help from another source. If we are to begin to learn to pray, we must realise that our position in life is like that of this needy man. Prayer will arise when men realise the urgency of their position in life. The man at midnight became a man of incessant, constant prayer to his neighbour because he was in a desperate situation. He knew the urgency of it and he knew from where alone his help could come.

The woman in the street pestering the judge had also discovered her critical position in life. She could not live unless the judge gave her justice. Her whole existence was at stake. She had no other alternative than to keep continually waylaying him with her shrill petitions for vengeance. So Jesus suggests that if we realised how much the life of our soul and our whole welfare depend on the things that can be won by prayer, and by prayer alone, we would indeed begin to pray. If we are to become men and women of prayer, we must find ourselves in a position of prayer—the position in which we realise our own personal need as the woman did, or realise vividly the need of our neighbour whom we are pledged to help as the man at midnight did.

It is not so difficult as we might think, to find ourselves in this position of the man who must pray. If we began to take risks for the sake of Jesus Christ, launching out more on faith in a Christian service that would tax all our energies and powers, perhaps then we would soon find ourselves with no power of our own, our own resources having failed, helpless on our knees with prayer at last becoming a reality. We might then find ourselves with others depending on what we had to give them, and yet with our cupboards empty and ourselves unable to meet the need, literally at midnight in desperate prayer to God to help us to meet the demands that the work had brought upon us. And if we were willing to face Christ's judgment on our own life more frankly, looking at ourselves more in the light of His life and His truth, we would find that our life is so poor, so empty, so unrighteous, that we would soon be on our knees imploring Him to fill us and to cleanse us and to renew us. Moreover, if we were more filled with the spirit of righteousness, and our conscience was more sensitive to the wrongs and injustices that are done in this world, if we realised more the tremendous volume of suffering that has been created by the wrongdoing of evil men upon this earth, we would find ourselves also crying day and night desperately with indignation to the Judge of all to avenge the wrongs on earth. This also is a position in which prayer would arise in our hearts.

If we are Christians, we live always in this position from which prayer should arise. For when a man lives by faith in Christ, he has indeed given up everything by which hitherto he may have lived and every other source of help but Christ. He has become an empty man with no resources, no powers of his own, no life of his own, and daily he must turn—in desperation sometimes he feels he has to turn—to Him from whom he lives. If a man is spiritually alive in Christ, he will not ask whether he should pray or not. He will realise that he simply has to pray if he is to live at all in the spirit. If men and women do not feel this about prayer, does it not mean that perhaps they are not alive in Christ? When a tadpole becomes a frog and starts venturing out of the water it is bound to find that even though it has never breathed crude air in its life, it has to begin to breathe now. So, when man truly comes to Christ, he finds that in order to live in Christ, he must pray.

Such is Christ's teaching about the position of the man who prays. Let us ask ourselves if we have begun to feel this vital and desperate need of the soul for God, for forgiveness, peace and divine strength, which drives us to true, importunate, life-winning prayer. Many of us say our prayers, but the important question is whether we pray when we say our prayers. Perhaps we need to go to the feet of Christ and say, 'Lord, teach me to pray. Help me to see my own shameful, desperate need of Thee and of Thy blessings, and help me to pray so that I may win it. Show me the desperate need of my friends and give me the fervent love that will inspire intense and winning prayer for them. Give me a vision of the sin and need of the world till I become a true intercessor on behalf of the needs and sorrows of all mankind.' When we know the desperation that inspires prayer, we may soon find ourselves truly praying.

The first step in prayer, then, is to realise how empty and hungry and desperate and helpless we are without prayer. We must ask God to put us in the position of the man who prays.

The Attitude of the Man who Prays

The central characters in these stories are two people who are fighting as for their lives, battling with all the force of will they have, to obtain their needs, and actually battling against the will of another. In all true prayer the will of the praying man is active and concentrated to an intense degree.

THE SELFISH NEIGHBOUR, AND THE WIDOW 85

We think often of prayer as being a matter of quiet and placid meditation. The setting of the life of prayer we imagine to be beautifully expressed in the hymn:

> O Sabbath rest by Galilee!
> O calm of hills above,
> Where Jesus knelt to share with Thee
> The silence of eternity,
> Interpreted by love!

Prayer, we imagine, is an exercise where the soul and the will are at ease and rest in God, but in coming to this conclusion we have allowed our imagination to go too far. This element of restfulness may be an element in prayer, but the main element in prayer is shown here. Prayer is a forceful and restless activity of the will. It is significant that in the New Testament it is during His hours of prayer, as in the Garden of Gethsemane and at the grave of Lazarus, that we see Jesus agonised and groaning within Himself. It was when He arose from prayer that His mind was at rest. 'Prayers are battles,' says Joseph Parker. Prayer was the battlefield of our Lord's life in which He won all His victories. 'In the days of his flesh . . . he offered up prayers and supplications with strong crying and tears.'[1]

There is a mystery here. The free will of man comes into action in the sphere of prayer to an intense degree. Prayer is the one great field for the unfettered activity of the freedom of the man who sees the desperate need of his own heart and who knows where alone that need can be met. Prayer involves a conflict of wills. It is the bringing of human free will to bear upon God in a meeting which can become, as in the case of Jacob, a real wrestling with God.[2]

THE THEME OF THE MAN WHO PRAYS

The theme running through the prayers of the man and woman shown in these parables is the definite and concrete need of the situations in which they are placed. The woman is praying probably about money. The man is praying about bread. These are very concrete and humdrum matters. There is not much room for courtesy or preliminary remarks or any literary frills in the petitions they utter. Their need is too desperate for such things to have any prominence. They mention all the

---

[1] Heb. 5.7   [2] Gen. 32

time their dire need and they keep on bringing this one matter before him whose help they seek.

When we go to pray we must not leave behind us the concrete needs of our own life. There is a misunderstanding to be cleared from certain minds on this point, for some in their prayers imagine that they must seek to forget about the world. Prayer to them is chiefly a retreat from the hard problems of life, and when they go to pray they try to divorce themselves from their daily life, shutting the whole of the world outside. Now this is surely to make prayer into a kind of playacting that reaches even the level of hypocrisy. When we pray to God, we must go to God as we are. We are worried men and women with all the needs of the world pressing in upon us, and we must talk to God frankly about our whole life's situation. Paul gave this advice to the Philippians when he said, 'Be careful for nothing; but in every thing by prayer and supplication with thanksgiving let your requests be made known unto God.'[1] All their anxieties are to be made the subject of prayer and their prayers are to be centred on these anxieties. We are to make the burden of our prayer the concrete problems of our own lives and the needs of others that are laid upon our hearts. We have to pray for our daily bread. God is our Father; if a thing matters to us, and makes us anxious or worried or desperate, it matters to Him, and we must not pretend when we go to Him that our needs are not what they really are.

There is, however, no suggestion here that we should pray for luxuries. Our prayers are for our needs. Perhaps other parts of the Scripture encourage us to pray for luxuries. The text, 'Delight thyself also in the Lord; and he shall give thee the desires of thy heart',[2] is indeed a challenge to pray for more than our needs, but no such encouragement is given in these parables for allowing either superfluous luxuries or ridiculous trivialities any prominence among the matters about which we should pray. Prayer is mainly for necessities. We must remember, of course, that Jesus is not here giving His whole teaching about prayer. There is room in true prayer for courtesies, for prayer is much more than asking for things. Prayer consists of thanksgiving, confession and adoration, as

[1] Phil. 4.6   [2] Ps. 37.4

well as petition. We need not be ashamed to confess, however, that at the centre of our prayers there is the matter of our concrete urgent need in daily life.

Some people seem to think that prayer itself is a luxury that is only to be enjoyed by certain fortunate Christians who are born with a natural faculty for praying and to whom it seems an easy matter. They themselves, they imagine, not being naturally religious, must be content to dispense with such extra dainties of the Christian life as are brought in with prayer and must be content with bread. An ordinary religion with not too much devotion is good enough for them. Prayer to them is a joyful, but all too expensive, extra luxury of the Christian life which they think they can do without. To Jesus Christ that view of prayer is nonsense. A Christian can no more dispense with prayer than he can dispense with his daily bread. Prayer is asking for bread for your soul's life. Prayer is a means of having the most concrete and desperate needs of life met victoriously, and if a man never seeks to win what can be won in prayer alone, then his life will suffer and others will suffer with him. Prayer is something we cannot do without. If we do not get our answer to prayer, we can do nothing except keep on praying. The only substitute for little prayer is more prayer, and the only cure for the despair and perplexity that come through prayer is to pray on.

The Difficulties besetting the Man who Prays

Jesus frankly admits here that prayer can be a difficult pursuit. He warns us that when we pray God may seem to us very like the selfish neighbour. We will be tempted to feel that He is sitting there in Heaven, lazy and comfortable, and does not understand our position. In fact, we may be tempted to feel that God has replied to us and has mocked us. In our first attempt to pray we will feel that whereas we asked for bread, God has given us a stone, and we are hungry still; whereas we asked for a fish, God has given us a serpent; and whereas we asked for an egg, He has given us a scorpion. Jesus understands our feelings and our human hearts and He knows perfectly the difficulties of prayer. Prayer, He warns us in the parable of the importunate widow, may seem to us the most God-forsaken, perplexing, worrying thing we undertake. When we pray we are to expect to feel like that woman, that the task we are at is hopeless, for the One we are speaking to is deaf, and hard and far away. We will feel that our prayers are feeble and foolish things to pit against all the resistance there seems to be in the beyond. No answer will seem to come. Like David, we will say, 'O my God, I cry in the daytime, but thou hearest not; and in the night season, and am not silent.'[1]

It is good for us to take this lesson to heart, and to be sober in our expectations of what a life of prayer is going to be like. It will be full of difficulties, and our faith must face them. God may seem to be regardless of our need, regardless even of human justice:

> I said, I will seek God, and forth I went
> To seek Him in the clearness of the sky:
> But over me stood unendurably
> Only a pitiless, sapphire firmament.

Such may be our feelings if we persevere in the prayer life. We must not be put off. We must steel ourselves against giving way to the changes of mood and feelings we will pass through. Whatever our feelings, we are to pray on. We must not judge by immediate answers. When no answer comes, we must go on praying. We are to expect delays. The judge would not listen to the woman at first, says Jesus, but all the while that nothing seemed to be happening the resistance was breaking down.

THE CONFIDENCE OF THE MAN WHO PRAYS

The answer to such desperate prayer is sure. It is absolutely guaranteed in the teaching of Jesus in these parables. '*Ask, and it shall be given you.*'

The answer may seem to be delayed. God may seem slow, as the selfish neighbour was slow in getting out of bed. But if even this man's selfishness and hard-heartedness were overcome by the persistent knocking of his neighbour, what of God who loves His children more than any earthly father? Shall He cast off one of His children hungry? What of God, who abhors evil and hates injustice? Shall not the Judge of all the earth do right when the cries of His people go up from earth pleading with Him to right the wrongs in His world? Yes, says

[1] Ps. 22.2

Christ, He will answer. '*If ye then, being evil, know how to give good gifts unto your children: how much more shall your heavenly Father give . . . to them that ask him?*' '*Shall not God avenge his own elect, which cry day and night unto him, though he bear long with them?*' If He seems to delay the answer, there are good reasons for the delay. He may be preparing us to receive a greater gift than we have ever thought of or asked for. 'For a small moment have I forsaken thee; but with great mercies will I gather thee. In a little wrath I hid my face from thee for a moment; but with everlasting kindness will I have mercy on thee, saith the Lord thy Redeemer.'[1]

Prayer is answered. The prayers of the man at midnight and the woman in the street were answered, and they were answered because they battled, because they put their whole will and all their powers and energies into their prayers. Let us be careful when we speak of prayer not to be too definite in asserting that 'prayer does not change the will of God'. These parables give us abundant justification for saying that prayer can change the will of God, or at least for saying, in the words of P. T. Forsyth, that 'it is the will of God that we should bend His will to ours through prayer'. Prayer is precisely the sphere where man has most freedom of will to assert his will, but it is the free will of the despairing man, the free will of the man who clings to God, not in pride or self-assertion, but in faith and true contrition.

David, in one of his psalms[2] tells us that God once upset the whole universe to answer his prayer. He was distressed nigh unto death: 'In my distress I called upon the Lord . . . and my cry came before Him, even into his ears.' And he goes on to describe what God did to answer his prayer: 'Then the earth shook and trembled; the foundations also of the hills moved and were shaken, because He was wroth. . . . He bowed the heavens also, and came down. . . . And he rode upon a cherub, and did fly: yea, he did fly upon the wings of the wind. . . . Clouds passed, hail stones and coals of fire. The Lord also thundered in the heavens. . . . He sent out his arrows, and scattered them; and he shot out lightnings, and discomfited them. . . . The foundations of the world were discovered. . . . He sent from above, he took me, he drew me out of many

[1] Isa. 54.7-8   [2] Ps. 18.6-16

waters.' This is the confidence of the man who prays. He believes that the Lord will upset the whole universe to answer the cry of one poor man who calls upon the Lord to deliver him.

THE TWO DEBTORS

And one of the Pharisees desired him that he would eat with him. And he went into the Pharisee's house, and sat down to meat. And, behold, a woman in the city, which was a sinner, when she knew that Jesus sat at meat in the Pharisee's house, brought an alabaster box of ointment, and stood at his feet behind him weeping, and began to wash his feet with tears, and did wipe them with the hairs of her head, and kissed his feet, and anointed them with the ointment. Now when the Pharisee which had bidden him saw it, he spake within himself, saying, This man, if he were a prophet, would have known who and what manner of woman this is that toucheth him: for she is a sinner. And Jesus answering said unto him, Simon, I have somewhat to say unto thee. And he saith, Master, say on. There was a certain creditor which had two debtors: the one owed five hundred pence, and the other fifty. And when they had nothing to pay, he frankly forgave them both. Tell me therefore, which of them will love him most? Simon answered and said, I suppose that he, to whom he forgave most. And he said unto him, Thou hast rightly judged. And he turned to the woman, and said unto Simon, Seest thou this woman? I entered into thine house, thou gavest me no water for my feet: but she hath washed my feet with tears, and wiped them with the hairs of her head. Thou gavest me no kiss: but this woman since the time I came in hath not ceased to kiss my feet. My head with oil thou didst not anoint: but this woman hath anointed my feet with ointment. Wherefore I say unto thee, Her sins, which are many, are forgiven; for she loved much: but to whom little is forgiven, the same loveth little. And he said unto her, Thy sins are forgiven. And they that sat at meat with him began to say within themselves, Who is this that forgiveth sins also? And he said to the woman, Thy faith hath saved thee; go in peace.

LUKE 7.36-50

Jesus told the parable of the two debtors to explain what lay behind the apparently strange behaviour of a certain woman towards Himself. She had interrupted Him as He sat at a meal in the house of Simon the Pharisee. Suddenly she appeared in the room and went up to Jesus, obviously intending to anoint Him with the box of very costly ointment she was carrying, but she was so overcome with emotion when she saw Him that she was unable to fulfil her intention in a calm and controlled manner; instead she burst into a fit of violent weeping, kissing His feet, washing them with her tears and wiping them with her hair. Only after this demonstration did she anoint Him as she had intended.

Jesus accepted it all calmly, showing no surprise and taking no offence. He understood perfectly what the woman meant, and offered neither rebuke nor restraint. He seemed rather to encourage her. But in the eyes of Simon the Pharisee who was the host this was shocking behaviour both on the part of the woman and on the part of Jesus. Simon had no objection to the ordinary intruders who were in the habit of coming into his supper room. It was a custom for friends of invited guests to seek them out at supper parties when they wanted to talk with them. Simon, like every decent householder of the time, had cushions laid around the walls for any such persons who cared to come and chat with the guests during the meal. His misgivings on this occasion were on account of the type of woman Jesus seemed to be encouraging to come around Himself. She was the worst imaginable, and Jesus was taking her effusive attentions as a matter of course! Simon felt disgusted. He had thought Jesus was a true prophet and that was why he had asked Him to supper. Now he was beginning to regret having done so.

But Simon did not know the whole story. Something he could not yet understand lay behind this woman's action and Jesus' response. Jesus seized the occasion and told a very short and simple parable in order to let Simon into the secret. '*Simon, I have somewhat to say unto thee,*' said Jesus. Simon replied, '*Say on.*' Jesus bade Simon take another look at the object which had offended him and asked him to give her case fresh consideration in the light of what He had now to tell him about her. He asked Simon to lay aside his prejudices and regard the situation in a new light.

THE REALITY OF THE FORGIVENESS OF SINS

As Simon was looking at this woman's strange behaviour and forming his own conclusions about what might lie behind it, Jesus told Simon about a certain man who had two debtors. One owed him an enormous amount, but had no resources with which to meet his creditor. He faced ruin. But his creditor, out of pity, cancelled all the debt and set him free. Thereafter he loved his creditor with an intensity measurable only by the greatness of the cancelled debt. '*There was a certain creditor which had two debtors: the one owed five hundred pence, and the other fifty. And when they had nothing to pay, he frankly forgave them both. Tell me therefore, which of them will love him most?*'

Jesus is here pointing out to Simon that this woman whom he is so greatly misunderstanding is like that debtor who has been forgiven a great debt. She has just undergone a great experience of the forgiveness of her sins, and that experience is the clue to her conduct. Her apparently exaggerated behaviour is merely a sign that her sins are forgiven. '*Her sins, which are many, are forgiven,*' Jesus said to Simon, and then it is as if He added, 'You can see that this is the case from her intense love.' The intensity of her love is a symptom of the intensity of the spiritual experience she had undergone deep in her soul. It has all been real, this experience of forgiveness. It has been as real and concrete an experience as her tears are real and concrete. Her whole outward bearing, her tears, her devotion, constitute a proof that through Jesus she has experienced real liberation from the guilt of sin.

Jesus is here deliberately advertising the fact that He has the power to solve for any man the problem of the guilt and bondage brought to the soul by sin, and that when He speaks to a soul saying, 'Thy sins be forgiven,' it is not mere talk; something really happens. Jesus was not anxious to advertise His power to cure physical disease and to work other miracles. In such cases He was not in the habit of saying, 'There, look and see what I have done!' but He was never hesitant about advertising far and wide that He could solve for men and women the consequences of their sin and cure the soul.

There was another occasion on which Jesus gave a proof to His audience that He had the power to forgive sins. When a paralytic man was brought to Him on a stretcher, the first words He spoke to the man were, 'Thy sins be forgiven thee.' The onlookers were angry at what they regarded as His presumptuous claim to be able to forgive sins, and they murmured against Him, accusing Him of blasphemy. But Jesus immediately gave them a sign that the forgiveness He had offered this man was a deep spiritual reality. He turned to the sick man and ordered him to get up and walk, and as He did so He told the onlookers to see in this physical miracle a proof that a far greater spiritual miracle had already taken place in the man's heart. 'But that ye may know that the Son of man hath power on earth to forgive sins!'[1] This, then, was the message Jesus sought to teach in speaking the parable to Simon. He has the power to forgive sins, and men do not need to wait till after death to prove the reality of this claim. His forgiveness can be experienced here and now.

To those who have awakened to the fact that the problems of the soul are even more urgent than the problems of the body, and that it is a far more difficult matter to heal wounded love than to heal wounded limbs, there is no more urgent need than some such proof as Jesus gave that God can cure where it is impossible for man to cure, that God can work in tormented human souls bringing a sense of deep peace and the assurance that all is well. To those who have seen something of the great gulf separating themselves from God because of their sin and who can never forgive themselves because of a past life that has seemed to involve the forfeiture of every claim to a blessed future, there is no greater need than the knowledge that God can indeed blot out the past in such a way that it will never again be remembered, that God can restore the tender and life-giving relationships that have become broken between Himself and His creatures through sin and ingratitude, and enable men to start again. Jesus gave Simon such proof of the reality of the forgiveness of sin as any truly awakened man might need. Simon did not feel that he required such a proof. He was not yet facing up to his real situation in life. Perhaps later on, when he began to face the reality of sin, he would begin to grope after what Jesus was freely offering him here.

Jesus does not leave us without signs to prove to us the reality of His forgiveness. Even today we can see around us liberated and renewed lives whose explanation can lie only in the fact that the living Christ has even now power on earth to forgive sins. But more than this He gives us. The Sacraments of Baptism and the Lord's Supper are signs given to us by Christ of the reality of the forgiveness of sins. The fact that we have been baptised is meant by Jesus to stand behind us all our days

[1] Mark 2.10

as a concrete symbol reminding us that we are washed by Him, that our past is buried and that in spite of all we may feel within us we have indeed risen again to new life. At every Lord's Table Jesus Christ Himself puts in our hands a piece of bread and a cup—tangible things of whose reality there can be no doubt—and it is as if He says to us, 'The forgiveness of sins, which I have shed My Blood and broken My Body to give to you, is as real as these symbols and is given now to your souls as this food to your body.'

A Rebuke to Half-hearted Devotion

Simon had sought to do Jesus a service by inviting Him to a meal, but the service had given insult to Jesus rather than honour. It was the common custom to provide at least water for the visitors to wash their feet. Simon had neglected even this little courtesy, not to speak of many other things he might have done to make Jesus Christ feel that He was indeed welcome and honoured. Jesus asked Simon to see in this woman an example, and a reproach to his own frigidity and lack of courtesy. '*Seest thou this woman? I entered into thine house, thou gavest me no water for my feet: but she hath washed my feet with tears, and wiped them with the hairs of her head. Thou gavest me no kiss: but this woman since the time I came in hath not ceased to kiss my feet. My head with oil thou didst not anoint: but this woman hath anointed my feet with ointment.*'

No doubt Jesus read Simon's whole attitude to life and to God written clearly in his conduct towards Himself at that meal. 'Cold civility', A. B. Bruce describes it. 'No heart, no cordiality, no spontaneity, no free play of natural affection: this in the matter of hospitality; and the same thing of course in all other departments of conduct, for the ruling spirit of a man reveals itself in all that he does.' How great the contrast between this behaviour and that of the woman! It is easy to criticise her but it is clear where Christ's preference lies. 'The woman's worship is an exhilarating spectacle,' says Marcus Dods. 'She creates an atmosphere it does one good to breathe, an atmosphere of high and true sentiment in which things are rightly estimated and conventionality disappears.'

Since Jesus holds up this woman's conduct to us as an example, and criticises with real, though indirect, severity the conduct of Simon, are we not meant therefore to examine ourselves? Of course He does not mean that we should deliberately cultivate amongst us and within us an effusive and emotional type of worship modelled on this woman's behaviour. Jesus did not expect from Simon the same type of clinging and demonstrative adoration as this woman gave Him. Simon was not made that way and Jesus does not ask us to be unnatural in our expression towards Him. But He did expect from Simon honour and true courtesy. Had Simon become His wholehearted disciple, He would have expected from him a no less wholehearted and spontaneous love, though one that found expression according to Simon's individual character.

There is no doubt that this spontaneity and wholeheartedness which Jesus missed from the attentions of Simon and found in the woman is also lacking from much of our Church activity in this generation. How exactly the picture of Simon the Pharisee fits us! Simon had responded to Jesus but to a very small extent. He had heard Him no doubt inviting men to enter the Kingdom of God and instead he had evaded the issue by inviting Jesus to supper. Instead of deciding, 'I will fit my life into the demands of this man and will be His slave for ever so that all that I have will be His', he had thought, 'Now this man would be an interesting addition to my supper table arranged for tonight. He can ask the blessing.' 'If Jesus Christ were to come today,' said Carlyle, 'people would not even crucify Him. They would ask Him to dinner, and hear what He had to say and then make fun of it.' Is it not only too true that the response of many of us to Christ has gone very little farther than an invitation to Him to come and bless the selfish arrangements that we have already made for our life—an invitation to Him to come and decorate our self-centred existence with a little of the thing men call religion? Moreover, in our desire to avoid too much 'enthusiasm' we put ourselves alongside Simon in his abhorrence of the conduct of this woman. In how few of our churches would an emotional outburst such as came from this woman at the feet of Jesus be really sympathetically understood, appreciated and welcomed! Perhaps this incident is recorded to encourage some of us to be less afraid of allowing our emotions to help us to form our response to Christ, and to remind the preacher of the Gospel that there is a very justifiable place for an appeal to the emotions in presenting Jesus Christ for men's salvation. It is a great vindication of the high place to which emotion is entitled in our faith that Jesus accepted and rejoiced over the behaviour of this woman and held her up as a rebuke to Simon the Pharisee.

The parable teaches that there is only one way to recapture in the midst of the Church such wholehearted devotion to Christ as this woman gave. We must become assured, as she was, of the forgiveness of sins. We must look at the Cross of Christ in which we see fully displayed the cost of that forgiveness. God has given His Son! Christ has given His blood! We must thus once more become debtors to Christ and realise how great that debt is; then, greatly forgiven, we will begin greatly to love. There is no other safe way of seeking to stir up enthusiasm in the Church over Foreign Missions or Home Missions or any good Christian cause than the way of presenting to men once more the Cross of Christ as the price God has paid for our sins. We will not get money or enthusiasm or devoted service from Simon the Pharisee, who thinks little of forgiveness, no matter how we may appeal to him on other grounds; but we will receive in Christ's name all that they have from those who, like the woman, realise how greatly they have been loved in the Cross of Christ. Let us then, in our practical approach to this matter, go to the root of the problem. There will never be any burning and lasting enthusiasm for anything in the Church till people realise that Christ has saved them, saved them from sin and death and Hell, and saved them at an infinite cost. The Cross, the place of forgiveness, is the place where all true and lasting devotion to Christ is born. The Cross is the place where true revival begins, where Church extension begins, and where missionary enterprise must begin in every generation. We cannot command men to love Christ. It is folly to tell men to stir themselves up to enthusiasm for this or that Christian cause. Love and enthusiasm can arise only as the spontaneous outcome of a faith that begins with the forgiveness of sins.

THE POWER OF JESUS TO CHANGE MEN'S LIVES

Simon thought that Jesus was being immoral in making it so easy for a woman like this to enter His company. Was He not likely to encourage sin by this apparently loose behaviour towards it? Jesus answered His thought, '*Seest thou this woman? . . . She loved much.*'

If we look at her as Christ desired Simon to do, we will see a sign that a remarkable transformation is beginning to take place not only in her inward feelings but also in her outward life. She brings to Jesus a box of very precious ointment and pours it over His feet. It is the ointment she had bought for her sinful uses and her own selfish adornment, but now she is consecrating it to the service of Him who has forgiven her. Her life has begun to take a new direction and she has found a new centre for her feelings and emotions. She who had deliberately sold herself to evil is now turned for ever from such paths and her body is now yielded as an instrument of righteousness unto God. Jesus is not ashamed or afraid of directing the world's attention to her as an example of His power not only to blot out the past but also to save from a life of uselessness and moral evil. She is now the servant of Christ and a life thus centred on Him will not turn again to evil. When Christ breaks men's bonds, they become His servants, bound to Him with a gratitude that is stronger than all the world's temptations. 'O Lord, truly I am thy servant,' cried the Psalmist. 'Thou hast loosed my bonds.'[1] The Gospel of the free forgiveness of God in Christ, that men are sometimes afraid to take seriously in all its implications because it seems to blur all moral distinctions between men, is nevertheless the only Gospel that in the end can produce such triumphs of salvation and redirect the energies of men in the paths of true righteousness.

[1] Ps. 116.16

THE PHARISEE AND THE PUBLICAN

And he spake this parable unto certain which trusted in themselves that they were righteous, and despised others: Two men went up into the temple to pray; the one a Pharisee, and the other a publican. The Pharisee stood and prayed thus with himself, God, I thank thee, that I am not as other men are, extortioners, unjust, adulterers, or even as this publican. I fast twice in the week, I give tithes of all that I possess. And the publican, standing afar off, would not lift up so much as his eyes unto heaven, but smote upon his breast, saying, God be merciful to me a sinner. I tell you, this man went down to his house justified rather than the other: for every one that exalteth himself shall be abased; and he that humbleth himself shall be exalted.

LUKE 18.9-14

'*Two men went up into the temple to pray.*' Both these men are often to be seen in this temple; and from all outward appearance, viewing them from a distance, both are very devout. One is a Pharisee most zealous in his devotions and full of good works. The other is a publican to whom something has obviously happened to make him religious. He was not at one time like this but now he is as zealous in his attendance at the House of God as any Pharisee. He tends to keep apart from the rest of the worshippers and his prayers are accompanied by much outward demonstration of repentance for his past life.

This parable is not just a story of what used to take place in the days of Jesus; it is a story of what takes place in every generation. Even today both the Pharisee and the publican go up to the temple to pray. It is true that the scene inside the temple is slightly altered. People today do not usually stand apart from others saying their prayers by themselves as was the custom in those times. Men of both the religious types represented by the Pharisee and the publican mingle with the congregation when they go up to the temple for their devotions. They find themselves sitting side by side in the pews in corporate worship. From all outward appearance there is even less difference today than in the days of Jesus between the man who would then have been classed as the religious Pharisee and the man who would have fallen into the class of the religious publican. Both types are today zealous devoted Church people. Perhaps one man is inclined to be a little more emotional in his religion than the other, but the other in his own way is also an enthusiast. It is difficult to judge between these men as they sit side by side in the pew listening to the sermon, or at the Lord's Table, or in the meetings of Church courts. Each is devout, each is loyal, each is regular.

Yet there is an infinite difference between the religions of these two men who find themselves thus regularly together in the same temple. In the parable Jesus, besides showing us the broad similarities, goes into details which show up clearly the great gulf that seems to separate so decisively in spirit these two men. He gives us the details of the prayers they uttered in their hearts in the temple. No one heard these prayers, for the Pharisee prayed '*with himself*', and the publican prayed in a corner by himself, but Jesus reports to us these inner prayers that no one else heard and the feelings of the heart that no one else could observe. He tells us the exact words and gives a clear indication of the emotions of each petitioner, then He adds a very significant phrase, '*this man went down to his house justified rather than the other*'. In other words, Jesus is here informing us that one of these men is a true citizen of the Kingdom of God and that the other is outside the Kingdom. These men belong to different worlds; there is an eternal barrier between them.

Thus the children of light and the children of darkness mingle not only in the business world and in the pleasure palaces but also in the temple, the place of worship. Jesus warned us that it would be very difficult, if not impossible, to distinguish clearly in this life between those who are without and those who are within the Kingdom of God. Two men may be each building a house. The outward structure of each house is alike, there is little difference in the speed and zeal with which each builder goes about his business, but down underneath the surface where no eye can see there is an infinite difference. One house is founded upon rock, the other is founded upon sand.

There are, of course, signs which help to indicate to men in a vague way whether, in dealing with a religious man, they are dealing with one who is genuine in his faith or not. Jesus taught that there would be 'fruits' by which we might be able to distinguish between a good tree and a bad tree. By a multitude of unconscious characteristic little ways men reveal the state of their hearts, and it is possible that as their friends get to know these two men, the Pharisee and the publican, better they will come quietly to certain conclusions about where they really stand in relation to God. But such conclusions are dangerous and uncertain. Only God can tell with certainty as men stand before Him in His house which are His true children and which are of another spirit. God judges between men according to the secret prayers which they spontaneously utter in the depths of their hearts when they bow before Him.

WHAT JUSTIFIES MEN BEFORE GOD

The man whom Jesus here describes as *'justified'* is a man who *'would not lift up so much as his eyes unto heaven, but smote upon his breast, saying, God be merciful to me a sinner'*. He has nothing to trust in but the mercy of God and he is looking nowhere but to the mercy of God for his help. He sees no good in himself that can be of any comfort to him. He has not even any fine religious feelings to trust in. He feels utterly wretched about his whole position before God and the more he thinks of it the worse he feels. There is only one thing which gives him hope —God is merciful. He has only one plea: *'God be merciful!'* His attitude is that of a man who is looking completely away from himself towards Him whose word is 'Look unto me, and be ye saved.'[1]

Because this is his attitude he is justified in the sight of God and his prayer is accepted. The New Testament teaches us that we are justified 'by faith alone'. Faith is the attitude that looks entirely away from the worst and the best that is in man to God alone. It is the act whereby a man, inspired by what he sees in God's mercy and finding nothing in his own character or feelings or intellect to give him any rest or comfort, lets go of the last shred of what he has hitherto held on to within himself, and thus commits his whole being to God. Faith is the acknowledgement in the presence of the merciful God that everything outside of this mercy is a false and worthless foundation to build upon, and that this mercy alone can be the starting point of the entirely new life that is required if a man is to be

[1] Isa. 45.22

saved. The publican in the parable had this faith. He had nothing more than this faith, but because he had this faith he was justified in the sight of God, and he was truly a citizen of the Kingdom of God. For there is only one way to enter that Kingdom. It is to cease trusting in ourselves, to realise how impossible it is that we should ever enter there by any effort of ours, however great, and trust in God's mercy alone. Only God's mercy can bring us to this point. God's mercy brought the publican to this state; he was in the temple seeking God's mercy because he had already been found and saved by God's mercy.

Here, then, is a message in which we can find a firm ground for confidence and hope. Jesus taught that this publican with his wasted powers and his godless past, which could only be a torment when he thought of himself, was nevertheless accepted by God and completely justified in His sight, because God's mercy enabled him to look away from himself to God alone. This was news indeed for His time. The people around Jesus thought that only the righteous and the good man could stand in the presence of God. 'Who shall ascend into the hill of the Lord? or who shall stand in His holy place?' asked the Psalmist in his day, and he answered his own question with an answer that everyone understood and approved of: 'he that hath clean hands, and a pure heart'.[1] But Jesus came and He reminded men that there was another answer to that question, for in this parable He gives us the picture of a man with impure hands and an unclean heart, standing in the holy place before God, and accepted by God because he has faith. In true penitence he is looking away from himself only to the mercy of God to save him. This is what alone justifies in the sight of God.

WHAT CONDEMNS MEN BEFORE GOD

Jesus' purpose in drawing the portrait of the Pharisee and in recording for us his secret prayer is to reveal the attitude that is condemned in the sight of God. He told this parable to *'certain which trusted in themselves that they were righteous, and despised others'*. He draws for them their own portrait in the Pharisee.

There is really only one thing wrong with the Pharisee: he

[1] Ps. 24.3-4

does not trust in the mercy of God alone and therefore he does not have faith. Faith rests in God alone but the Pharisee has much in his own life on which he imagines he can base a good deal of confidence. He fasts twice a week, he gives away either to charity or religious purposes one tenth of his income, he fulfils more than the strictest requirements of the law of God. The man is a perfect zealot in the pursuit of doing good; he has a burning passion to win for himself a place in Heaven. But in reality there is no hope for him unless he changes his whole attitude and outlook, for his trust is misplaced. He is trusting in himself, in his good works, his charity, his zeal, his character. In his prayers his mind dwells on these things rather than on God. This is what marks the Pharisee as being far from the Kingdom of God.

This is why he despises others, and holds himself aloof and apart, especially from those who he imagines have not the character that he himself possesses. This also is a serious fault but it is merely the outcome of the fact that he has not let God's true light shine into his heart to reveal him to himself and to destroy, once and for all, all self-confidence. Unless a man has been humbled at the feet of God he will never be truly humble towards his fellow men. George Eliot shows true insight in Maggie Tulliver's angry outburst against her brother Tom. Maggie describes Tom's cruelty to her from childhood and goes on to attack in him the cause of that inward hardness— his self-righteousness. 'You have always enjoyed punishing me—you have always been hard and cruel to me; even when I was a little girl and always loved you better than anyone else in the world, you would let me go crying to bed without forgiving me. You have no pity; you have no sense of your own imperfections and your own sins. . . . You are nothing but a Pharisee. You thank God for nothing but your own virtues; you think they are great enough to win you everything else. You have not even a vision of feelings by the side of which your shining virtues are mere darkness!'

The Pharisee is so like the best of us that none of us can feel comfortable when we read about him. There is no suggestion in the parable that he is a deliberate hypocrite. He believes in prayer and he acknowledges that his virtues come from God. His defect is simply that he imagines that he has good ground on which to stand before God, ground other than His eternal mercy which receives sinners. He has not allowed his self-confidence to be destroyed by the vision of God's holiness and love.

Jesus Christ alone can give us the vision by the side of which our shining virtues become mere darkness. 'Depart from me,' cried Peter when he saw that vision, 'for I am a sinful man, O Lord.'[1] He alone can destroy within us that false confidence in our own selves which makes it impossible for us to have faith in God—and without faith it is impossible to please God.

What Alone can Comfort Men as they Stand before God

If it was Jesus' purpose to teach any other lesson in this parable besides those already indicated, it may have been this further lesson: that we should not lay too much stress on our religious feelings. The Pharisee had beautiful religious feelings when he went to the temple. He felt right with God and with life. So comforting were his religious feelings that he felt sure he was in the Kingdom of God; his heart told him so. But his heart told him a lie. His feelings deceived him utterly. He stood condemned before God, yet he felt he was accepted. The publican, on the other hand, thought he was all wrong. He felt no sweet feelings of peace within; he did not even feel forgiven. He was miserable when he came to the temple and he went back home as miserable as he came up. His heart, had he believed his heart, sought to tell him that he was condemned in the sight of God and that there was no hope for him. But his heart told him a lie. His feelings deceived him no less than in the case of the Pharisee. He stood justified before God yet he felt he was condemned.

We must not, therefore, try to use our religious feelings as a source of comfort. We must find our comfort nowhere else but in the thought of God's goodness and mercy, and no matter what we feel within ourselves, never take our eyes off Him who has been lifted up to draw us ever to Himself.

[1] Luke 5.8

THE GOOD SAMARITAN

And, behold, a certain lawyer stood up, and tempted him, saying, Master, what shall I do to inherit eternal life? He said unto him, What is written in the law? how readest thou? And he answering said, Thou shalt love the Lord thy God with all thy heart, and with all thy soul, and with all thy strength, and with all thy mind; and thy neighbour as thyself. And he said unto him, Thou hast answered right: this do, and thou shalt live. But he, willing to justify himself, said unto Jesus, And who is my neighbour? And Jesus answering said, A certain man went down from Jerusalem to Jericho, and fell among thieves, which stripped him of his raiment, and wounded him, and departed, leaving him half dead. And by chance there came down a certain priest that way: and when he saw him, he passed by on the other side. And likewise a Levite, when he was at the place, came and looked on him, and passed by on the other side. But a certain Samaritan, as he journeyed, came where he was: and when he saw him, he had compassion on him, and went to him, and bound up his wounds, pouring in oil and wine, and set him on his own beast, and brought him to an inn, and took care of him. And on the morrow when he departed, he took out two pence, and gave them to the host, and said unto him, Take care of him; and whatsoever thou spendest more, when I come again, I will repay thee. Which now of these three, thinkest thou, was neighbour unto him that fell among the thieves? And he said, He that shewed mercy on him. Then said Jesus unto him, Go, and do thou likewise.

LUKE 10.25-37

Jesus told this story to a lawyer who twice interrupted Him, first with a question about theology and then with a question about one of the practical problems of life. He interrupted Jesus because he wanted to start a religious discussion along certain familiar lines. These men loved discussion, especially about practical problems such as the meaning of suffering, or how to keep the Sabbath day. They discussed even the urgent social problems of their day. But they did nothing about such problems except discuss them, and they always tried to evade action and responsibility by the kind of answers they gave.

For instance there was the problem, 'Who is my neighbour?' God's law said: 'Thou shalt love thy neighbour as thyself.'

Some people took that seriously and said that it meant they were obliged to help everyone in need. The lawyers discussed the problem and justified themselves for ignoring the full force of the commandment by saying that the word 'neighbour' meant only a fellow Jew, and even that only under certain restricted conditions. This answer relieved them of many unpleasant obligations towards those whom they excluded from their definition of the word. They could talk very cleverly to prove their case, arguing even from Scripture in order to evade their duty. This lawyer in particular felt so sure of his ground that he was ready to justify his lack of concern for his neighbour even before Jesus. Indeed he sought to force Jesus into argument about it.

To end all further discussion Jesus told this story in which the answer to the question, 'Who is my neighbour?' shines out so clearly that not even the lawyer could argue against the meaning which Jesus intended. No man was ever so clearly faced with the unwelcome and plain truth he was seeking to evade. After Jesus told the story the lawyer had no argument left and he allowed Jesus the last telling word: '*Go, and do thou likewise.*'

We are all tempted like this lawyer. The world around us is full of desperate and crying need. It is in order to force us to face such need realistically that we are given the commandment, 'Thou shalt love thy neighbour as thyself.' But instead of throwing ourselves into action we discuss the problems dispassionately. We try to think out reasons why God should allow suffering; we discuss whose fault a thing is and where relief should first come from; we scarcely think of starting to do something where the problem most acutely confronts us, in the case of our neighbour. Life with all its horror and misery is for many of us a mere spectacle. We look on it as on a play at the theatre. We discuss the plot, we allow it to stir our feelings, we can even discuss these feelings, but we do not act, for we are not supposed to act in a theatre. No less than the lawyer do we need to listen again and again to the parable of the Samaritan.

OUR NEIGHBOUR AND OURSELVES

Jesus begins by showing us the actual situation in which we often find our neighbour in real life: '*A certain man went down from Jerusalem to Jericho, and fell among thieves, which stripped him of his raiment, and wounded him, and departed, leaving him half dead.'* This lawyer thought he was living in a world where he could sit and argue about who is one's neighbour, and where it could be decided in calm and logical discussion whom one is to help and whom one is to pass by. Christ made him face a more real world of murderous strife and ugly reality, where the path of life is strewn with men whose souls and bodies are maimed and bleeding because of the ruthlessness of the order of things. In facing the lawyer with such a world in this parable He is in effect saying to him all the time, 'This is life as it really is.' Jesus took this lawyer out of the comfortable security of the synagogue and set him down on the road from Jerusalem to Jericho—a road which the lawyer knew to be so dangerous and infested with robbers that part of it was called 'the Way of Blood', and it is as if He said, 'That is the road of life.' Jesus showed him the mutilated body lying there by the roadside, and it is as if He was saying, 'That is the kind of thing you will meet continually on life's way. There you have your neighbour!' Jesus is saying as He tells this story: 'This life is a grim and tragic affair where there are frequent helpless casualties in the ordinary course of events, and any man in need laid at the side of your daily path of life, as this half dead man was laid by the path of the Levite and the priest, *he* is your neighbour. *He* is the man God commands you to love.'

He is not a very pleasant-looking man, our neighbour. He cannot do anything for us in return for our help to him. It is a dirty, unpleasant job loving him, one that will put our lives out of gear and spoil our plans for our pleasure. It is going to mean sacrifice to love our neighbour, but such is the situation that we dare not leave him and pass him by, for if we do his blood may be upon our heads. Such is life, such is our neighbour; and to love this man, our neighbour, is what God means by the command: 'Thou shalt love thy neighbour as thyself.'

This unpleasant picture of life and our neighbour is followed by a still more unpleasant one—a picture of ourselves as we act daily in the midst of life: '*And by chance there came down a certain priest that way: and when he saw him, he passed by on the other side. And likewise a Levite, when he was at the place, came and looked on him, and passed by on the other side.*'

Dr Alexander Whyte used to tell a story about George Meredith and one of his friends. When Meredith's novel *The Egoist* was published, one of Meredith's friends read it with eagerness, intending to send an early congratulation to the author, but he seemed to see in the unlovely character of the hero a strange likeness of himself, and in disappointment and anger he said to the author, 'It is too bad of you, Meredith— Willoughby is me!' 'No,' replied Meredith, 'Willoughby is all of us.' Do we not feel about the priest and the Levite in the parable what they felt about Willoughby? Here we see ourselves as we act in daily life. We find it so hard to face up to the needs of our fellow men and the demands these needs make upon us that our lives are full of subtle evasion. We are always prone to pass by on the other side. We are even glad at times if we can avoid contact with those who might make unpleasant demands upon us. How easy it is to avoid our neighbour by burying ourselves in pleasure, or in work.

Yet though we evade our neighbour and his need, we cannot evade our responsibility. The priest and his fellow temple-worker are shown up in an ugly light in this parable, and in that light we see ourselves. They are shown up as potential murderers. Let us face the truth. We have not lived in the way of love or even in the way of duty, and if our hope lay in being judged as to whether we had loved our neighbour we could have no hope of standing before God and inheriting eternal life. This is the truth about ourselves.

HIMSELF

'But a certain Samaritan, as he journeyed, came where he was: and when he saw him, he had compassion on him, and went to him, and bound up his wounds, pouring in oil and wine, and set him on his own beast, and brought him to an inn, and took care of him.'

Jesus gives a perfect description of Himself in the guise of the Samaritan. *'When he saw him, he had compassion on him, and went to him.'* Never did *He* pass by on the other side. He always *'went'* wherever He knew there was suffering and need, even when He knew He could if he wished avoid the contact. How significant in the Bible are the verses which tell us that Jesus went! When Jairus came to Him and told Him of his daughter at home on the point of death and besought Him to come

'Jesus arose, and followed him'[1]—right into the midst of the need and the scene of tragedy. Jesus 'stedfastly set his face to go to Jerusalem',[2] right into the midst of the stronghold of the enemy. The disciples wished Him one day to send the multitude away. It was the easier way, and it was a perfectly legitimate method of evading responsibility for their welfare at a juncture when to continue with them might mean becoming really 'involved'. But Jesus faced squarely all the demands of the situation. 'They need not depart,' He said. 'Give ye them to eat'[3]—and He fed them. Jesus always faced the need of men.

'*And when he saw him, he had compassion on him, and went to him.*' Here again Jesus describes Himself. In this short phrase from the story before us we are given a clue to all that lies behind the coming of the Son of God into this world. The answer to the question of '*Cur Deus Homo?*—Why did God the Son become Man?'—can be given in these few simple words: He saw and had compassion and came. The older commentators are not far from the true interpretation of this parable, for they labour to compare this helpless, mutilated man on the road with Humanity, lost in sin and corruption and doomed to death; then they compare the act of the Samaritan with that of God stooping in Christ to raise us up once more to health and freedom. In the book of Ezekiel the prophet likens God's people to an unwanted child cast into the open field unswaddled and unwashed. 'None eye pitied thee . . . to have compassion upon thee.' Then God's compassion for man is described. 'And when I passed thee by, and saw thee polluted in thine own blood, I said unto thee when thou wast in thy blood, Live . . . and I spread my skirt over thee, and covered thy nakedness: yea, I sware unto thee, and entered into a covenant with thee, saith the Lord God, and thou becamest mine. Then washed I thee with water . . . and I anointed thee with oil. I clothed thee also with broidered work, and shod thee with badgers' skin, and I girded thee about with fine linen, and I covered thee with silk. I decked thee also with ornaments . . . and I put a jewel on thy forehead . . . and a beautiful crown upon thine head. . . . And thy renown went forth among the heathen for thy beauty: for it was perfect through my comeliness, which I had put upon thee, saith the Lord God.'[4] No doubt Jesus had this

[1] Matt. 9.19 [2] Luke 9.51 [3] Matt. 14.15-16 [4] Ezek. 16.5-14

passage in mind in telling the story of the Good Samaritan as a description of His own saving work for mankind.

OUR DUTY

'*Go, and do thou likewise*,' said Jesus to the lawyer after the man had heard the story. '*Go, and do thou likewise*,' He also says to us. 'I have been a neighbour to *you*. I have shown you what love is like. I have picked you up out of your lost and wretched condition and made a new man of you. Go, and do thou likewise.' The parable gives us a pattern for a life of love lived out of gratitude to God in this world; and the pattern is perfectly plain and clear.

We must ask no questions about the merit or worth of those whom we serve in love. The Samaritan asked no such questions. All we are told about the man who was the object of his mercy is his terrible need. We are not told whether this victim of cruelty, whom the Samaritan helped, was a good or a bad man. We do not know his nationality or his station in life. He was probably a Jew, and here we have a Samaritan loving a Jew with such love in the midst of a world where these two races were at mortal and constant enmity. Such is love. It draws no bounds to its outgoing. It does not ask the question 'Who is my neighbour?'

We must make no excuses. The two ecclesiastics in the parable made excuses for their omission of duty, and they were good excuses. They were very busy men, both of them, on their way to serve God in His temple. If they touched this man they would become ceremonially unclean and would be unable to function in the House of God. Robberies were becoming very frequent on this road and if you started helping one victim, there was no knowing in what you would involve yourself. In any case it was quite likely that others more capable of rendering help would soon be coming along. We can see the line their thoughts took. But the Samaritan, busy man as he was, could also have manufactured excuses. Love makes no excuses.

We must be sane and practical. Notice how much thought and practical commonsense were combined with the compassion of the Samaritan. He had even an emergency first-aid kit with him, and he did not forget to pay the innkeeper. But there is no undue extravagance or gushing show of emotion.

There is only one source from which a love like this can flow into the human heart. '*He had compassion.*' All this was the expression of a compassion that was there in the heart. We cannot force ourselves into this kind of activity by merely resolving, 'I will act as this man acted.' Our concern must be to let the love of God come into our own hearts to live there and ever prompt and direct and inspire us.

After reading this parable we can no longer imagine that our salvation rests on anything other than the forgiving mercy of God, for the parable places us so clearly alongside the priest and the Levite that we know we cannot inherit eternal life by loving our neighbour. But the parable in showing us the Good Samaritan picking up the broken man tells us plainly that there is everlasting hope for each of us, when such a One is here to lift the fallen and to restore the lost, and it shows us the way in which, out of gratitude to Him who has so loved us, we too must act towards our brethren who have fallen by the wayside.

THE UNPROFITABLE SERVANT

But which of you, having a servant plowing or feeding cattle, will say unto him by and by, when he is come from the field, Go and sit down to meat? And will not rather say unto him, Make ready wherewith I may sup, and gird thyself, and serve me, till I have eaten and drunken; and afterward thou shalt eat and drink? Doth he thank that servant because he did the things that were commanded him? I trow not. So likewise ye, when ye shall have done all those things which are commanded you, say, We are unprofitable servants: we have done that which was our duty to do.

LUKE 17.7-10

There is much evidence in the parables of Jesus of the extreme poverty and terrible social conditions in which men lived at that time. We read of beggars lying at the gate of the rich and of people in debt pleading for time to pay or being cast into prison. We read too of how within ordinary households the cupboards could be so empty that there was nothing to set before the chance visitor when he called in, and of how the finding of even one small coin could cause exuberant rejoicing. These were times of scarcity and life was by no means easy for a large section of the community. It was hard to be poor.

If it was hard to be poor, it was far worse to be a slave. In those grim days slaves had to do much more than the full day's hard work out in the fields which was the usual lot of the ordinary freeman. The ordinary man, when he had finished the daily toil by which he earned his bread, knew that then he was at least able to relax. He had some kind of a home to go to and he could expect a certain amount of attention and a rest. But the slave, on the other hand, after a hard day's work, enough to tire any man, had no such prospect of rest when he came into the house in the evening. There was no one to serve him and give him friendly attention and a meal. He had no choice but to forget his hunger and weariness, gird his robes about him and go and make himself ready to serve his master indoors no less arduously than he had already done outside, for there were now meals to prepare. The slave expected this extra service.

It was his daily routine, for after all he was the slave. Moreover, he never expected a word of thanks from the master for this additional toil, and he was seldom given one. He could take comfort only by saying to himself, 'Why should I expect praise or reward? It is but part of my lot as a slave. It is my duty in the station of life in which I was born.' Thus, in this parable, Jesus describes the life of the slave in His day.

We must not imagine, because Jesus describes with such sympathetic feeling and picturesque familiar detail the conditions of the slave in His day, that He therefore approved of poverty or slavery. No such conclusion is justified. Jesus was merely taking His illustrations from the scenes and experiences that the common people of the day knew best. In the parables He related stories of these conditions without passing judgment on the system and outlook which produced them; but in other parts of His teaching it is obvious that His purpose was to bring men to such a knowledge of the mind of God and into such a relationship with God that the mentality that upheld such conditions of dire poverty and slavery described in the parables would disappear.

The lessons which this particular parable teaches are on the nature of the service of God in this world, the temptations which men are likely to undergo in this service and the attitude of mind which alone can prevent God's servants from giving way under such temptations.

THE SERVICE OF GOD DEMANDS THE COMPLETE SURRENDER OF THE WHOLE OF MAN'S LIFE

'*Which of you, having a servant plowing or feeding cattle, will say unto him by and by, when he is come from the field, Go and sit down to meat? And will not rather say unto him, Make ready wherewith I may sup, and gird thyself, and serve me, till I have eaten and drunken; and afterward thou shalt eat and drink?*'

There is no end to the practical obligations men take upon themselves in becoming the servants of God. The Christian is the slave of the need of the world and he must always be ready to serve that need as the slave in the parable is always ready to serve the need of his master. As for the slave, so for the Christian, there is no release from duty. The Christian must expect to be the one on whom is laid all the extra work, including the dirty work that others sometimes leave because they do not like doing it, and he has no right to allow his personal preferences or his natural feelings of exhaustion or repulsion to enter as a deciding factor in determining the service he renders to God's people and to God's Church and thus to God Himself. No limit can be set to that service. Its obligations can never be defined with precision. They can be defined by only one word, 'love', and to seek to unfold the meaning of that word in practical terms in daily life is to take up a never-ending task. Love 'endureth all things'. Love 'never faileth'.[1] Love can be called upon at all times and is ready to seize each opportunity for sacrifice.

The obligations of a Christian cannot be written up as a list of duties after the fulfilment of which a man can sit down and say, 'There! I have done my work, my conscience is clear, I now deserve a rest.' Just when a man is tired and feels that it is time to resign for he has done enough, the demand of love is renewed. He sees opening before him an urgent situation which his further service alone can meet. A case of human need is laid at his feet by God and a voice seems to call him to arise and work on yet a while. Dr Grenfell somewhere describes how these extra demands were gradually laid on him in his work at Labrador. His work as a doctor took him to a home where the mother and father both died within a short time. Since there seemed to be no responsible relative, he found that in addition to his medical services he had to make arrangements for the funeral and conduct the burial service. Then he found himself faced with a fresh problem. There were the orphans to be cared for. He found himself with 'five little mortals sitting on the grave mound. We thought that we had done all that could be expected of a doctor, but now we found the difference. It looked as if God expected more.' Such is the way God lays the service of love upon His servants, and He seems to expect more and more.

This hard service is made all the more difficult by the fact that in the midst of it the servant of God is tempted to feel that God does not care for him, nor does He understand the feelings of weakness and weariness that come over the best of His servants. In the parable Jesus deliberately makes the master of

[1] 1 Cor. 13

the slave appear neither to understand nor to sympathise with the feelings of the slave. The master appears as a typical slave-owner, hard and stern. He gives no indication to the slave of whether he thinks the man has worked well. Not a word of thanks passes his lips. '*Doth he thank that servant because he did the things that were commanded him?*' Jesus, in portraying the slave-owner thus, does not mean us to infer that God is in reality like him. He means rather to warn us that from our point of view God will *seem* to behave like that hard man towards us while we are in the midst of all the toil we have to undertake for His Kingdom. In the midst of our hard overwork God may give no sign that He is thankful for or even interested in the progress of the work we are doing, no sign that He is looking on with appreciation.

Jesus Himself became in this world not a free man but a slave. Paul says of Him, 'He made himself of no reputation, and took upon him the form of a servant.'[1] In His lowly guise He undertook the shameful task of bearing the world's sin upon a Cross. This task no one else could do, and it fell to Him. 'All we like sheep have gone astray; we have turned every one to his own way; and the Lord hath laid on him the iniquity of us all.'[2] His whole life was an extra service of love, and the Cross was that love to the uttermost. And in the midst of this service Jesus felt the sense of weariness and frustration that he describes as belonging to the slave. He too found Himself suffering in obscurity and was tempted to ask if His Heavenly Father understood. On the Cross He cried, 'My God, my God, why hast thou forsaken me?'[3] When Jesus calls us to such service as He describes in this parable He is not calling us to any experience of hardship which He Himself does not understand. When He calls on us to take up our cross, it is merely to follow Him in the path of His Cross.

ONLY THROUGH A SENSE OF INFINITE INDEBTEDNESS TO GOD CAN WE MEET THIS DEMAND

The slave in the parable was saved from despair and bitterness and enabled to fulfil with cheerfulness and without breakdown the tasks set before him, because he always said to himself, 'I am a slave. I have no choice but to serve always and with

[1] Phil. 2.7   [2] Isa. 53.6   [3] Matt. 27.46

all my energy. It is a debt I owe to the master. In sacrificing my life for him I am bringing him no profit that is not his just due.' The slave never allowed his mind to dwell much on the greatness of the amount of toil which had been exacted from him. He remembered only that he belonged to his master in the bonds of slavery.

In the attitude described in this parable we can meet the most severe temptations that come our way in our Christian work. We too are tempted to despair and bitterness, and to renounce the service that brings us under what seems at times hard and unrelieved bondage. We begin to feel as Moses felt when he smashed the two tables of stone against the rocks—a token of his hasty determination to resign the task that he felt was too much[1]—or like Elijah in despondency under the juniper bush praying that he might die, for he felt he had had enough of the service of God.[2] We are as human as these men were. Our flesh is weak, and our wills rebel under too much strain. There are indeed times when only one thought will keep us to our task. That is the thought of our indebtedness to Him whom we serve, and in the light of whose love we have no rights at all.

'*So likewise ye*,' says Jesus after describing the patient devotion of the slave, '*when ye shall have done all those things which are commanded you, say, We are unprofitable servants: we have done that which was our duty to do.*' We must always remember that towards God, no matter how much we have done, we are always in debt. The God we are serving may at times seem to our tired imagination to be One who sits unmoved and exacts an unfair measure of toil from exhausted men, but in reality He is a God who has given all and counted no cost too much that it might be possible for us, instead of living in eternal bondage to evil, to serve Him with willing love and with all our powers for ever. He is the One who in Jesus girded Himself in a slave's garb to serve us. Our response to such a love can be nothing less than the giving of everything with a whole heart. Before such a love we are always merely unprofitable servants. In giving God our all we are giving back nothing more than the least part of a mere fraction of what we owe to Him for redeeming us. Therefore, whatever we do, however devotedly we pour out

[1] Exod. 32.19   [2] 1 Kings 19.4

our lives in sacrifice to Christ and spend our all on Him, it is no more than we ought to do in response to His Sacrifice, and therefore we cannot resign from the service of Christ. 'The love of Christ constraineth us,'[1] cried Paul. He felt the love of Christ gripping him and forcing him to the task. From the bonds that this love brought over his heart there could be no escape.

The slave in the parable was saved also from pride by remembering the bonds that made him a slave. We too are faced by the temptation to grow proud in the midst of the work, to let our minds dwell even for a little while on how much we have done for God, especially in comparison with others. We may be tempted even to start self-consciously counting up the hours and money we spent in extra service and begin to feel pleased and to flatter ourselves that we are indeed of some significance. Such a thought and attitude creeping in and developing would indeed spoil our service and take away its value in the sight of God. It would make our very sacrifice self-centred and thus hateful in the sight of Him we are seeking to serve. There is only one way to save ourselves and our service from this taint: that is again to remember our debt to God. In this Paul is again our example. Always he regarded himself genuinely as an unprofitable servant. 'Less than the least of all saints',[2] 'chief of sinners',[3] 'not worthy'—these are the phrases he is in the habit of using about himself. Speaking of his work he says, 'Though I preach the gospel, I have nothing to glory of: for necessity is laid upon me; yea, woe is unto me, if I preach not the gospel!'[4] Always he felt that his own work was worth nothing because always he was conscious of the greatness of the redeeming love of Christ beside which no Christian can glory in anything else. In the light of this love Paul was able to forget the things that are behind, even the things about which the ordinary man is tempted to say to himself, 'Well done!'

There is one final thought on which we can close our study of the passage. It is because we have been delivered from a slavery to evil far more bitter than that described here that we become such slaves to Christ. We are set free from sin that we may yield ourselves thus to Him. Such bondage as we now have to Him is glorious freedom compared with that from

[1] 2 Cor. 5.14   [2] Eph. 3.8   [3] 1 Tim. 1.15   [4] 1 Cor. 9.16

which we have been delivered; and it is but a faint prelude to a service beyond into which no weariness can enter, nor temptation to doubt.

THE LABOURERS IN THE VINEYARD

For the kingdom of heaven is like unto a man that is an householder, which went out early in the morning to hire labourers into his vineyard. And when he had agreed with the labourers for a penny a day, he sent them into his vineyard. And he went out about the third hour, and saw others standing idle in the marketplace, and said unto them; Go ye also into the vineyard, and whatsoever is right I will give you. And they went their way. Again he went out about the sixth and ninth hour, and did likewise. And about the eleventh hour he went out, and found others standing idle, and saith unto them, Why stand ye here all the day idle? They say unto him, Because no man hath hired us. He saith unto them, Go ye also into the vineyard; and whatsoever is right, that shall ye receive. So when even was come, the lord of the vineyard saith unto his steward, Call the labourers, and give them their hire, beginning from the last unto the first. And when they came that were hired about the eleventh hour, they received every man a penny. But when the first came, they supposed that they should have received more; and they likewise received every man a penny. And when they had received it, they murmured against the goodman of the house, saying, These last have wrought but one hour, and thou hast made them equal unto us, which have borne the burden and heat of the day. But he answered one of them, and said, Friend, I do thee no wrong: didst thou not agree with me for a penny? Take that thine is, and go thy way: I will give unto this last, even as unto thee. Is it not lawful for me to do what I will with mine own? Is thine eye evil, because I am good? So the last shall be first, and the first last: for many be called, but few chosen.

MATTHEW 20.1-16

How varied are the pictures Jesus gives of Himself in these parables! He pictures Himself in one parable as a king ruling over his subjects; in another as a judge sitting upon his throne of judgment; in another as a host entertaining his guests; in another as a good Samaritan helping his needy fellow-traveller; here He is an employer of labour setting out to hire labour in the marketplace of this world. There are those who will confess that before they knew Him as King or Judge or Host or Saviour they were at least conscious that He was seeking to employ them. The things of Christ were vague and unreal to them.

They were sure of little in their faith, but they somehow felt themselves challenged to go and throw themselves into some form of Christian service for the sake of fulfilling the command of Jesus Christ, and that was the start of the road with Christ that led them ultimately to real and living communion with God. Because of this, the picture of Christ that most appeals is that of the man who goes out into the marketplace to lay hold of men and say to them, '*Go ye also into the vineyard.*'

This parable has indeed a most up-to-date background. It speaks of employers and employees, pictures the scene at the labour bureau, shows us men involved in a wage dispute. It should therefore appeal to us even more vividly than those parables in which Jesus is speaking about kings and royal banquets.

CHRIST OFFERS WORK AND A REWARD FOR WORK DONE

Christ likens His Kingdom to a place where there is work to be done. It is remarkable that He should do so, for in other parables He likens His Kingdom to a feast where there is no work to be done, to which an invitation is the highest and most gracious privilege which can be bestowed on a man. One does not work at a feast; one sits down to partake and enjoy.

We need not imagine that there is a contradiction here and that the teaching of one parable cancels the other. Both parables are true. It is true that the Kingdom of God is like a great banquet where everything is already prepared and nothing need be added. God does not need man's labour or help to bring in His Kingdom. But it is also no less true to say that the Kingdom of God is like a vineyard where there is hard work to be done for the Master. God needs nothing, nevertheless He allows man to work for Him. God allows man, even here on earth, to set his hand to the tasks of building and planting for eternity. Paul can speak of Christ's people as being 'labourers together with God'.[1] In the Kingdom of God there is work waiting for us to do.

Moreover, there are rewards given for work done. This parable was spoken in answer to a question asked by Peter in the name of the twelve. Peter felt that he and his fellow disciples were due a reward for what they had given up, and for

[1] 1 Cor. 3.9

the toil they had expended for the sake of the Kingdom of God. He asked Jesus about it. 'Behold, we have forsaken all and followed thee: what shall we have therefore?' Jesus did not rebuke Peter for asking about this; instead He promised him a very handsome reward. 'And Jesus said unto them, Verily I say unto you, That ye which have followed me, in the regeneration when the Son of man shall sit in the throne of his glory, ye also shall sit upon twelve thrones, judging the twelve tribes of Israel. And everyone that hath forsaken houses, or brethren, or sisters, or father, or mother, or wife, or children, or lands, for my name's sake, shall receive an hundredfold, and shall inherit everlasting life.'[1] Jesus then added this parable which tells of the Kingdom of God as a sphere where there is a reward for work done. We need not therefore be ashamed to expect and hope for a reward for serving Jesus Christ. We are sometimes told that we should serve God with no thought of any reward, but Jesus encourages us here and elsewhere to think about what we will have in return for serving Him.

God is no man's debtor. 'My people shall never be ashamed.'[2] We shall never be ashamed of the reward He gives us for patient faith and well-doing; it will be more glorious than all we could hope for, because it is a reward given by the grace of God. Paul tells us that he made the thought of this reward a source from which he drew ever fresh inspiration for his activity as an Apostle. At the end of his days he thought of this reward with gladness in his heart: 'I have fought a good fight, I have finished my course, I have kept the faith: henceforth there is laid up for me a crown of righteousness.'[3] In one place he urges his people to faithfulness by pointing out that whereas in the world men labour for a 'corruptible crown',[4] Christians are people who toil for an 'incorruptible' reward.

This parable teaches that Christ can save us from labouring and dying in vain. In the spheres of this world's life much of our labour appears to be in vain; much is trivial. Many enterprises that have challenged men's sacrificial efforts seem in the end to produce no lasting result. Men can toil in vain because they are pouring out their lives in some cause that is not of God and for which there is no reward. There is only one sphere in which it can be said with absolute confidence, 'Your labour is

[1] Matt. 19.27-29   [2] Joel 2.27   [3] 2 Tim. 4.7-8   [4] 1 Cor. 9.25

not in vain',[1] and that is the Kingdom of God. It is to save us from a life of uselessness and frustration that Christ comes into the marketplace of this world to seek our labour for His vineyard. In that vineyard not the least effort is allowed to go for nothing.

It is in free competition with other interests that Christ comes to seek our labour. No man can stand long in the marketplace of this world before being pestered with claims for his service. How many movements calling for our loyal support, how many 'personalities' seeking a flock of admirers, how many 'causes', 'leaders', 'isms' there are in this world! How many voices are sounding imperiously and passionately around us, each calling for our time and devotion and claiming to be the true director of labour! Christ is not the only one who is busy in the marketplace of this world. The Devil is also busy, for he does not wish Christ to have men's service. It is a wonder of unsurpassable grace that in the midst of all the babel of voices offering us terms, calling for our service, we hear also the voice of Christ, who comes and says, 'Go into my vineyard. I too have work. I also give rewards.'

Working in Christ's vineyard does not necessarily mean working in the direct employment of the Church and resigning our jobs in civil life. To stay where we are, to serve Him in the secular sphere of life, looking to Him and doing all for His glory, may be working in His vineyard. The Kingdom of God is not identical with the Church. The great matter is that we should be working for His sake under His commission, for all other labour is in vain. But it is possible that these words, '*Go ye also into the vineyard*', are meant to come to us as a challenge to serve Him in His Church. We are right to speak of the Church especially as 'the Lord's vineyard'. It is nothing short of a tragedy when gifted men refuse office in a Church which seems desperately to require the service of their gifts because they are so busily occupied in the service of agencies which seem to have little connexion with the Kingdom of God.

CHRIST IS PARTICULARLY INTERESTED IN THOSE WHO ARE DOWN AND OUT

'*And when he had agreed with the labourers for a penny a day, he*

[1] 1 Cor. 15.58

sent them into his vineyard. And he went out about the third hour, and saw others standing idle in the marketplace, and said unto them; Go ye also into the vineyard, and whatsoever is right I will give you. . . . Again he went out about the sixth and ninth hour, and did likewise. And about the eleventh hour he went out, and found others standing idle, and saith unto them. . . . Go ye also into the vineyard.'

There is something unusual about this employer. Other employers, anxious to have the best labour, seek for men of worth and standing capable of giving a good return for their wages, but this one does not seem to care about that. He is concerned to employ the idlers and wasters as much as those who have a reputation for good work. He seeks as employees those whom the world casts off and deems useless. Neither the wages nor the capacity of men for working nor the amount of work they accomplish seems to matter. This man is employing labour because he is interested in men and cannot bear to see them wasting their lives. He is continually visiting the market-place to make sure that no one is standing idle. Even at the eleventh hour he goes out for the disappointed people, for those who are the 'cast-offs' from other vineyards, and he approaches all the idle with the same invitation, the same message and the same offer, 'Go, work in my vineyard, and I will reward you.'

Is this not typical of Jesus Christ? He is especially interested in the wasters, the idlers, the useless and unfortunate, and the cast-offs of the world. Paul perfectly described the preference of Jesus in recruiting for His Church when he wrote: 'Ye see your calling, brethren, how that not many wise men after the flesh, not many mighty, not many noble, are called: but God hath chosen the foolish things of the world to confound the wise; and God hath chosen the weak things of the world to confound the things which are mighty; and base things of the world, and things which are despised.'[1] Of course we must not imagine that the owner of this vineyard is not also interested in the capable people. He goes out early in the morning so that he can have the best as well as the worst. When the rich young ruler came to Jesus, we read that 'Jesus beholding him loved him'.[2] He saw something in the man that made him want to have him; he was naturally what the world would call 'the

[1] 1 Cor. 1.26-28   [2] Mark 10.21

best type'. But the rich young ruler turned away from Jesus. Christ is not always successful in getting the 'best'. Usually men are not ready for Christ till they have come up against disappointment and failure, and have been, as it were, cast out of other vineyards. Most of us are simply idlers and wasters till we receive that gracious personal invitation from Him whose wish it is to see men in His fold. If we happen to find ourselves in God's vineyard it is not through any merit of our own. It is simply because we happened to be idling in the marketplace when Christ passed by, and He came to us in His mercy and chose us. And if we find ourselves, at the end of our life, in the position of receiving a reward for the work we have done, it is not because of our own merit, but simply because He sought us out in our uselessness. Even at the eleventh hour He comes for men, this employer of labour. The dying thief on the Cross turned and looked at Jesus and said, 'Lord, remember me when thou comest into thy kingdom.' Jesus said to him, 'Today shalt thou be with me in paradise.'[1]

Christ Rewards Men in Accordance with His Own Ever Gracious Will

Our parable has a sequel even more remarkable than the story itself. Pay hour came along at six o'clock and the men came to get their wages. First of all came those who had worked only since five o'clock. They were not tired, for they had done little. They received a denarius—one penny. Then came those who had planted and dug since three o'clock. Then came those who had been at it since noon. Then those who had been at it since nine o'clock and before, and they all received the same reward—one denarius. There was no trouble till it came to the turn of those who had worked all day. Probably they had begun to hope that they would receive more than their agreed wages when they saw that the employer was generous enough to give a whole day's pay to those who had worked only one hour. But their expectations were dashed. One penny! It was the sum they had agreed to, true, but these other fellows had got that amount and they had worked only one-twelfth of the time! They put in their protest. '*These last have wrought but one hour, and thou hast made*

[1] Luke 23.42-43

them equal unto us, which have borne the burden and heat of the day.'

The Master's answer was severe and reproving. *'Friend, I do thee no wrong: didst thou not agree with me for a penny? . . . Is it not lawful for me to do what I will with mine own? Is thine eye evil, because I am good?'* Do not bring your worldly reasoning and the distinctions that hold in this world into the sphere of the Kingdom of God or the Church of Christ! In the world, because the principle is 'justice', the one who works longest should get most pay, but here in the Kingdom of God the principle is not 'justice' but 'grace', 'mercy'. In the world merit counts and ability must be paid for. We are justified, therefore, in making comparisons. But here in the Kingdom of God we are working according to no such principles, simply under the good pleasure of Him who is the Lord of Grace. Those grumbling workers had forgotten that they were working in the Kingdom of God and not in the kingdom of this world. They had forgotten that they were in the vineyard only because the Master was good. They had forgotten that in this vineyard everything —even the reward—is decided by the grace and kindness of God and that no man has any 'rights' in relation to God or to his fellows.

How different the rules are when we turn from the world and enter the Kingdom of God! Here there are no rules at all. God has been infinitely kind to us. How can we thank Him that He has redeemed our life from wastefulness? We may think He has given us a hard piece of work to do in His vineyard and has made the task of another comparatively easier, but we will not complain; we will try not even to compare. He may have given us an unimportant part to play and given another man some part that gains more fame and prominence and is of more apparent worth. Will our eye be evil because God is good? Shall we start counting up the hours we work? Shall we bring the spirit of the world into a sphere where things are decided not by mathematics and justice but only by grace— the grace that has saved us? Envy, the evil eye, can have no place in the Church or in Christian work.

When the Kingdom of God is finally established, everything will be decided by the grace of God. Some look forward to a Kingdom of God on earth where everything is ordered on principles of perfect justice and equality. Such is not the Kingdom of God that Jesus spoke about. It is another Kingdom, not of this world, where the first are last and the last are first, where the humble are exalted and the high places are filled by those whom the world deemed idlers and wasters. But no one is envious, because everything is decided by the grace of God, the infinite redeeming love of Christ, and men have forgotten themselves and their claims in the praise of this glorious love.

THE TALENTS

For the kingdom of heaven is as a man travelling into a far country, who called his own servants, and delivered unto them his goods. And unto one he gave five talents, to another two, and to another one; to every man according to his several ability; and straightway took his journey. Then he that had received the five talents went and traded with the same, and made them other five talents. And likewise he that had received two, he also gained other two. But he that had received one went and digged in the earth, and hid his lord's money. After a long time the lord of those servants cometh, and reckoneth with them. And so he that had received five talents came and brought other five talents, saying, Lord, thou deliveredst unto me five talents: behold, I have gained beside them five talents more. His lord said unto him, Well done, thou good and faithful servant: thou hast been faithful over a few things, I will make thee ruler over many things: enter thou into the joy of thy lord. He also that had received two talents came and said, Lord, thou deliveredst unto me two talents: behold I have gained two other talents beside them. His lord said unto him, Well done, good and faithful servant; thou hast been faithful over a few things, I will make thee ruler over many things: enter thou into the joy of thy lord. Then he which had received the one talent came and said, Lord, I knew thee that thou art an hard man, reaping where thou hast not sown, and gathering where thou hast not strawed: and I was afraid, and went and hid thy talent in the earth: lo, there thou hast that is thine. His lord answered and said unto him, Thou wicked and slothful servant, thou knewest that I reap where I sowed not, and gather where I have not strawed: thou oughtest therefore to have put my money to the exchangers, and then at my coming I should have received mine own with usury. Take therefore the talent from him, and give it unto him which hath ten talents. For unto every one that hath shall be given, and he shall have abundance: but from him that hath not shall be taken away even that which he hath. And cast ye the unprofitable servant into outer darkness: there shall be weeping and gnashing of teeth.   MATTHEW 25.14-30

We ourselves who are members of the Church of Jesus Christ are referred to here in this parable by the phrase '*his own servants*'. The fact that He refers to us in this way should remind us that we are greatly privileged in being chosen by Him and in being given by Him responsibility in the affairs of the Kingdom of God. There are many in the world whom the call to His service does not seem to have reached, and upon whom the responsibility of furthering the Kingdom does not seem to have been laid. It may be a mystery to us why God seems to pass by so many people, perhaps better equipped for the work than ourselves. But the fact remains that we have not escaped as they have. We have been confronted by Christ, and challenged by Him into His service. We have heard Him clearly saying to us, 'Ye shall be witnesses unto me',[1] 'Go ye and teach all nations',[2] 'Ye are the light of the world'.[3] Thus we have been called as '*his own servants*'.

SERVANTS IN PARTNERSHIP

'*The kingdom of heaven is as a man travelling into a far country, who called his own servants, and delivered unto them his goods.*' A man carrying on the business of a trader, in order to promote the interests of his trade, chooses men to work for him. He trusts them. He puts his talents into their hands with perfect confidence and leaves them free from supervision to do the necessary trading. They are not really servants, they are partners. This is how God acts for the furtherance of His Kingdom. There are men in the world of business who refuse to trust anyone else with partnership or responsibility, carrying their whole business on their own shoulders. 'You cannot trust anyone nowadays,' they say. God does not act so. He has important business indeed, for He has all the business of the Kingdom of God on His hands. He calls His own servants and entrusts them with His affairs.

It would be contrary to the teaching of Scripture generally to conclude from this parable that God out of necessity requires our help and that He cannot do the work of His Kingdom without us. God is God and has all power to do what He wills. As He made the world in a moment by the Word of His power, saying, 'Let there be,' and there was, so God could bring in His Kingdom in a moment by the same direct Word, without any other help. He does not need us, our cleverness, our willingness, or our talents.

Stradivarius, the violin-maker, was wrong when, in reply to a critic who told him that if God had really wanted violins He

[1] Acts 1.8   [2] Matt. 28.19   [3] Matt. 5.14

would have made them Himself, he said, 'No, not even God could make my violins without Stradivarius.' God can do precisely what He wills, with or without Stradivarius or anyone else. He is able to create another Stradivarius if He wishes. He does not need men if He wills to do without them. Nevertheless, God does not will to do without men. He does not choose to make violins without Stradivarius. He does not choose to bring in His Kingdom without our co-operation and our service. He acts as if He were a man so busy that He cannot look after His own affairs and must seek the help of others if His business is to be carried on. So He takes men into partnership while He goes away to busy Himself elsewhere. It is a mystery that can be explained only by His love that God should choose and use men such as us for the furtherance of His Kingdom, and should make His reputation and His apparent success depend so much upon our faithfulness.

Our responsibility is real. In a certain area in Africa missionaries had come and had taught about God and Christ, had healed disease, and had had to withdraw from the field. They had left behind a few converts among whom was a boy who contracted an illness and suffered great pain. He had been told by the missionaries that God loved him, and he still believed it. An older man laughed at him for his belief. 'Look at all the pain and disease you are suffering,' he said. 'How can you go on saying God loves you when He is doing nothing for you?' 'Yes, He does love me and He has done something for me,' replied the boy. 'He knows that I need help, and He has told other people about me and given them the power to help me, but they have forgotten.' If we do not fulfil the task He trusts us to do, God's name is blasphemed and His purposes are hindered. God is not playing a game with us in taking us into partnership but is really binding Himself, and His cause on earth, with us for better or for worse.

Our responsibility is also great and glorious. It is the furtherance of the everlasting Gospel that even the angels would be happy to proclaim. It is the completion of the work for the sake of which Jesus Christ died on the Cross.

EQUIPMENT FOR THE TASK

'Unto one he gave five talents, to another two, and to another one; to

every man according to his several ability.' The trader made sure that every man entering his service had sufficient talents for all the tasks to be faced for his business in this world. In the same way, God never gives a task without assuring equipment. Pharaoh ordered the Israelites to make bricks and refused to give them straw, but when God appoints men to tasks within His service He gives them the personal equipment necessary for the task. When the men of Asher were sent to inherit their portion of the land of Canaan, the word God spoke to them was, 'Thy shoes shall be iron and brass; and as thy days, so shall thy strength be.'[1] Their task was to be hard, for the sphere into which God had sent them to serve was an area where travelling was difficult and there were bare and rocky mountain paths to negotiate. But God knew the nature of the task, and He assured their equipment: 'Thy shoes shall be iron and brass.'

We are apt to think when we read this parable that the 'talents' which God gives men for the furtherance of His work are simply the natural gifts with which each man is born. We think in this connexion especially of the gifts of personality, of powers of thought, and of musical and artistic ability. There may be some truth in this interpretation, for the Church, under the providence of God, can make use of the natural gifts of men. Why should not God use genius to further Christ's Kingdom? We should be careful not to discourage those who have great natural gifts, yet whose help we might be tempted to refuse because they seem 'unspiritual'. It is possible that the very purpose for which God has endowed them with these extraordinary talents is that they may be put to the service of His Church. Natural ability can be an endowment in the service of the Kingdom of God. Our training colleges and divinity halls are a continual testimony to the fact that we believe in enlisting and developing the natural gifts and abilities of men in the service of the Word of God.

But woe to the Church that comes to depend on the natural capabilities of its members and that waves its flag too joyfully when genius joins its ranks! 'Cursed be the man that maketh flesh his arm, and whose heart departeth from the Lord.'[2] Woe to the preacher whose mainstay in his ministry is his own cleverness of mind and his own eloquence and personality!

[1] Deut. 33.25   [2] Jer. 17.5

Even supreme natural ability, thrown into the service of God by the most zealous of His servants, is not enough. Far more is required as equipment for the Church than ability and training. A special endowment or talent is required if our efforts are to be of real value in the work of God. The New Testament tells that Christ loved His Church and that He endowed His Church with such 'spiritual gifts'. It speaks of Christ as ascending and giving gifts to men.[1] In the ceremony of ordination, as a symbol that such endowment from above is required, the hands of the Presbyter or Bishop are laid upon the head of the minister to be ordained, suggesting that Christ is seeking to bestow upon His servant a power greater than his own in the task to which he has been called.

The fact that Christ is seeking to endow us with these supernatural gifts should encourage us to undertake with boldness tasks beyond our natural powers. It is impossible to explain the rise and expansion of the Church in the early days except by asserting that the early Christians received new powers and new gifts from Christ beyond all their natural abilities. It was through the gift of such new powers that Peter became a great Apostle and a great leader, and was able to preach on the day of Pentecost with such effect that three thousand souls were added to the Church. The Holy Spirit had endowed him with the power of speaking in the name of Christ and he became a true witness. We ourselves must constantly pray that such spiritual gifts may be given to the Church and that God will raise up continually men and women with such talents as shall supply what is lacking in our common service. This equipment the Church needs far more than a knowledge of modern methods, far more than money, far more than buildings. Our office-bearers and Church courts and Church leaders require also to pray for insight and wisdom and ability, for even in their decisions a supernatural insight is required if the Church is to be governed rightly. God will not leave His Church without ample gifts for His work if we seek them in faith.

FREEDOM AND SCOPE FOR THE TASK

After he gave these men the talents he '*straightway took his journey*'. We read in the first sentence that it was a journey

[1] Eph. 4.8

'*into a far country*'. He endowed his servants, went off to some far distant place, and left them without any oversight or compulsion, free either to fulfil their trust or not. He did not stand over them saying, 'Now, I am going to see that you work.' In using these men he used them as free agents.

Today God seems to leave us free to do what we like with the gifts and talents He has given us. We can waste them and let them lie idle, or we can use them for our own glory and not for His. It is easy for gifted people, especially for people with truly spiritual gifts, to thwart God's immediate purpose in their endowment by burying their talents or by using them in a perverse way. God has hidden Himself so carefully from us, and made Himself so invisible, that if there is any carelessness in our hearts about God's business we are almost encouraged to decide to wait for tomorrow and to let things slide.

If God remained more visible here amongst us and we saw Him as He really is, we would all be His devoted servants. 'Why are there so many more attending church this month than last?' the visiting minister once asked the beadle in a little country place where he had been worshipping. 'Ah,' said the beadle, 'the Laird has come back this month!' There was a compulsion to go then. They knew that the Laird expected it, that he counted the numbers and reckoned who were there, and they were afraid of him. But God keeps out of sight. He goes and stays away, leaving us perfectly free. It has pleased Christ that the Church should depend upon the free will of His people in response to His great love.

It is noticeable that the master in the parable leaves no instructions about what is to be done with the talents. There is no fixed pattern given of how the men are to trade with their gifts. Each man is left to use his own imagination within the sphere of legitimate trading. Christ means that there should be ample room in the service of the Gospel for personal initiative, imagination and opportunism in the use of gifts. There is danger in our modern zeal to run the work of Christ according to the best methods. We are keen on introducing a definite pattern of modern technique in such matters as running clubs and teaching Sunday School classes. We try to train ability to work in prescribed channels. But we must beware lest we fetter imagination and enterprise, and the exercise of individuality, through the multitude of our training schools. David might not have been allowed to slay Goliath in his own way had he lived today. He might have been compelled to attend a training school, to learn the most modern and up-to-date methods of doing the job. Let us remember that what matters fundamentally in the exercise of a ministry in Church and Sunday School is that we should have individuals with gifts, each seeking to exercise these gifts for the glory of God according to his peculiarly individual genius. Of course there must be order and decency. We must not allow individualism to run riot. But we must beware lest through overmuch training and direction we quench the Spirit of God.

This Means Danger!

There must be risks in trading. Money must be put out in order to circulate and to bring in gain. In business life we hear of failures through over-boldness in speculating, but in the sphere of the Kingdom of God it is not the reckless man who is shown up as a failure; it is the cautious man. It was the man who had one talent and was over-cautious who failed to do his lord's will. There is only one attitude to take up when we seek to trade for God. We must launch out in faith. We do not have to read deeply into the Scriptures to discover that the men who were the greatest servants of God were the men who took great risks of failure, loss and shame; men who almost became a laughing-stock amongst other men. If Abraham had been careful, or if Moses had been careful, they could never have been the great leaders in the service of God. We must be prepared to take risks for Him, believing that He approves of ventures of faith. 'Lord, if it be thou,' cried Peter in the storm, 'Bid me come unto thee on the water.' Jesus answered 'Come!'[1]

The men who had been given five talents and two talents respectively launched out in faith. They traded to the good pleasure of their master, without thought of results, reward, or possible success or failure, and they were able at the end of the day to say, 'Look, master, thy talents have gained more!' But the other man was careful. He had a wrong idea of the master and his will. He did not see that if he honestly traded, taking risks, the master was loving enough to understand. He thought,

[1] Matt. 14.28-29

'He might not understand if I lost; he is a hard man. He expects a good return for every penny! I will be very careful! I will make sure that I have wherewith to please him!' And so he buried his talent and came with confidence on the day of reckoning. '*Lord, I knew thee that thou art an hard man, reaping where thou hast not sown, and gathering where thou hast not strawed: and I was afraid, and went and hid thy talent in the earth: lo, there thou hast that is thine.*'

The wrathful reply of the master proves that if God hates anything, it is the spirit that does not believe and that will not go forth in trust, abandoning all, to His service. God wills that men should take risks with their gifts, throwing them into circulation like bread cast upon the waters, and it is those of us who have few talents who are most prone to the sin of holding back. We think our talents are so small that we do not matter, and so we shirk our responsibilities. 'The sin of sins in my service,' Christ says here, 'is to try and preserve and safeguard what I have given, so that on demand it can be produced exactly as it was.'

There is a hint given here of how men can be helped to put their talents to best use. '*Thou oughtest therefore to have put my money to the exchangers*,' said the master, '*and then at my coming I should have received mine own with usury.*' He should have co-operated with others. Many of us do not have the initiative and imagination necessary to put us in the first two classes, but there is always the Church with its fellowship (and its methods!). It is in the Church in fellowship with others that we find a sphere of trading in the service of God in which our gifts can find circulation with profit.

'*Well done, good and faithful servant,*' said the lord to those who had traded well. '*Enter thou into the joy of thy lord.*' He is no hard man. It was only the wicked imagination of the slothful servant that made him appear to be a hard man. It is to the froward that God shows Himself froward, but to those who believe, who will launch out in faith with the gifts He has given, He is ever gracious, never failing to appreciate the least service, rewarding all with His love an hundredfold.

THE POUNDS

A certain nobleman went into a far country to receive for himself a kingdom, and to return. And he called his ten servants, and delivered them ten pounds, and said unto them, Occupy till I come. But his citizens hated him, and sent a message after him, saying, We will not have this man to reign over us. And it came to pass, that when he was returned, having received the kingdom, then he commanded these servants to be called unto him, to whom he had given the money, that he might know how much every man had gained by trading. Then came the first, saying, Lord, thy pound hath gained ten pounds. And he said unto him, Well, thou good servant: because thou hast been faithful in a very little, have thou authority over ten cities. And the second came, saying, Lord, thy pound hath gained five pounds. And he said likewise to him, Be thou also over five cities. And another came, saying, Lord, behold, here is thy pound, which I have kept laid up in a napkin: for I feared thee, because thou art an austere man: thou takest up that thou layedst not down, and reapest that thou didst not sow. And he saith unto him, Out of thine own mouth will I judge thee, thou wicked servant. Thou knewest that I was an austere man, taking up that I laid not down, and reaping that I did not sow: wherefore then gavest not thou my money into the bank, that at my coming I might have required mine own with usury? And he said unto them that stood by, Take from him the pound, and give it to him that hath ten pounds. (And they said unto him, Lord, he hath ten pounds.) For I say unto you, That unto every one which hath shall be given; and from him that hath not, even that he hath shall be taken away from him. But those mine enemies, which would not that I should reign over them, bring hither, and slay them before me.

LUKE 19.12-27

'*A certain nobleman went into a far country to receive for himself a kingdom, and to return.*' All the big decisions of state in those days were made in Rome, in the far country of Italy. It was quite common for local governors or statesmen or noblemen to be called upon to go to Rome to be interviewed by Caesar or the Senate about affairs of state. Sometimes this meant that a man was about to be deprived of his public office, but sometimes it meant that he would come back with promotion. He might come back even with authority to assume a throne and become a king. One particular case of this kind was fresh in the memory of Jesus' hearers. Herod the Great, before he died, divided up his estate among his sons, but it was a condition of the will that the Emperor in Rome should approve of what he had decided. Archelaus, one of Herod's sons, had therefore to go to Rome and receive his royal commission at the hands of the Emperor before he could assume real authority. The proceedings outlined in this story were thus familiar to the audience Jesus was addressing.

This story makes us think of Jesus Christ Himself. It fits into the pattern of the events by which He worked out the salvation of mankind. After He died and rose again, Jesus did not assume immediately the manifest power and place as Lord of this earth to which He had won the right. He went away. He ascended to Heaven, there to await the good pleasure of the Father before He should return. It is as if Jesus has gone into a far country to receive the Kingdom, to come again one day with power, when all things in earth, as well as in Heaven, shall be put under His feet and His Kingdom will be manifestly established. Through reading in the parable the events of the Gospel history we are given a key by which the meaning is opened to us.

THE UNACKNOWLEDGED CROWN RIGHTS OF JESUS CHRIST

Our Lord spoke this parable to warn the disciples of the state of affairs which might prevail upon the earth in every generation. As they were nearing Jerusalem on His last journey the disciples thought that the Kingdom of God would now suddenly appear and that all men would acknowledge the true Messiah in Jesus. Our Lord warns them in telling this story that in the meantime His crown rights will be acknowledged in Heaven, but on this earth which is destined to be His peculiar possession and domain the majority of His subjects will seek to resist His rule, saying, '*We will not have this man to reign over us.*' The nobleman in the story receives his kingdom at the court in the far country but the people of his own land reject him. So it is with Jesus. His royal claim is acknowledged everywhere except on this earth.

The cry of the men of His own generation, '*We will not have this man to reign over us*', has been echoed in many hearts in every age. There are still multitudes in this world for which Christ has died who cannot see the passion and death of Christ as an act of redeeming love which should claim and constrain them to absolute obedience. They cannot see Him as divine at all. They cannot see meaning and significance in talk about a Kingdom of Love established by suffering in a world where sheer force seems to have the power always to decide ultimate issues. In any case they feel uncomfortable before the demands for self-denial and for new standards of life with which Jesus confronts them. '*We will not have this man to reign over us.*'

All this does not alter the real situation. Jesus Christ is Lord even though this earth does not acknowledge Him, and even now He Himself on the throne of all power is controlling all things in Heaven and earth for the fulfilment of His purposes. For the decision as to who is Lord is taken not on this earth but in Heaven, where Christ has gone. Even though the sacrifice by which He has saved this world remains unacknowledged, nevertheless His right to rule has been established. He has put every man eternally in His debt; He has made every living man His bondslave by right. His worst enemy, the man who lives only to blaspheme His name, can henceforth live only on His bounty and by virtue of His passion. And He sits now at the right hand of God, controlling all things, and awaiting the good pleasure of the Father till He shall return.

'OCCUPY TILL I COME'

Though the majority of the subjects of the nobleman in the parable hated him, there were, however, some in the land who believed in his worth and in the validity of his claim. He had at least ten apparently faithful adherents, and before he went he gathered them together and said, 'Hold this kingdom for me.' '*And he called his ten servants, and delivered them ten pounds, and said unto them, Occupy till I come.*' In giving them each a pound, he was giving them a very small amount compared with the wealth of a kingdom. They could hardly be expected to do much in a spectacular way with a pound. We can nevertheless understand the policy which the nobleman was following. He was not going to leave the realm which he claimed void of all connexion with his name during his time of departure. Having a right to this kingdom he was thus staking his claim to it before he departed to the court which would decide the issue. The pound was very little, it is true. Perhaps he could not at present afford more. But it was a pledge between him and his followers to bind them to his service. In accepting the pound they were entering his service and giving acknowledgment that they believed in his claim.

In spite of the decision of the world of His own day not to allow Him to reign, Jesus, like the nobleman, had a few who had recognised His true Lordship and whom He could leave to claim the earth for Himself. 'We beheld His glory,'[1] writes John. There were a few who saw His glory in the miracles He did. Where others, looking at His miracles, saw only the usual sensationalism produced in every generation by wonderworkers seeking popularity and felt that the most likely explanation lay in His having allegiance with evil powers, these few, on the other hand, saw in the miracles true signs of the glory of Christ and of the reality of His Kingdom. There were a few who caught glimpses of His royalty even in His human bearing, for to them there was that about His humanity itself that was never seen in man before, and occasionally men seemed to see His glory almost as a flash of radiance that seemed to light Him up to their inner minds so that they became convinced that in dealing with this man they were dealing with the Son of God. It happened in this way to those who saw His transfiguration on the mountain,[2] and to Peter when he fell at His feet, crying, 'Depart from me, O Lord.'[3] Even at the Cross, though many saw nothing there except that which would form the subject of ironical comment, the dying thief beheld Him as a king and cried, 'Lord, remember me when thou comest into thy kingdom.'[4]

Before He left this earth Jesus gathered round Him those who had believed, and said, 'All power is given unto me in heaven and in earth.'[5] He told them to stake and maintain His claim to be Lord of all men. The words of the nobleman, '*Occupy till I come*', sum up the last command and promise of Christ to His followers. 'Go ye into all the world,' He commanded them.

What does the one pound which was given to each follower signify? What did Jesus give to His servants, before He ascended, as a pledge between them and Himself? Commen-

[1] John 1.14 [2] Matt. 17.1-5 [3] Luke 5.8
[4] Luke 23.42 [5] Matt. 28.18

tators are divided in the answers to this question. They are agreed, however, that the pound does not stand for the varied and distinctive gifts of personality and ability such as are signified by the talents in the superficially similar (but very different) parable in St Matthew's Gospel. Some think that by the pound is meant the Gospel, which is certainly given to each member of the Church as a trust to be traded with. It seems more likely, however, that if the pound stands for anything in particular, it should be interpreted as signifying the gift of the Holy Spirit. As the risen Jesus sent out His disciples, He breathed on them and said, 'Receive ye the Holy Ghost.'[1] Paul speaks of Christians as being 'sealed with that holy Spirit of promise, which is the earnest of our inheritance',[2] likening the Spirit, in the same sentence, firstly to a seal by which Christ's disciples are marked as belonging to Him, and secondly to an 'earnest', or pledge, which is a small preliminary gift, the foretaste of much greater things to follow. The early disciples were to go forth to claim this world for their Master in an antagonism no less subtle and determined, no less prepared for violence than that which had crucified Him. They required some such pledge to encourage and reassure them.

This parable defines clearly our own task as Christians in this present world. Christ has given to each of us a pound to trade with as our pledge, for each of us has been baptised in His name and sealed by His Spirit. We must occupy this earth till He comes. We must seek to uphold the crown rights of the Redeemer, even though those may not be acknowledged by the majority of men. 'All things are yours; whether the world, or life,'[3] wrote Paul, reminding the Corinthians that they must claim the whole realm of the world's life for their Master. It does not suit those who have such a claim to make to be apologetic or timid in their approach, or in the words they use in the name of their Lord. Nor must they give way to the thought that, in view of the unsettled conditions that so constantly prevail everywhere on earth, it is therefore hardly worth while putting every effort and sacrifice into the immediate task. We are given in the parable a picture of a few servants setting quietly and determinedly about their occupation of trading and capturing the markets of the realm for their master because they

[1] John 20.22   [2] Eph. 1.13-14   [3] 1 Cor. 3.21-22

are confident of his approaching triumph, and all this takes place in the midst of a land where there is open armed rebellion, where all seem to be proclaiming loudly, '*We will not have this man to reign over us,*' and where there is no sign of any peaceful settlement of the problem. It is precisely under such world conditions that the servants of Christ are expected to go about their task of trading diligently to win men to His cause. The attitude upheld for highest praise in this particular parable is not so much the attitude of dauntless courage that won for the early Christians the crowns of martyrdom, but rather the attitude of patient unwearied welldoing in steady hard self-sacrificing work in the name of Christ in a world full of strife, violence and atomic bombs. It is this attitude which is rewarded when the Lord comes back with power to His Kingdom.

It required great faith on the part of the servants in the parable to go forth and trade for the master under such conditions as prevailed in the land in those days. They could not have accomplished the task without a firm belief that their master had right as well as might on his side. It requires like faith for any man to serve Christ acceptably in this world. Jesus told this parable in His day to remind His followers that conditions in this world would not be ideally suited for those who would enlist in His service. The Kingdom would not suddenly appear here and now. They would be left, as if alone, with a challenging task requiring much courage and power of endurance, in a turbulent and antagonistic world. They would be able to fulfil the task appointed only if they kept a firm faith that the right and the might were on His side.

THE SECRETS OF MEN REVEALED AND JUDGED AT HIS RETURN

In the parable the servants were rewarded according to the measure of their success, which, of course, was proportional to their faith. '*And it came to pass, that when he was returned, having received the kingdom, then he commanded these servants to be called unto him, to whom he had given the money, that he might know how much every man had gained by trading. Then came the first, saying, Lord, thy pound hath gained ten pounds. And he said unto him, Well, thou good servant: because thou hast been faithful in a very little, have thou authority over ten cities. And the second came, saying, Lord, thy pound hath gained five pounds. And he said likewise to him, Be thou*

THE POUNDS 141

also over five cities.' They have been faithful in little. They have believed wholeheartedly in His coming and in His right, and according to their faith they have had success and have been rewarded.

One man among the original ten recipients of the pound, however, on the day of reckoning proves that he had no faith in the master. '*And another came, saying, Lord, behold, here is thy pound, which I have kept laid up in a napkin: for I feared thee, because thou art an austere man: thou takest up that thou layedst not down, and reapest that thou didst not sow.*' He accuses the master quite bluntly of being a usurper, a man who steals what is not his by right simply because he is hard and has all power. His speech implies that he believes the lord to have no right to this kingdom, and to have acquired it by sheer force and rapacity; for, he argues, the master has neither sowed nor laid down anything in proportion to what he has acquired in the kingdom and expects from his servants. This man has lost all faith in the real right of the master to true sovereignty. He has allowed his mind to be influenced, no doubt, by the talk of the rebellious in the land, who spread abroad a propaganda of hate against the rightful king. He had not, it is true, joined in the open rebellion. He acknowledged that the master had the power to win the day even though he was a usurper. He compromised, and wrapped his pound in a napkin, for he felt that it might be useful to prove that he had at least been afraid to throw it away. Perhaps he did not admit even to himself that this line of argument was going through his mind, but when the master came, in the confusion of the moment, he found himself blurting out the truth.

So the truth about men's attitude to the Lord comes out when Jesus comes to face men and reckon with them about their lives. Men begin to read their own hearts aright in the presence of Christ. They begin to discover in all their crudity the evil motives which have controlled their behaviour but which they have all along sought to hide even from themselves. Then they begin to give utterance to the wicked thoughts and sentiments which have so long dominated them. They never misquote their hearts in the presence of Christ. They confess, to their own shame and confusion, their real attitude to Him, and out of their own mouths they are judged.

Jesus Christ searches the hearts of men thus and brings to light the hidden things of their darkness for the purpose of passing true and fair judgment upon them. He tests men by the thoughts about Himself that are behind their actions, by the motives and secret inspiration of these deeds. Let us never give way to faithless thoughts that He is a hard man. Such thoughts poison faith and paralyse action. It is a lie that He seeks to gather where He has not laid down and to reap where He has not sown, for He has laid down His life on the Cross, and sown in agony and death all that was most precious to Him, that men through His grace may freely inherit the untold riches of His Eternal Kingdom.

THE TRAGEDY OF THOSE WITHOUT

THE RICH FOOL

And one of the company said unto him, Master, speak to my brother, that he divide the inheritance with me. And he said unto him, Man, who made me a judge or a divider over you? And he said unto them, Take heed, and beware of covetousness: for a man's life consisteth not in the abundance of the things which he possesseth. And he spake a parable unto them, saying, The ground of a certain rich man brought forth plentifully: and he thought within himself, saying, What shall I do, because I have no room where to bestow my fruits? And he said, This will I do: I will pull down my barns, and build greater; and there will I bestow all my fruits and my goods. And I will say to my soul, Soul, thou hast much goods laid up for many years; take thine ease, eat, drink, and be merry. But God said unto him, Thou fool, this night thy soul shall be required of thee: then whose shall those things be, which thou hast provided? So is he that layeth up treasure for himself, and is not rich toward God.
LUKE 12.13-21

THE DANGER OF DEVELOPING A FALSE SENSE OF SECURITY

'*The ground of a certain rich man brought forth plentifully.*' Most of us imagine that to possess wealth is a good thing, and when we read these words at the beginning of this parable we exclaim, 'Fortunate man!' When we hear of people inheriting fortunes we say, 'Lucky people!' When we hear of men winning rich prizes through their own industry and skill we are willing to admit that we would gladly be in their places. We think of the sense of security and the relief from financial strain that wealth could bring, of the desirable things it could purchase, of the opportunity it would give for doing good, and after considering all this we conclude that it is good to be rich.

Jesus taught otherwise. As James Denney points out, He taught that men should be afraid to become rich. How hardly shall they that have riches enter the Kingdom of God! 'It is easier for a camel to go through the eye of a needle, than for a rich man to enter into the kingdom.'[1] This parable is designed to show how riches and good fortune in life tend to lead not to

[1] Mark 10.24-25

blessing but to tragedy. Here we discover one of the great differences between the thinking of Jesus Christ and our own.

Our Lord is quite explicit about the reason why He regarded the possession of wealth as undesirable. To possess wealth gives a man a false sense of security. Jesus spoke of the 'deceitfulness of riches'.[1] When a man possesses riches he is deceived about his position in life. He receives a deference and flattery from others which gives him a false view of his own person. He tends to begin to feel independent, to rely on and trust in his riches rather than in God. He feels safe apart from God and forgets that he may die at any moment.

The rich man in the parable is an illustration of this. When his ground began to bring forth plentifully, he took an inventory of his possessions and found them enormous, almost embarrassing, and he began to say within himself, 'At last I can be at ease.' When he surveyed his balance sheets, and looked over the huge new barns he had built and the enormous stocks he had laid up, he said to himself, '*Soul, thou hast much goods laid up for many years: take thine ease, eat, drink, and be merry.*' How secure he felt, and how settled he considered himself! He did not need God now; he did not need prayer; for he had so much else. He did not think of the possibility of death and then the Judgment Seat; he had so many pleasant things to absorb him. Calvin says, 'He lengthened out his expectation of life, in proportion to his great riches.' He felt his riches to be his bulwark against all evil.

It was a false sense of security. Life is never secure for anyone. This rich man was no more secure in his health and wealth than the starving diseased beggars in the village streets who were dying at the rate of twenty a day. The hand of God would find him as easily as it finds anyone else. Death would pick him up out of his snug surroundings as easily as it picks up the frailest of God's creatures that come forth one day to die the next. God has made life apart from Himself fundamentally insecure. He has made it so that there is no satisfying rest for man but in Himself, and anything that gives man a sense of security and pleasure and ease apart from God is therefore evil.

It has been pointed out that it is usually material wealth that

[1] Matt. 13.22

gives man this false sense of security, but if a man is rich in anything apart from God—rich in talents, brains, ability, popularity—he is no less in danger than this rich man. Man must never try to settle down and take his ease until he has faced the questions raised by the thought of his soul, his sin, his eternity, and the Judgment Seat of God. Anything that makes him shelve these questions—and earthly good fortune can do this—is to him a curse and not a blessing. 'What shall it profit a man, if he shall gain the whole world, and lose his own soul?'[1] This therefore is why prosperity is so often bad for us and this is why earthly affliction and privation, evil things though they may seem in themselves, are sometimes good for us. We must be continually disturbed, continually prevented from feeling at ease in this life, if we are to learn to trust in God.

THE FOLLY OF PLANNING WITHOUT GOD

This rich man in the midst of his security made clever and admirable plans. '*He thought within himself, saying, What shall I do, because I have no room where to bestow my fruits? And he said, This will I do: I will pull down my barns, and build greater; and there will I bestow all my fruits and my goods. And I will say to my soul, Soul . . . eat, drink, and be merry.*'

According to the way of the world this is wise, sensible planning. In spite of all his wealth, he was a prudent and practical man, no fool in worldly wisdom. He insured against every contingency. He had heard of many as rich as himself who had gone bankrupt through not having proper storage accommodation, and he was not going to be caught out in that way. His plans embraced the distant future. There is much that is admirable in this rich man and in his outlook. There was nothing in him of the miser who never enjoys his wealth. '*Take thine ease, eat, drink, and be merry.*' He knew when to retire, and he made careful and detailed plans to enjoy his wealth at his ease; he had every good earthly reason for hoping to see them fulfilled.

His plans were spoiled because God had another intention. This wise rich man had not consulted God, and his plans were spoiled because he had considered the welfare only of himself. His plans, inspired by selfish ambition, were all folly, because

[1] Mark 8.36

God has the final decision, and this is God's world. The man said to himself, 'I will plan wisely and strategically; I will do this and this and this.' 'Thou fool,' said God. 'I have other plans, and no man can force his own will in My world.'

We are all keen to try to master our circumstances and become lords of our own destiny. We try to manœuvre people and things in ways to suit our own ends and get our own will done. But this is a ridiculous game to play in this universe. It may succeed for a time, as it succeeded for a time with this man, as it succeeded with Hitler for a time. But what folly it proves to be in the end! God had His will in the matter of this rich man's life, and the rich man had forgotten this one factor in the situation—the will of God. '*Thou fool,*' God said to the clever planner, and spoilt all his plans. How foolish to plan ahead, to dream dreams and see visions, to seek to execute one's dreams and visions, and to leave out of account the one thing that matters—the will of God. It is a simple matter for God to thwart our plans. One word from God and this rich, wise man was a fool. Caesar Borgia was a great schemer and a successful and subtle diplomat. He made shrewd and careful plans to achieve, on the death of his father, Alexander, a *coup d'état* that would result in his being master of Italy. He told Machiavelli that he had prepared for every eventuality on his father's death. But one thing destroyed his schemes. On his father's death he happened to be ill and not one of his plans could be put into action. He had planned so cleverly, but God said, '*Thou fool!* I have other plans.' We must beware of the folly of planning for self in the midst of a world where God has the final decision in all things.

THE TRAGEDY OF HAVING NO RICHES OF SOUL TOWARDS GOD

On that night on which God took his soul—and God took it for judgment—this rich man had no riches towards God. Jesus explicitly draws our attention to this. '*So is he that layeth up treasure for himself, and is not rich toward God.*' He had plenty of riches heaped up on earth, but, as the old proverb says, 'There are no pockets in a shroud.' '*Thou fool! This night thy soul shall be required of thee: then whose shall those things be, which thou hast provided?*' He had not even friends to whom he could leave his goods, so soulless had been his life. He was a poor lonely soul in the end, this rich man. From the point of view of the world he had been a success and his funeral was attended by the big men of the land. He was officially mourned as few others, but how pathetic is his life seen from the point of view of his death. How pathetic his success in view of the end.

God requires then that we should have riches towards Himself. He demands an inward righteousness which the world cannot always see but which is always before Him. He looks for riches in the heart and soul: '*This night thy soul shall be required of thee.*' A man's life is surely a tragedy and a failure if he has been a success in everything else but in the end he lacks this one thing that matters. When the rich young ruler came to Jesus He looked at him and loved him, and said, 'One thing thou lackest: go and sell that thou hast, and give to the poor, and thou shalt have treasure in heaven.'[1]

How can we succeed in giving heed to the warnings of Jesus in this parable and in keeping ourselves alive to all the issues this story raises? This present life is so absorbing to us that we are as easily fascinated by the things of this world and led astray as this man was. There is only one answer. It is Jesus Christ who speaks these warnings, and in speaking them He offers Himself as Saviour. He Himself can save us from the danger, the folly and the tragedy so vividly shown up in this story.

It is by His Cross that He saves us from the danger of sleeping the sleep of death in false security. He 'gave himself for our sins, that he might deliver us from this present evil world'.[2] The Cross, when we understand its meaning and hold it before us, shatters all the fascination of the spells the world may have thrown over our souls. The Cross delivers us from the ways of the world by revealing to us in all its brutal details the outcome of these ways. The Cross reveals the vanity of all human glory by revealing to us the glory of the love of God set shatteringly against all the pride of man. No man can constantly remember Calvary and live under its shadow and at the same time mould himself according to the pattern set by the careless life of this world.

Christ can save us too from the covetous self-centredness

[1] Matt. 19.21, Mark 10.21   [2] Gal. 1.4

that plans only for self, only in the end to find each plan thwarted, and to reap bitter disillusionment. Paul claims that Christ has delivered him from self. 'I am crucified with Christ: nevertheless I live; yet not I, but Christ liveth in me.'[1]

Above all, Christ can make us rich towards God, for He can clothe us in that righteousness and truth and love in which God takes delight. Let us not imagine that these riches towards God here referred to consist merely in the earthly character we develop as we walk through this life. This heavenly treasure is, rather, Christ Himself as He gives Himself to us. Paul speaks of 'Christ in you, the hope of glory'.[2] If God were to look on any of us as we are in ourselves, or as we could make ourselves, how would we stand? 'If thou, Lord, shouldest mark iniquities, O Lord, who shall stand?'[3] But Christ gives Himself to us through faith in Him, and when the Father sees Christ in us He sees us as indeed rich, and fit to inherit all things.

[1] Gal. 2.20   [2] Col. 1.27   [3] Ps. 130.3

DIVES AND LAZARUS

There was a certain rich man, which was clothed in purple and fine linen, and fared sumptuously every day: and there was a certain beggar named Lazarus, which was laid at his gate, full of sores, and desiring to be fed with the crumbs which fell from the rich man's table: moreover the dogs came and licked his sores. And it came to pass, that the beggar died, and was carried by the angels into Abraham's bosom: the rich man also died, and was buried; and in hell he lift up his eyes, being in torments, and seeth Abraham afar off, and Lazarus in his bosom. And he cried and said, Father Abraham, have mercy on me, and send Lazarus, that he may dip the tip of his finger in water, and cool my tongue; for I am tormented in this flame. But Abraham said, Son, remember that thou in thy lifetime receivedst thy good things, and likewise Lazarus evil things: but now he is comforted, and thou art tormented. And beside all this, between us and you there is a great gulf fixed: so that they which would pass from hence to you cannot; neither can they pass to us, that would come from thence. Then he said, I pray thee therefore, father, that thou wouldest send him to my father's house: for I have five brethren; that he may testify unto them, lest they also come into this place of torment. Abraham saith unto him, They have Moses and the prophets; let them hear them. And he said, Nay, father Abraham: but if one went unto them from the dead, they will repent. And he said unto him, If they hear not Moses and the prophets, neither will they be persuaded, though one rose from the dead.

LUKE 16.19-31

There are two scenes in this parable. In the first, upon earth, we are shown Lazarus lying miserable at the gate of the rich man, whom we shall call Dives. The scene soon changes and in the latter half of the parable we are taken to the world beyond, where we are shown Lazarus now in bliss, and Dives now suffering the torments of Hell fire.

It should disturb us profoundly that Jesus in the second part of this parable should have thus vividly pictured for us the torments of a man in Hell. He knew the facts about the world beyond, and if there were no such state or place as Hell, surely He would have refrained from drawing this realistic picture of the torments and remorse of a man caught in its toils, even though it were used only for the purpose of illustrating other truths which He wanted to teach. In spite of much confident talk about universal salvation and the impossibility of a God of Love ever condemning men to everlasting torment, those who read this parable, and consider fully the implications of the fact that it was spoken by Jesus Christ, will find it impossible to be dogmatic in asserting that in His picture of Hell Jesus is describing something that to Him did not really exist.

But Jesus did not tell this parable to teach us about Hell. He told it to teach us about life; and it is a startling fact that this story, so awful in its sequel in the world beyond, is so true in the equally grim picture it paints of this life on earth in its opening scene. This parable shows us very plainly what life is like—our modern life today—and it shows us very clearly the duty in which we fail so miserably.

A GRIM PICTURE OF HUMAN LIFE

'*There was a certain rich man, which was clothed in purple and fine linen, and fared sumptuously every day: and there was a certain beggar named Lazarus, which was laid at his gate, full of sores, and desiring to be fed with the crumbs which fell from the rich man's table: moreover the dogs came and licked his sores.*' That is what life is like and always has been like. Some people seem to have every privilege and a superfluity of this world's goods. Others at their side seem to be deprived of most of the things necessary for earthly health and pleasantness of existence. Privileges, talents and riches seem to be badly distributed. In all its aspects life is made up of the 'haves' and the 'have nots'. There are the rich and the poor, the west end and the east end.

It is nobody's fault in particular, this Dives and Lazarus situation on earth. Lazarus was not at fault for being so poor; we read of no crime or sin that brought him to that sorry state. And it was not Dives' fault that he was rich. Jesus deliberately omits any hint that Dives had no right to be rich. However this man obtained his wealth, whether by birth, or by business, or by good fortune, it was all obtained honestly. Therefore it was neither Dives nor Lazarus who brought about the situation described by Jesus in the first scene of this parable. It simply happened to be so. Dives would have been a poor man had he been born as Lazarus. Lazarus would have been a rich man had he been born as Dives.

This still 'just happens' today. Some are born naturally gifted, others have no talents to speak of. Some are born temperamentally fit for the struggle for existence, others are born quite unsuited for it. All such natural differences, which no legislation can prevent, are bound to lead to the formation of 'class' in any society, however governed. We must never cease trying to prevent this happening. Let us pray and work always for the abolition of 'extreme differences of wealth and poverty', but let us remember that, however we dream and legislate and coerce and plan, we will always have privilege flourishing alongside poverty, the man of prosperity living next door to the man of ill fortune. Perhaps not even in our generation will the saying of Jesus become out of date: 'Ye have the poor with you always.'[1] In the book of Deuteronomy[2] there is given a piece of legislation designed in the days of Moses to abolish extremes of wealth and poverty in Israel. At the end of every seven-year period every man in debt was to have his debt freely cancelled and forgotten by the creditor. Surely this was a most effective method of levelling capital? But immediately following this law for the prevention of poverty comes this other command. 'If there be among you a poor man of one of thy brethren within any of thy gates in the land . . . thou shalt not harden thine heart, nor shut thine hand from thy poor brother: But thou shalt open thine hand wide unto him.' Moses was wise. He says first, 'We shall legislate so that there will be no poverty. We shall abolish want.' Then he adds, 'But in spite of all our efforts there *will* be poverty, therefore let us encourage charity.'

Here, then, in this grim picture we have a true portrayal of life as it is. Where is our place in this scene? Do not let us imagine that this is a story concerning only the very wealthy and the very poor in material things, so that we can fold our hands and decide that since we are in neither class we can evade the challenge of its disturbing message. We are very prone to evade the message we do not want these stories of Jesus to teach us. Fosdick tells of an American Sunday School teacher who, after teaching his boys the message of the parable

[1] Mark 14.7 [2] Deut. 15

of the good Samaritan, asked what lesson they had gained from it for themselves. Immediately one boy answered, 'What I get out of it is that when I am in trouble my neighbour ought to help me!'

As far as this parable is concerned, we dare not place ourselves anywhere but alongside the rich man. Is there anyone in our land who is not rich even in material things when we take a wide view over the whole world? 'See,' says a modern writer on this passage. 'You may be rich in love, friendship and honour which have come a-flying to you on all sides. Perhaps you have somehow in and about you, without any effort on your part, a something which makes folk like to have you around or like to be around you, insomuch that you never feel lonesome or forsaken.' Yes, you may be rich and you have not realised it. And you may have some poor Lazarus at your gate and you have not realised it. 'Some thoroughly boring person who perhaps talks incessantly when you meet, because he is so miserable at heart and his misery makes him nervous. You try to avoid the person but somehow he or she keeps cropping up. Lazarus! Repulsive, intolerable, unloved. Lazarus, who has to comfort himself with crumbs and dogs, so despised, needing a friend, and he is laid at your gate.'

Yes! This parable gives us a grim picture of life as it is—of *our* life as it is. Here Jesus is addressing you and me.

THE NEED FOR PERSONAL COMMUNICATION BETWEEN RICH AND POOR

The parable is so told by Jesus as to make the duty of the rich man in this situation quite obvious—so obvious that it does not need to be explicitly mentioned in the story. The duty of Dives was obviously to give personal attention to Lazarus. He should have looked at him, spoken with him often. He should have got to know him, and by personal interest and friendship and giving helped to brighten and alleviate the poor man's lot. But he did not do this. It was the dogs who took a personal interest in Lazarus, being, like Balaam's ass, wiser than their master. The dogs were Lazarus' friends; Dives passed him by.

Notice that even though Dives passed by Lazarus so carelessly, there is no suggestion that in other respects he was not a generous and charitable man. It is likely that this man Dives cared very much for the poor as a class and for his fellow men in general. His name was no doubt found near the top of every list of subscribers to charitable funds. Where others gave a little, he gave much. He may have been a leading citizen working for the community, or even an ardent social reformer. He omitted only one thing. Lazarus happened to be his neighbour and he did not love his *neighbour*, for love involves personal interest and communication. He was in such a hurry to do good to humanity in general that he passed by his neighbour who was in need.

Are we not tempted to imitate him? It is easy to profess love for the distant and to embrace humanity as a whole but hard when it comes down to the unpleasant details of our needy neighbour's wretched state. It is hard sometimes to love even those who live under the same roof as ourselves. But surely this is the crucial test. Is our love and service worth anything if it does not come down to the level of Lazarus and his horrible sores? Tolstoy was an apostle of love. Few have had more love for humanity than he, but his wife wrote of him, 'What amazing understanding in his writings of the psychological life of the people, and what lack of understanding and indifference to the life of the people nearest him,' and she adds these words, 'I do not believe in his goodness and love of humanity.' Dr McNeile Dixon, after making this quotation, writes, 'The love of the distant is an easy thing. We know less about far-off folk. They involve us in fewer duties and responsibilities.' Yes, we are like this rich man. It is as if God, setting his life so near to Lazarus, had said to Dives, 'See! I lay this beggar at your gate. He is your personal concern. Become his friend,' and it is as if Dives answered, 'Not so, Lord! It shall be done through the local poor relief association,' and passed Lazarus by.

HE WHO PASSES BY THE POOR IS MISSING SOMETHING HE MAY ETERNALLY REGRET

For the remainder of the story the scene is shifted to represent the afterlife, and we have a strange picture of Lazarus in Paradise resting in Abraham's bosom, and of Dives burning in Hell, his tongue gasping for moisture. Dives sees Lazarus afar off, and realises too late that Lazarus could be of help to him.

'Father Abraham,' he cries, 'send Lazarus!' But Abraham replies, 'It is too late. There is a great gulf between you two that cannot be crossed now. You should have befriended Lazarus in the other life. You had your opportunity there, and had you taken it you would not be without his help now.'

The two parts of the parable combine to teach us (a lesson admirably brought out in a sermon of Dr Denney) that Dives after all needed Lazarus as much as Lazarus needed Dives, and the tragedy of most rich people is that they wake up too late to the realisation that they need their fellow men. Lazarus may be at our gate daily and in him God is seeking to make up to us what we most lack in life, if we will only stoop to seek to find it in Lazarus. Indeed, Christ is somehow waiting for us there in poor Lazarus, the Christ who can be our wealth into all eternity. Might this not be why we are missing so much of the joy and satisfaction and divine companionship that our Christian faith is supposed to give us, but which we do not experience—and we wonder why? The reason is that we are trying to shield ourselves from Lazarus who has the very thing to give us that we thirst for. When Marie Antoinette was married she ordered that all the beggars should be cleared from the streets along which her wedding procession was to drive. She wanted no such ugly and sad sights to spoil her bliss. Such an attitude can only ensure the exclusion of all true bliss from our life for ever, and of the Christ who was there Himself among the despised and rejected of men.

When the rich man awakened to the stern reality of his situation in Hell he thought of his brothers. He had five brothers and he did not want them to miss what he had missed. He called out to Father Abraham, '*I pray thee, therefore, father, that thou wouldest send him to my father's house: for I have five brethren; that he may testify unto them, lest they also come into this place of torment. Abraham saith unto him, They have Moses and the prophets.*' They have the Scriptures! Dives protested that these were not enough but if one went from the dead they would listen. '*If they hear not Moses and the prophets,*' said Abraham, '*neither will they be persuaded, though one rose from the dead.*'

Let us take note that all the warnings we need are given to us in the Scriptures, if we will read them. They are given to us plainly even in Moses and the prophets. Our whole duty is set forth there so plainly that we need no man from the dead to tell us of it. We do not even need this parable if we have Moses and the prophets. This parable simply brings out in a vivid fashion what is written in the Old Testament about that duty, and we know that we have failed miserably to do that duty.

But there is more shown in Moses and the prophets than simply our duty. Moses and the prophets in the Scriptures tell us also of One who can save us when we have failed in that duty. They tell of a sacrifice for the trespasses and omissions of men who tremble at the Word of God and who are contrite of heart, and who walk through this world in that penitence and fear. Moses and the prophets lead us to the Cross of Christ, where alone any man who knows what they teach about our duty can find forgiveness and peace of heart. They lead us to Christ who can save.

But Christ when He saves us points away from Himself and says 'Go! I send you forth,' and our duty is not obscure; it is perfectly plain. It begins with Lazarus, for 'Thou shalt love the Lord thy God with all thy heart, and with all thy soul, and with all thy mind, and thy neighbour as thyself.'

THE WICKED HUSBANDMEN, AND THE BARREN FIG TREE

Hear another parable: There was a certain householder, which planted a vineyard, and hedged it round about, and digged a winepress in it, and built a tower, and let it out to husbandmen, and went into a far country: and when the time of the fruit drew near, he sent his servants to the husbandmen, that they might receive the fruits of it. And the husbandmen took his servants, and beat one, and killed another, and stoned another. Again, he sent other servants more than the first: and they did unto them likewise. But last of all he sent unto them his son, saying, They will reverence my son. But when the husbandmen saw the son, they said among themselves, This is the heir; come, let us kill him, and let us seize on his inheritance. And they caught him, and cast him out of the vineyard, and slew him. When the lord therefore of the vineyard cometh, what will he do unto those husbandmen? They say unto him, He will miserably destroy those wicked men, and will let out his vineyard unto other husbandmen, which shall render him the fruits in their seasons.

MATTHEW 21.33-41

He spake also this parable; A certain man had a fig tree planted in his vineyard; and he came and sought fruit thereon, and found none. Then said he unto the dresser of his vineyard, Behold, these three years I come seeking fruit on this fig tree, and find none: cut it down; why cumbereth it the ground? And he answering said unto him, Lord, let it alone this year also, till I shall dig about it, and dung it: and if it bear fruit, well: and if not, then after that thou shalt cut it down.

LUKE 13.6-9

The interpretation of the first story is obvious. The vineyard is the Jewish nation. The householder who so carefully planted it out and hedged it in and made everything ready for the time when it should bear fruit is God, who chose the Jews to be His peculiar people, who protected them from their enemies, nurtured them in His truth, and trained them in His ways as no other nation had been protected and nurtured and trained. The husbandmen to whom the vineyard was let are the Jewish leaders in succeeding generations. The series of messengers who were sent by the householder to receive the fruit of the vineyard at the time when it might be expected to bear fruit, and who were despitefully treated and stoned and killed, are the prophets who were given to Israel by God in succeeding generations to speak His Word, to demand trust in Him and to call for obedience, and to remind them of One who was yet to come after them. The Son who with amazing trust and love on the part of God was sent as a confident last appeal to this nation, even though for generations it had shown hatred and contempt of all His previous representations, was Jesus Christ Himself.

This parable, then, is full of plain speaking on the part of Jesus. He told it to the partly hostile crowds who flocked round Him in Jerusalem during the days before His crucifixion. His hearers would know exactly what He was meaning, for they had been accustomed to think of their nation as the Lord's vineyard. The Pharisees and scribes and priests would be angered by His scathing description of the behaviour of their predecessors in office.

Jesus closed the parable with a fearful warning to everyone present. Alas! what their forefathers have done to the prophets may soon find its awful climax and culmination in what they themselves are going to do to Jesus Christ the Son of God. '*But last of all he sent unto them his son, saying, They will reverence my son. But when the husbandmen saw the son, they said among themselves, This is the heir; come, let us kill him, and let us seize on his inheritance. And they caught him, and cast him out of the vineyard, and slew him.*' Jesus is here stating plainly that He is the Son of God, One greater than all the prophets. He is foretelling to his hearers that they are going to kill Him, for even now the plotting for this purpose had started. Thus far He read their minds and the situation in which He found Himself, and then He finished with a further prophecy. 'Therefore say I unto you, The kingdom of God shall be taken from you, and given to a nation bringing forth the fruits thereof.'[1] If they fulfil their intention to slay Him and thus to thwart His ministry among them, the privileges which they have enjoyed for centuries will be taken from them. They are going to be denied the fulfilment of the very purpose for which God had raised them up as a nation. Their whole national history will be

[1] Matt. 21.43

henceforth a story of hopeless frustration. But God will not be thwarted in His will to have fruit from His vineyard after such preparation and such waiting. Others will be called into the vineyard to fulfil the task the Jewish nation has refused, and to act as faithful stewards to yield to God His fruit in its season when He shall call for it.

CHRIST FREES MAN FROM BONDAGE TO HIS OWN PAST

One of the great truths taught in this parable is that in spite of the long and dreadful history of the past there was nothing to prevent the Jewish leaders from receiving Christ and from yielding to Him obedience and reverence if they so willed. The owner of the vineyard, knowing their past history, could nevertheless say of the husbandmen, '*They will reverence my son.*' He felt that no matter how they had behaved in the past they would and could undergo a complete change of attitude and heart when they were confronted by his son.

We naturally think that the owner of the vineyard behaved foolishly. We imagine that the past always determines the future. When we think of the extent and strength and determination of human wickedness, we sometimes feel that there are men whom nothing can change. Such is their past record and such is the hardness of their attitude that they seem bound up with evil for ever and sure to reject even Jesus Christ. When we realise how stubbornly and consistently we ourselves have resisted the will of God in our own past life, and made our selfish choice of ways, and yielded to our unruly passions, we are apt to regard ourselves as hopeless of radical change. But if such were the case there would have been no point in God's sending Jesus Christ into this world. It was to a world of men confirmed and hardened in wickedness, as these vinedressers were, that Christ was sent. But He was sent with hope by the Father, because when He comes on the scene of human life He brings with Him a new freedom to men to choose to yield to God in spite of the past, and to make new and unforseeable decisions for love and righteousness. Apart from Christ human wickedness is dreadful indeed and every man is hardened against God. Apart from Jesus Christ we are forced to use the word 'hopeless' in connexion with all optimistic schemes for the bringing in of the Kingdom of God. But when Christ comes into the human situation He gives men the power to break the law of sin and death that has hitherto been the iron rule of their behaviour.

Therefore no human situation can ever be called 'hopeless' if Christ is at hand to step into it. Even the situation at Jerusalem during the week before Christ was crucified was not yet 'hopeless'. The very fact that Jesus told this parable to the Jews in Jerusalem as a last appeal in the hope that they might yet repent and receive Him meant that they could even now crown Him as their true King if they would. In spite of their dreadful past history, which branded them as a confirmed and deliberate anti-God community, nevertheless nothing had been finally decided. 'You have killed or rejected every prophet and for generations you have been consistent in your hatred of your true Lord,' Jesus is saying, 'yet even now the question of the future is open and will be decided not by the past but by what you do to me.' Only when men give a decision about Jesus Christ Himself do men give a final decision about their destiny.

There is nothing irretrievable with Jesus Christ. Our attitude can therefore be hopeful and optimistic when we face this world in the name of Christ with the Gospel that proclaims His loving and gentle appeal to men. Even those who may seem to have decided that evil is to be their good and that good is to be their evil have finally decided nothing before we go to them with the appeal of the Gospel. God's thoughts are not our thoughts and even of such men God's thoughts may still be, '*They will reverence my son.*' Our Lord here suggests that words such as these arose in the mind and heart of the Father before He sent His Son into this world. The decision of men when faced by the claim of the Gospel of Christ is determined not by the bondage of evil habit that is the legacy of their own past but by the gracious constraining appeal of His love, which can, if it is allowed, overwhelm and conquer the most determined and hardened opposition. No man when faced by Jesus Christ is bound to react according to the fixed rules that have hitherto determined his behaviour.

Therefore we can have hope even for ourselves. Our own past life may tell a sorry tale of violence done regularly to those quiet influences and gentle voices by which God long ago sought from us what today He is still seeking through His Son. That past can be forgotten, for what matters is that Christ stands before us today and there are two possibilities before us. We can yield to Him our lives, thus fulfilling the purpose for which He created us, or we can reject Him as He was rejected by His people in Jerusalem. But today's decision need not be determined by the past!

In Yielding to Christ Man Discovers and Fulfils the Purpose of his Creation

If the Jewish nation had received Jesus Christ with reverence, and had yielded to Him what He had demanded, they would, in spite of their wicked history, have fulfilled the destiny for which they had been raised up as a nation. Jesus in speaking this parable is pointing to Himself as the One in whom they can discover and fulfil their true national destiny. 'Behold in ME,' He is saying, 'the whole purpose of your existence. This nation was created and preserved and trained through the centuries to receive Me and to yield to Me the fruit of its obedience and devotion. In yielding such to Me now you will be yielding the harvest which My Father has sought from you from all eternity and you will be fulfilling the thrilling purpose of His eternal love towards you. In rejecting Me you will be missing all that you were meant to have and to fulfil and all your past national history will have been in vain.'

When Jesus Christ comes to us today through His Word as He came to the Jews in His flesh, He makes the same demand upon us and His coming gives to us the same thrilling opportunity as it gave to the Jewish nation in those critical days in Jerusalem. The first question in the Shorter Catechism is, 'What is the chief end of man?' This parable gives the answer: 'The chief end of man is to receive and reverence the Son of God when He comes with His claims and promises.' No man can really understand why he is alive and what is the meaning of the way God has dealt with him until he looks at Jesus Christ, and the realisation comes, 'I was made to belong to HIM. In Him I was created, and in responding to Him I yield to God the fruit of His care and love for me throughout all my life. In Jesus Christ therefore I find and fulfil the meaning of my life.'

It is only when Jesus Christ comes to us and demands response of us that we can know the answer to the question, What is man? and that we can understand why we have been endowed with such wonderful powers of will and mind and feeling. We were made for Him. Left to ourselves we remain restless and unsatisfied in the quest of the meaning of our life. It is only when we come to Him who says, 'Come unto me, all ye that labour and are heavy laden, and I will give you rest,'[1] that we find lifted from us the heavy burden of all the unanswered and tormenting questions about our own meaning and destiny.

IN REJECTING CHRIST MAN REVEALS THE TRUE MEANING OF HIS SIN

It was only when the husbandmen took the son and cast him out of the vineyard, and, with full knowledge of who he was, slew him, that they finally revealed in its full significance their true attitude towards the owner of the vineyard and the spirit which had been ruling in their hearts from the very start of their persistent refusal to yield fruit to those appointed by the owner.

On a first reading of the parable we might be tempted to conclude that all that was wrong with these men could be defined by one word, 'selfishness'. Rather than deliver to the messengers the harvest of the vineyard, they decided that they would use the profits of the whole concern for their own self-centred aims. They preferred to work for themselves rather than for the benefit of the owner, and they did not like being reminded by the messengers who called for the fruit that neither the vineyard nor the harvest of it belonged to them.

If we read a little more deeply, however, into the story of the vinedressers, we shall see that from the start these men were possessed of a spirit of much more sinister significance than merely one of self-centredness. If they kept for themselves the fruit of the vineyard it was because a spirit of intense hatred against the owner had from the first possessed their hearts. They resented interference from him because they considered him an enemy. Their strong hatred for the owner finds its first expression in maltreating his messengers, then in stoning and

[1] Matt. 11.28

killing them, and gradually it develops in its expression till when faced with the son of the landlord they say to one another with glee and satisfaction, '*This is the heir; come, let us kill him!*' They find malicious pleasure in this act of violence and shame, for they know that it is their opportunity of letting their resentment find its vent in a way that will injure to the quick the one they hate. This then is what lies behind their selfish conduct. It is only a symptom of this spirit of hatred that has taken possession of their hearts.

Sin is this hatred of God that finds its expression in self-centredness, in breaking the law of God, in a multitude of distorted ways of living and of using God's benefits, and that ultimately crucifies Jesus Christ. We cannot define sin satisfactorily, therefore, by such phrases as 'selfishness', or 'a missing of the mark', or 'a breaking of the law'. The Shorter Catechism itself misses the mark when it defines sin as 'any want of conformity unto, or transgression of the law of God'. The true nature of sin is something that can be defined only as a poison in the heart—a spirit of enmity against a loving God. This is what is behind all 'sins'. No matter how trivial the transgression may seem, the inspiration behind it is this thing Sin which is revealed in the Scripture as hatred of God.

The Cross of Christ proves all this to us. The coming of Jesus Christ to confront man in His flesh and to demand the fruit that was God's due was the crucial test of the attitude of man towards his Maker. That attitude was revealed for what it truly is in the hatred of the men who rejected Jesus and exulted in His shame and crucifixion. And their attitude is typical of our own. A man in a dream saw Christ tied to a whipping post and a brutal soldier scourging him with a heavily studded whip. He shuddered as he saw the cruel hand of the soldier flaying the back of his victim till heavy and painful marks appeared and the blood flowed. At last he could stand it no longer and rushed forward to stop the agony. But just then the soldier turned round to face him and the dreamer recognised his own face in that of the brutal executioner. It was he himself who had crucified the Lord! Do we not feel the same about ourselves when we read the story of how they crucified Jesus, scourged Him, derided Him and forsook Him? It is ourselves we are watching as we watch those who crucified Him!

Every type of sin is represented around the Cross of Christ. The Cross is the work of pride, of envy, of disbelief, of selfishness, of lust, of carelessness. And every type of sin is shown up in that Cross to be simply this: hatred against the God who is crucified there by man! Whatever may be the form our besetting sin takes, that is nevertheless simply the *form* our sin assumes. All the varied forms of sin are alike symptoms of the fact that deep down in the heart of man there is the spirit which crucified Christ. All sins are inspired by the spirit of hatred against God which is typified in this parable by the hatred of of the vinedressers for the owner whose son they took such delight in slaying.

THE LONGSUFFERING LORD

The setting of the parable of the barren fig tree is very similar to that of the parable we have been discussing.

'*A certain man had a fig tree planted in his vineyard; and he came and sought fruit thereon, and found none. Then said he unto the dresser of his vineyard, Behold, these three years I come seeking fruit on this fig tree, and find none: cut it down; why cumbereth it the ground? And he answering said unto him, Lord, let it alone this year also, till I shall dig about it, and dung it: and if it bear fruit, well: and if not, then after that thou shalt cut it down.*'

Here we have a fig tree in the same position of privilege as the wicked husbandmen, frustrating the design of its owner by refusing to bear fruit at the time of fruit. It is threatened with the same fate as that which must come to the wicked vinedressers. The vinedressers will be cast out of the vineyard and their position given to others unless they repent; the fig tree will be uprooted unless it bears fruit. Both parables thus prophesy the possible rejection by God of the Jewish nation. God cannot allow His special ground to be cumbered by a deliberately fruitless tree, or His special experiment to be wilfully spoiled by wicked men when He can get others to fulfil His purposes. Both parables therefore warn the Jewish nation of its approaching doom. But in the parable of the barren fig tree Jesus announces that one more chance is to be given to the Jewish nation even though they have committed such crimes of violence and deliberate malice against the person of the Son of God. For one more year the fig tree is to be specially cared for.

One last desperate attempt is to be made to enable it to yield its fruit that it may be saved. Jesus is here teaching that the Jewish nation is to be given one more chance under new conditions, even after the fulfilment of such an act as that of the crucifixion of Jesus.

We know what Jesus meant by this from the actual course that events took after He was crucified and rose again. The Gospel of the redeeming love of God in the Cross calling for faith and repentance was taken to the Jews as well as to all the world. It was preached in their marketplaces and in their synagogues by the Apostles, who wherever they went tried first to convert the chosen race whose representatives had slain the Christ in their name. God sought to retain this people within the vineyard even after they had cast out the Son and slain him. For a whole generation He called them patiently to repentance for their deed; it was only then that the doom that Jesus predicted fell upon them, and Jerusalem was destroyed and the nation scattered abroad to be homeless for centuries to come.

There does come a stage in affairs when God can no longer withhold His judgment, but He withholds that final act as long as He can. His judgment fell upon the Jewish nation only *after* they had had time to see and understand the full consequences of their sin in the Cross of Christ, only after they had had ample opportunity to repent in the light of the terrible deed that had been the issue of their rebellious career as a nation. Before God judges men He allows them to see in the Cross of Christ what their sin has led to. He asks whether they approve or repent, and He passes final sentence only on those who with open eyes and deliberate choice and approval hold on to those ways that have brought them to such shame.

WARNINGS TO ALL

THE UNFORGIVING DEBTOR

Then came Peter to him, and said, Lord, how oft shall my brother sin against me, and I forgive him? till seven times? Jesus saith unto him, I say not unto thee, Until seven times: but, Until seventy times seven. Therefore is the kingdom of heaven likened unto a certain king, which would take account of his servants. And when he had begun to reckon, one was brought unto him, which owed him ten thousand talents. But forasmuch as he had not to pay, his lord commanded him to be sold, and his wife, and children, and all that he had, and payment to be made. The servant therefore fell down, and worshipped him, saying, Lord, have patience with me, and I will pay thee all. Then the lord of that servant was moved with compassion, and loosed him, and forgave him the debt. But the same servant went out, and found one of his fellowservants, which owed him an hundred pence: and he laid hands on him, and took him by the throat, saying, Pay me that thou owest. And his fellowservant fell down at his feet, and besought him, saying, Have patience with me, and I will pay thee all. And he would not: but went and cast him into prison, till he should pay the debt. So when his fellowservants saw what was done, they were very sorry, and came and told unto their lord all that was done. Then his lord, after that he had called him, said unto him, O thou wicked servant, I forgave thee all that debt, because thou desiredst me: shouldest not thou also have had compassion on thy fellowservant, even as I had pity on thee? And his lord was wroth, and delivered him to the tormentors, till he should pay all that was due unto him. So likewise shall my heavenly Father do also unto you, if ye from your hearts forgive not every one his brother their trespasses.

MATTHEW 18.21-35

This parable would make an exciting and satisfying drama if it were staged or filmed. There is great variety of scene. We first meet our principal character in an audience chamber in the king's palace, then we follow him out into the streets of the city, then into the dungeon. There is swiftness of action and great melodrama in this story. We experience, as we read it, exciting changes of mood. Our feelings are stirred now to pity, now to indignation, and at the end there is a feeling of satisfaction as the just consequences of the whole unfold themselves. But this interested delight in the parable for its dramatic worth, and these feelings of satisfaction, can come to us only if we view it as a piece of play-acting in which we ourselves are not involved. If, on the other hand, we view this parable as a challenging message addressed to us, it leaves us more perturbed than perhaps any other of the parables of Jesus. It leaves us with anxious questions in our hearts, and perhaps that is how Jesus meant it to affect us.

THE RECKONING EVERY MAN MUST MAKE WITH GOD

When we ask what it is that makes a man a citizen of the Kingdom of God, this parable furnishes us with its own particular answer. A citizen of the Kingdom of God is one who has made a full reckoning with God over the question of sin and guilt.

'*Therefore is the kingdom of heaven likened unto a certain king, which would make a reckoning with his servants.*'[1] Jesus draws here the picture of a king in a certain kingdom, who seeks to meet with each of his subjects. The meeting has to be personal; they are to be brought before him one by one. The meeting must be frank. The matter to be discussed between the king and his subjects is the settlement of past debts and past crimes. All outstanding matters between this king and his subjects have to come under review. If they have complaints to make or accounts to render to the king, these will be examined, but in this parable it is the king who has all the main accounts to render. There are many people who have been running into trouble. There are judicial sentences that must be executed. Arrears of debt too have been piling up. In this realm things have been getting slack. The king is determined that no longer must any such matters be outstanding. Reckoning must be made between himself and his subjects.

Jesus intends by this picture to teach us that God is seeking to reckon with us, each one personally, about the matter of our sin and guilt. In the New Testament Christians are addressed as the 'called of God', and this word 'called' simply means those who have each had a personal meeting with God in which they have heard His challenge and received His mercy. When Jesus Christ dealt with men and women He always preferred to do so in a face-to-face meeting. A woman once

[1] Substituting R.V. translation for A.V.

came behind Him in the crowd and by touching the hem of His garment tried to steal a blessing from Him without this personal interview. But Jesus immediately cried, 'Who touched me?' and trembling she had to face Him.[1] In this interview it was frankness that mattered. Jesus would do nothing for any man or woman who did not tell Him all the truth. Think of how, when the woman at the well of Samaria sought blessing from Him, He first of all, before she received the blessing, forced her to be frank with Him by Himself revealing openly all the shameful side of her life. Today, God in Jesus Christ seeks with us this same personal frank interview. He seeks to reckon with His people. A citizen of the Kingdom of God is one who has been through this interview with the King and who has nothing outstanding to be settled between himself and his Lord.

In the reckoning described in the parable the debt was revealed in its full proportions and the cost of payment stated in all its severity: *'And when he had begun to reckon, one was brought unto him, which owed him ten thousand talents. But forasmuch as he had not to pay, his lord commanded him to be sold, and his wife, and children, and all that he had, and payment to be made.'* Ten thousand talents is an enormous debt. Adam Clarke, in his commentary on this parable, reckoning it out in terms of talents of gold, calculated that the sum owed by this subject to his king was equal to the annual revenue of the British Empire in his day. We can see why Jesus, for the purpose of forcing home His lesson, made it such a sum. He wanted to impress upon us that when men reckon with God, and are brought into His presence, no one can stand upon his feet. The debt we owe to God is so enormous that no man can face the thought of his life being revealed and his worth frankly stated in the sight of God. 'If thou, Lord, shouldest mark iniquities, O Lord, who shall stand?'[2] Jesus was always seeking to help men to realise the hopelessness of their position in this reckoning before God. Is this not why He put in the forefront of His teaching the Sermon on the Mount, with all its precepts impossible to our attainment, that sermon whose clear statement of what we owe to God brings us into a position of shame and almost hopeless despair? On another occasion He warned us that 'every idle word that men shall speak, they shall give account thereof in

[1] Mark 5.25-33   [2] Ps. 130.3

the day of judgment'.[1] Where can we stand if God takes into account all our wandering thoughts, all the words we speak when we are off our guard?

The man then is condemned, and this debt is a most serious matter. Nothing in it can be glossed over or reduced. But at the same time as the debt is revealed, the man is freely forgiven. He falls on his face in despair, and when he pleads for mercy the debt is cancelled. The whole adverse account of the past is torn up before his eyes. Every trace of the things that can be reckoned against him is destroyed because the one with whom he is dealing is not only just but merciful and compassionate.

God, in reckoning with man, is frank with him. Even when God is going to forgive sin, He reveals its hideous nature and sinister proportions. Think of the story of how Joseph, after he rose to his high place in Egypt, treated his brothers when they came to him to buy bread. Joseph was ready and longing to forgive his brothers from the start, but before he forgave he started a long and agonising process to test them, to see whether they were repentant. For day after day, week after week, they were forced to undergo experiences that brought back to their minds the clear details of the crime they had committed against their younger brother and made them sick unto death in the agonies of remorse. In the process of being forgiven these men had their sin revealed. Before their burden was lifted they were made to feel it as a crushing, terrible load. This is God's way, for He is holy and just as well as loving, and in forgiving the sins of men in Christ through the Cross, He reveals in the same Cross the awfulness of the debt to be paid. There at the Cross we see the cost of all our rebellion against God, but there at the Cross God in revealing the debt meets it and cancels it before our very eyes.

A Warning against Leading a Double Life

'*The same servant went out.*' The scene shifts. He goes out of the presence of God, this man who on his knees has received so freely of the mercy of God, and no sooner has he gone out on to the street than he meets another servant, and he is forced now to reckon with his fellow man.

We too have to go out from the presence of God on to the

[1] Matt. 12.36

hard street of daily life. We too have the same two very different worlds to face and the same two different problems as this man had. We have our reckoning with God, and we also have our reckoning with our fellow men. We have our life of worship and prayer to live in secret with God, and then we have to go out from our church services and our prayer closets and live our life in this world. If it is a hard matter to face God frankly and reckon with Him on matters that are secret between Him and ourselves, it is no less difficult a matter, after we have faced God, to have to go out and reckon with life and its problems. What a difference there seems to be between the atmosphere we breathe when we worship in the church, listening at the feet of Jesus to His Word or sitting at the Lord's Table to partake of His benefits, and the atmosphere in the streets of this world where everything seems to clamour in our ears, 'Don't be a fool. Forget here what you learned at the feet of Jesus!' How hard it is to take this Gospel, which in church we confess to be the truth on which we stake our eternal destiny, and apply it to daily life! How hard it is not to find ourselves living a double life! 'You cannot be a Christian in business life today,' one man says. 'You cannot be a Christian and a soldier,' another man says. 'How can I be a Christian and a newspaper reporter?' a man once said. 'It is my job to get all the sensational details of cases which I know will do harm and bring sorrow to other people in their publication, and then I go to church and I am told that I must be loving to everybody!'

In the man spoken of in the parable Jesus gives us a vivid illustration of how easy it is for us to slip into a double and hypocritical way of acting. This man became different when he left the presence of the king. When he met his fellow servant in the street he went up to him and seized him by the throat and shouted, 'Pay what you owe!' In his reckoning with his fellow man he was seeking to settle affairs on an entirely different principle from that which had held in his relation to the gracious king whose bounty he had received.

The biggest difference of all between the way things are done in the sphere of the Kingdom of God and in the world is that before God everything is decided by His gracious and loving will. The basis of everything is free forgiveness. It is the weak and the helpless who are most encouraged in the Kingdom of God. It is the man who has cast himself down at the feet of God who is raised up. There are no rigid principles by which God acts. But in the world it is *principle* that holds all the time. Justice! Equality! No work, no food! To each according to his merits or his usefulness to society! It is the strong and the righteous who flourish in the world. It is the fittest who survive. The weak and the broken and the wasters have little chance. This world is ruled by the principle that each man must pay his debts, and if he cannot he must face up to the consequence of his folly like a man. Bearing all this in mind, the action of the man in the parable whose conduct we are discussing is not so bad as appears on a superficial reading. He did not say, 'Pay *me* that thou owest.' This is a mistranslation in the Authorised Version. He said, 'Pay what thou owest.' He was not acting out of selfishness or for reasons of spite or vengeance, he was merely acting on the principle of justice. He was acting according to the way of the men of the world. He could have justified himself before his fellow men for his action, and there is indeed much to be said for his behaviour. This world would go to pieces if people thought they could get off without paying their debts. If we had not seen this man a few minutes before on his knees in the king's palace pouring out his gratitude to his king for cancelling so freely such a great debt, we would not be able to pick any holes in his behaviour or raise our voices against him. What shocks us about the man's behaviour is its duplicity. It seems unbelievable that such contradiction should be found in one man.

We are meant to examine ourselves. In all our dealings with men on the streets of this world on week days we must remember that on Sunday we sang and prayed before God as those whose eternal destiny was decided not according to strict principles of justice and fairness, but by free and wholly undeserved forgiveness of sins. This thought must surely modify our desires to adhere to strict principles in exacting the service or the debt that other people owe to us. A Christian has no right to lay aside all trace of his inward Christian experience when he deals with men on the streets of daily life. He must at least show signs that reflect the light of his experience of the grace and goodness of God into his business and social and family life.

The One Unpardonable Inconsistency

When we think all this over we sometimes find it hard to see any consistency at all in our life. 'O wretched man that I am!' we cry, 'who shall deliver me from the body of this death?'[1] We know that only through death can we be delivered from this strange tension, this pull between two different worlds that we cannot harmonise. We live ashamed of all this, for from the world we turn back to God in confession and repentance, and because we live ashamed, ever groaning with this as a burden, ever seeking to get rid of the compromise, we trust that God in His mercy will pardon us.

We are like Naaman, the Syrian. From the land of Israel he had to go back to the land of Syria, and he knew that in his life in Syria he would have to bow down in the house of Rimmon, the god of the Syrians, even though he now believed that Rimmon was an idol and that there was only one true God, the God of Israel. He went back to face his life in Syria, but as a token of his belief in Elisha's God he took with him two mules' burden of the earth of Israel, and he prayed to God that when he bowed down in the house of Rimmon the Lord would pardon his compromise, and God did so. There is no way for us to free our life from compromise while we live in this flesh. Not even the most fervent believer in Christian perfection can renounce to this extent the life of the society in which he lives.

Our only hope of salvation must lie in the assurance that the merciful God will pardon all our inconsistencies as time and again we turn back from the streets of the city to His temple to make our confession in penitence before Him. But we must not take such forgiveness for granted and we must remember the teaching of this parable that there is one form of inconsistency for which there can be no hope of pardon. That is the utter inconsistency of the unforgiving spirit. It is the deliberate and conscious cultivation of the two-faced attitude, this double life against which Jesus is warning us in this parable. And to enforce His warning He adds a sequel to the parable in which He shows how terrible can be the consequences of one particular form of such inconsistency.

'*So when his fellowservants saw what was done, they were very sorry,*

[1] Rom. 7.24

and came and told unto their lord all that was done. Then his lord, after that he had called him, said unto him, O thou wicked servant, I forgave thee all that debt, because thou desiredst me: shouldest not thou also have had compassion on thy fellowservant, even as I had pity on thee? And his lord was wroth, and delivered him to the tormentors, till he should pay all that was due unto him. So likewise shall my heavenly Father do also unto you, if ye from your hearts forgive not every one his brother their trespasses.'

'*If ye forgive not every one his brother!*' '*Shouldest not thou also have had compassion?*' Unforgiveness! Lack of compassion! If we come out of the church of Christ having spent an hour in meditation upon the breadth and length and depth and height of the love of God which we profess has saved us from sin, and then proceed to act in everyday life on a policy that is dictated by business methods overriding compassion, then let us beware! If we can rise from the Communion Table and continue to keep up our cool and distant behaviour towards those we considered had done us a wrong, then let us beware! For there is this one form of inconsistency that God will not pardon. There is this one characteristic that excludes men from the Kingdom of God and brands them as citizens of one world only, doomed when this world ends to unutterable loss. We cannot be forgiven by God and at the same time remain with an unforgiving spirit towards our fellow men. 'If ye forgive men their trespasses, your heavenly Father will also forgive you: but if ye forgive not men their trespasses, neither will your Father forgive your trespasses.'[1]

Jesus Christ told us that there was a chance even for the publicans and harlots, even for the Pharisees, to get into the Kingdom of God, but he tells us frankly that there is no chance for the unforgiving. We cannot be unforgiving and forgiven. This form of inconsistency God will not pardon. This was the really serious element in the conduct of the unforgiving servant.

There can be no settlement with God unless a man settles with his fellow men under the inspiration of the forgiving love that he has experienced in the presence of God. The man in this parable had not really *settled* with his king. In that interview in the king's palace he had only made a reckoning with him. There can be no final settlement with God until it is re-

[1] Matt. 6.14-15

vealed what a man's settlement with his fellow men is to be. It is good to be certain on religious matters, and to be able to say, 'I have made my peace with God: I have had my sins forgiven,' but there is only one way to seal that assurance and to turn the reckoning into a full and final settlement; that is to manifest towards our fellow men in our daily manner of living the forgiving love we have received in secret with God.

The purpose of the king in making his merciful reckoning with his servants was that the spirit of mercy might be spread abroad through all his realm. It was his desire that all those who had been at his feet and had received such a free and gracious pardon would go out and act likewise in the world, and that a fellowship should be created in his realm, based on this same mutual forgiveness. He knew what life was like outside his palace; he knew that it was hard and cruel, and that every man stood up for his rights and acted on principles rather than from personal considerations of love. His aim was that all that should be altered and that the spirit of mercy should be spread abroad. He does not, it is true, in this story say to the servant, 'Now go out and do and act as I have acted towards you.' What could have been more obvious? What more certain than that, if a man has really opened his heart to the grace of God, his whole outlook will change and he will now act differently towards his fellow men?

If we find it hard to forgive, if, like Peter, to whom this parable was spoken, we find that we can forgive seven times, but no more than seven times, let us go back to the place where we made our reckoning with God—the Cross of Jesus Christ, where we see all our debt revealed and at the same time cancelled, through the almighty, wonderful and suffering love of God. Let us meet Him there and let us not be too much in haste to go out of His presence.

THE WISE AND FOOLISH VIRGINS

Then shall the kingdom of heaven be likened unto ten virgins, which took their lamps, and went forth to meet the bridegroom. And five of them were wise, and five were foolish. They that were foolish took their lamps, and took no oil with them: but the wise took oil in their vessels with their lamps. While the bridegroom tarried, they all slumbered and slept. And at midnight there was a cry made, Behold, the bridegroom cometh; go ye out to meet him. Then all those virgins arose, and trimmed their lamps. And the foolish said unto the wise, Give us of your oil; for our lamps are gone out. But the wise answered, saying, Not so; lest there be not enough for us and you: but go ye rather to them that sell, and buy for yourselves. And while they went to buy, the bridegroom came; and they that were ready went in with him to the marriage: and the door was shut. Afterward came also the other virgins, saying, Lord, Lord, open to us. But he answered and said, Verily I say unto you, I know you not. Watch therefore, for ye know neither the day nor the hour wherein the Son of man cometh. MATTHEW 25.1-13

'*Then shall the kingdom of heaven be likened unto ten virgins, which took their lamps, and went forth to meet the bridegroom.*'

Each of these ten virgins looked like the other. Each had a lamp, and each was dressed to fit into the general scheme designed by those who planned the wedding. Each claimed to have been invited. Each acted alike, and it was a pretty ceremony they were engaged in. They were acting as the bridal party at an eastern wedding, gathered, as was the custom, by the wayside to meet the bridegroom when he came to claim the bride.

The outcome of the story proves that five were false and foolish women trying to pass off a piece of trickery that was bound ultimately to be discovered. They had had no real personal invitation from the bridegroom to meet him, but were there because the excitement and the trappings and the rôle of bridesmaid appealed to them. They were not genuine in their purpose to meet the bridegroom for his own sake. Yet no discovery of their fraud was possible until the hour of his coming.

THE WISE AND FOOLISH VIRGINS

The imitation was perfect. They had all adorned themselves alike and trimmed their little lamps alike. All had professed to be genuinely waiting for the great event, and when the bridegroom delayed coming and everyone grew weary of waiting, they all lay down in similar postures, wise and foolish mingled together, and slept an apparently peaceful sleep with their lamps beside them—a pretty picture of slumbering, yet waiting bridesmaids—so much alike!

But there came an hour of decision when the foolish five failed to keep up their false appearance. Suddenly their folly and hypocrisy were shown up to their shame and confusion. It had been easy to succeed in their play-acting at the start, but during that sudden hour of crisis after the long and trying hours of waiting such deception became impossible to sustain.

The bridegroom came at midnight and the wise, who were ready, calmly trimmed their lamps. The foolish looked at their lamps and they had no oil. '*Give us of your oil,*' they said to the others. '*Not so,*' replied the others, '*Go and buy for yourselves.*' And while the foolish ones went to buy oil to make their preparation for the feast, the doors were shut. They were shut before the foolish virgins had time to gather their wits together and think out what to do. It was too late now to mend their ways and go back to the past, too late now to review the situation and determine that next time they would be prepared. There was to be no next time. The door was shut, and shut for ever. '*Watch therefore, for ye know neither the day nor the hour when the Son of man cometh.*'

THE FALSE AMONG THE TRUE

One of the most remarkable features of this parable is the ease with which, almost up to the very end, the foolish virgins were able to keep up the appearance of being thoroughly prepared and genuine. A few borrowed clothes and a little clever acting and everyone seemed taken in—even the other bridesmaids! So quick and easy was their first success that they began to feel very confident of their ability to win their way into the wedding feast and to pass any test that might be applied. So confident were they that when it came to the time of sleeping, they slept soundly amongst the others.

There are such imitators and borrowers in the Church of

today. Men hear tell of a Kingdom of God, a coming King, a Heaven of Blessedness, a pilgrimage to the Beyond. They feel that it is good to be in on this. It takes their fancy just as the idea of a wedding procession took the fancy of the five foolish virgins. They are thus emboldened to join in with those who speak of these things. And when they find themselves Church members they can strictly imitate the behaviour that is typical within the Church. They zealously observe all the ceremonies and services of Christianity. Genuine Christianity can be imitated.

This imitation extends not only to regular churchgoing and devout forms of worship but even to a simulated enthusiasm. The very keenness that others manifest in all the varied activities of the Church they can reproduce. Moreover, this imitation can extend even to the realm of inward religious experience. Men seeing others undergo religious experiences can induce within themselves religious emotions and feelings similar in every respect to those undergone by others in a genuine experience of the living Christ, and yet in their case the whole 'experience' may be nothing but a sham, because in it there is no such personal dealing with Christ. During religious revivals there are always among genuine cases of conversion spurious ones. There are those who seem to have the correct emotions and feelings, yet time reveals the sham. The religious imitator is busy even here!

This matter of imitating and borrowing from the genuine children of God extends even farther than the field of the Church. In the midst of the life of the world at large, the children of this world manage to imitate very well the personal and social morality of the true children of the Kingdom of God. It is difficult to distinguish believers from unbelievers in the midst of a society that has been leavened by the Christian Gospel, and where there is a high prevalent standard of morality. Even those without faith in God can shine with Christian virtues in such a society. Atheists can be charitable, apparently humble, charming, self-controlled men, sometimes morally better than many Christians, but this does not mean that they are therefore genuinely in the Kingdom of God. Their virtue has no foundation in faith, nor does it have a living root from which it can grow. They are simply borrowing

THE WISE AND FOOLISH VIRGINS

virtue from others by reason of their inherited environment and tradition. It is a superficial virtue that is no less easy to acquire than it was for the false bridesmaids to borrow their dresses.

In view of this aspect of the teaching of the parable, it is well that we should ask ourselves if we are indeed 'genuine' in our profession and in the activity in which we participate when we move in the midst of the fellowship of the Church. John Bunyan tells us that there was a time when he was zealous in his observance of religious duties and loved to join in religious talk and argument. But one day in the midst of a company of godly women he discovered that he himself in his own heart was a stranger to the experiences they were discussing. In the midst of our religious activity, our hymn-singing, our confession of faith, we should ask ourselves the question which Jesus put to Pontius Pilate, 'Sayest thou this thing of thyself, or did others tell it thee of me?'[1] In the parable, what distinguishes the genuine from the false is the personal relationship which they have with the bridegroom and the invitation they have received from him. Only that religion is genuine and lasting which arises in response to a call that is felt to come from Jesus Christ Himself, and which has at its heart a personal relationship with Him.

THE CERTAINTY OF THE EXPOSURE

The parable shows how ruthlessly and unerringly the falsehood and the folly of the imitators were exposed. The ten virgins underwent each a long period of trial and disappointment. So long did the bridegroom tarry that all lay down and slept, and it was not till the last hour, the midnight hour, that he came. By the time he came the borrowed resources of the foolish virgins had failed during the long sleep and their lamps had gone out. All this was a prelude to the great exposure and separation that was now soon to take place.

For the purpose of separating the genuine and the imitators, God brings testing experiences upon His Church. He is never in a hurry and His testing processes are sometimes slow. The slow passing of time itself is a searching test which reveals that many who start the Christian life with a boundless enthusiasm

[1] John 18.34

excelled by no one have no true staying power because they have no true faith. With the mere passing of the years lights that once seemed to be burning brightly wilt and gradually flicker out.

It is to be noticed, however, that these foolish virgins managed to endure the long test without complete disaster. Though their resources were strained and their lamps had begun to flicker, they held on till midnight, and even then were able to keep up appearances. It was only in the sudden crisis that came after the long test that the great exposure was made. '*At midnight there was a cry made, Behold, the bridegroom cometh; go ye out to meet him.*' Then there was a whirl of excitement and in the crisis each one seemed suddenly to be left to her own resources and imitation became impossible. It was impossible now for one to borrow from another. '*Give us of your oil*,' said the foolish to the wise. '*Not so*,' was the reply. No more borrowing or imitation was possible after this point. In the sudden crisis the pretence was fully exposed, for all sudden crises have a way of throwing us on our own resources and exposing our hidden weaknesses. We can think of how France cracked in 1940. We speak of the sudden fall of France, but it was no sudden collapse. It was the outcome of a process that had been going on for years. 'No nation,' writes Ruskin, 'ever had, or will have, the power of suddenly developing under the pressure of necessity faculties it had neglected when it was at ease.'

The great crisis which will reveal all false imitation in the midst of the Church and society is the coming of Jesus Christ. And that day, the day of Christ's coming, will be a day of revelation. God will then judge the secrets of men by Jesus Christ. We must ask ourselves, Supposing He came now in this present time to confront us, how would we behave? With confidence and assurance, or with complete confusion? There is only one way to avoid such shameful exposure as is described so vividly in the parable, and that is to face up now to the exposure to which Jesus Christ seeks to subject us. When we begin to ask ourselves whether we are really genuine in our faith or not, we may find that we cannot answer with certainty. When Jesus at the Last Supper said to the disciples, 'One of you shall betray me,' they began each to say. 'Is it I?'[1] None

---
[1] Mark 14.19

THE WISE AND FOOLISH VIRGINS 183

was sure of himself. When Peter *was* sure of himself, events proved to him that he was in the wrong. But God knows for certain who are His. God searches our hearts, and no one can ever hide falsehood from His sight. He seeks in a gentle way today to reveal to men in secret all those things which must come to the light in the day of His judgment unless they are faced now and frankly confessed in secret before Him. Like the Apostle Peter's, our confidence lies in the fact that the Lord 'knoweth all things',[1] and if in anything we are 'otherwise minded',[2] He will reveal even this to us. Before God there is only one fatal attitude—that which seeks deliberately to conceal what is false when God is seeking to reveal it, and to postpone the day of reckoning. The Christian will always genuinely do one thing. He will pray the prayer of the Psalmist, 'Search me, O God, and know my heart: try me, and know my thoughts: and see if there be any wicked way in me, and lead me in the way everlasting'[3]; and having perhaps given up his own self-examination in despair, he will fall back on the trust that God in His mercy will answer this prayer.

THE SHUT DOOR

In the parable, at the hour when the final exposure was made it was no longer possible for the foolish virgins effectively to make up for their neglect of opportunity. '*While they went to buy, the bridegroom came; and they that were ready went in with him to the marriage: and the door was shut. Afterward came also the other virgins, saying, Lord, Lord, open to us. But he answered and said, Verily I say unto you, I know you not. Watch therefore.*' They woke up *then* to the urgency of their situation, but it was too late. It is a dreadful picture of bitter unavailing remorse. How foolish they had been to spend their energy and time in sustaining the imitation and to waste their precious opportunities in taking sleep when they might have been busy searching for the precious oil and preparing themselves genuinely to meet the bridegroom!

The picture is certainly true to ordinary life as we see it around us. Daily we see men and women wakening up to find that the door they might have entered, had they only been prudent a year or two previously, is now closed. There are

[1] John 21.17   [2] Phil. 3.15   [3] Ps. 139.23-24

many who have cause to regret that at school they never acquired skill in certain branches of knowledge which it is now impossible to acquire. There are many who have cause to regret bitterly their silence when words that might have been spoken in time to bring blessing and comfort to others can never now be heard or appreciated.

The picture suggests that there may come a time when it is impossible for men to repent. In the two descriptions given in the New Testament of the Day of Judgment, a characteristic of both is that there is no last moment pleading or change of mind on the part of those who are judged. Jesus speaks here of a door that closes, separating the true from the false, and separating them for ever. The foolish virgins used their golden opportunities only for sleep.

The ending to the parable is intensely tragic. It almost seems too harsh to be reconciled with other parts of the teaching of Jesus. But it is His teaching. We must remember that this ending came to His hearers only as the climax to a whole career of pretence in the face of constant warning. 'No soul will ever be lost,' said Pusey, 'which has not had the Father throw His arms around him, and look into his face with the eyes of love, and yet has deliberately rejected Him.' God forbid that we should sleep, on the day of opportunity, and play a game with life! God forbid that we should play a game with Jesus Christ! Let us seriously face up to the fact that one day it might be too late to do what we might have done to save our souls. We are fond of saying, 'It is never too late to mend.' Jesus Christ says here plainly that one day it may be too late to mend. '*Watch therefore, for ye know neither the day nor the hour when the Son of man cometh.*'

THE SHEEP AND THE GOATS

When the Son of man shall come in his glory, and all the holy angels with him, then shall he sit upon the throne of his glory: and before him shall be gathered all nations: and he shall separate them one from another, as a shepherd divideth his sheep from the goats: and he shall set the sheep on his right hand, but the goats on the left. Then shall the King say unto them on his right hand, Come, ye blessed of my Father, inherit the kingdom prepared for you from the foundation of the world: for I was an hungred, and ye gave me meat: I was thirsty, and ye gave me drink: I was a stranger, and ye took me in: naked, and ye clothed me: I was sick, and ye visited me: I was in prison, and ye came unto me. Then shall the righteous answer him, saying, Lord, when saw we thee an hungred, and fed thee? or thirsty, and gave thee drink? when saw we thee a stranger, and took thee in? or naked, and clothed thee? or when saw we thee sick, or in prison, and came unto thee? And the King shall answer and say unto them, Verily I say unto you, Inasmuch as ye have done it unto one of the least of these my brethren, ye have done it unto me. Then shall he say also unto them on the left hand, Depart from me, ye cursed, into everlasting fire, prepared for the devil and his angels: for I was an hungred, and ye gave me no meat: I was thirsty, and ye gave me no drink: I was a stranger, and ye took me not in: naked, and ye clothed me not: sick, and in prison, and ye visited me not. Then shall they also answer him, saying, Lord, when saw we thee an hungred, or athirst, or a stranger, or naked, or sick, or in prison, and did not minister unto thee? Then shall he answer them, saying, Verily I say unto you, Inasmuch as ye did it not to one of the least of these, ye did it not to me. And these shall go away into everlasting punishment: but the righteous into life eternal.

MATTHEW 25.31-46

Jesus Christ spoke often about Himself, and He spoke in very exalted terms. He 'knew of no more sacred task than that of pointing men to His Own Person'. If we heard any other man speaking so often and so seriously about himself we should feel forced to class him as self-centred, but with Jesus we feel differently. We are conscious that we belong to Him; He concerns us vitally. Therefore we feel that it is a matter of the utmost importance that we should know who He is. When He speaks about Himself He is speaking not for His own sake but for ours; He is telling us what we need to know if we are to understand the meaning of this world, of this life and indeed of our own existence each as an individual. Let us listen, therefore, to what this parable teaches about Himself, for here He makes His greatest personal claims with such clarity and definiteness that they cannot be evaded by those who would learn of Him.

CHRIST AS THE JUDGE OF ALL MANKIND AT THE LAST DAY

'When the Son of man shall come in his glory, and all the holy angels with him, then shall he sit upon the throne of his glory: and before him shall be gathered all nations.'

When the prophets of the Old Testament looked into the future and prophesied of the things that would come to pass, they saw the future of the world dominated by the great figure of One who would come from God with mighty power to put all things right and bring in the final triumph of God. They looked for a glorious Messiah. When Jesus, however, looked into the future He did not say, 'A Messiah will come.' He said, 'I Myself will come again.' *'The Son of man shall come in his glory, and all the holy angels with him . . . and before him shall be gathered all nations.'*

There are two comings of Jesus Christ spoken of in Scripture. When we celebrate Christmas we celebrate the first coming, the first advent. Then we rejoice that the Messiah came in His humiliation, clothed in our flesh and blood. We rejoice that our Redeemer, the Son of God, came in His lowliness, in the form of a man like ourselves, as one who had to toil and travail, as one who could suffer want and pain and thirst and temptation, as one who could be plotted against, spat upon, maltreated, despised, and killed. He came thus disguised in lowly form—in the form of a babe in a manger. This is what we confess with gladness when we repeat the first part of the Apostles' Creed: 'I believe in God the Father Almighty, Maker of heaven and earth; And in Jesus Christ His only Son our Lord, Who was conceived by the Holy Ghost, Born of the Virgin Mary, Suffered under Pontius Pilate, Was crucified, dead, and buried.' We believe all this about Jesus. He came! But we believe more. We believe also in a second advent of

THE SHEEP AND THE GOATS 187

Jesus Christ—an event just as sudden, just as wonderful as His first advent. 'He ascended into Heaven,' continues the Creed, 'And sitteth on the right hand of God the Father Almighty; from thence He shall come.'

The second advent will be a coming in glory. 'From thence He shall come to judge the quick and the dead.' His first coming was for the purpose of saving mankind. That is why He took such a lowly, appealing form—the form of a carpenter, of a lowly, approachable teacher, patient with His pupils, of a king meek and lowly and riding upon an ass, of One with whom men can make friends. Had His first coming been a coming in His true glory, majesty and manifest divinity, we could not have made friends with Him; we would rather have been consumed and tortured in His presence by the awful radiance of His holiness. We could not have been saved had Christ at His first coming come 'in the form of God'[1]; but he did not come thus. For our sakes He concealed His glory and came in 'the form of a servant'.[2] His first coming was a preparation for His second coming, which will be in order to judge. On that day He will not come disguised, incognito, in the form of an ordinary and friendly man, but in the form of the true and righteous Judge and King over all creation.

But Jesus Christ also comes to us today. He is a living reality to multitudes who have been confronted by Him in personal encounter, have heard His voice, and have felt His challenge and His saving power. When we ask in what form He comes to us today to have dealings with us, we are forced to confess with joyful adoration that He comes still to us in a form no less gracious and lowly than was His form as He lay in the manger, or stood before Pontius Pilate, or allowed Himself to be led to the Cross. Today when Jesus Christ comes His advent is accompanied by no overwhelming signs that the Lord of all glory is here. No visible rays of eternal light break astonishingly upon the gaze of man when Christ comes to work on this earth, and to challenge and save His people. He comes as Christ the Spirit, who comes to meet us as we gather in the fellowship of His Church and listen to the Word of the Bible and take in our hands the elements of bread and wine at the Lord's Table. Here is the lowly form in which we meet today

[1] Phil. 2.6 [2] Phil. 2.7

with Jesus Christ—the form of Bible and Sacrament! It is all part of the humiliation He suffers for our sakes that He is still content to work in this world through such lowly instruments to give men time and room and opportunity to repent and to receive His friendship. But He will come one day suddenly in His full and manifest glory—the glory which He had with His Father before the world was.[1] Then we shall see Him as He is, and all nations will be brought before Him for judgment.

If we have not entered into His friendship in these days when His forgiving love is so freely offered to us in such a way that we can receive it for our salvation, how will it stand with us on that day that is to come? A man was once arrested on a criminal charge. He sought the help of a friend who was a distinguished lawyer and asked him to plead his case in court. But on that very day his friend had been raised to the bench. 'Yesterday,' he said, 'I might have been your advocate. Today I can only be your judge.'

CHRIST AS THE JUDGE OF MEN TODAY

The parable teaches that all who come to the Judgment Seat to receive final sentence have been previously encountered by the Judge. 'I have seen you before,' He in effect says to each one of them. 'I met you once during your life on earth and during My humiliation. I met you once when I was hungry, thirsty, naked and imprisoned. You had an opportunity then of making a decision about Me. Do you not remember?' This is no meeting for the first time between Jesus Christ and those who come before Him. The same Jesus who sits on the throne has been wandering about the earth among men as one naked and hungry and poor. In this form He has confronted every man. In this encounter every man has judged himself by the decision then made. In this picture of the Last Judgment there are no advocates present. There is no calling of witnesses to testify to the moral worth of any man's life, no summing up of cases for and against those who stand at the Bar. The cases are all decided beforehand. Jesus looks at one man, recognises him, and says, 'Depart from me! I know you, for when you were faced by Me in My humiliation you passed Me by.' He looks at another man, and says, 'Come, ye blessed of My Father,

[1] John 17.5

for when I confronted you as one friendless and humble, you opened your heart in response.' A process of judgment has been going on all through the previous ages, leading up to the final revelation of where men stand with relation to the Eternal Christ. As Jesus the Judge in His humble disguise moved about the earth, challenging in a quiet secrecy the whole range of human life, men of all nations have judged themselves by their response to Him often in the ordinary situations of life. On the Judgment Day no decision has to be made. There takes place then merely a separation according to the decision each man has already made. The Judge has no difficulty in recognising at a glance those who are to be acquitted. An eastern shepherd has no difficulty in recognising which are the sheep and which are the goats when he looks over his flock. It is implied here that a man's destiny is written all over him before he comes for the final reckoning. Today then Jesus Christ is confronting men and women in the midst of a great hidden process of judgment. Jesus taught that if men received those who preached His Gospel they would receive Him; if they rejected those who brought His message, they would at the same time reject Him. He promised to confront men personally through the preaching of His Apostles, and to judge men by their reaction to the living Word they would speak. Through the preaching of the Gospel, the living Christ fulfils His purpose to sift out the hearts of men and bring them to the hour of decision.

But all men do not hear the Gospel, and the question is frequently asked, 'Will a man be damned because he has never heard the preaching of the Gospel and consciously made a surrender to Christ?' Our text suggests that even where the Gospel is not spoken, even in places where the name of Jesus has never been named, Christ is nevertheless there at work confronting men for judgment in a hidden way that is a mystery. Christ, through His incarnation, has linked Himself with the whole human race, especially with the sufferings of the poor and the outcast. Has He not borne all these sufferings in His own body? Christ can come to be mysteriously present to challenge and judge men even where His Word is not preached. Men who do not hear the Word of God preached by His Church do not for that reason escape the challenge of Jesus Christ. Karl

Heim, writing on the matter, says, 'Christ ... is the invisible "Thou" towards whom all the actions of men, even those which they are not aware of, are directed. He is the invisible brother of all men. All men have to reckon for ever with Him even when they do not know it. ... In a mysterious way Christ partakes of all the history of mankind. He is present unseen in the fiercest wars, on the fields of battle, in revolutions, in the establishing of nations. ... The whole of human history right to the end is a continuation of the Passion of Christ.'

Men are not always conscious that this process of judgment is going on in this world, and that their situation in life is so critical. Those who were set on the right hand for glory were surprised when it was revealed to them that they had made such great and eternal decisions during their earthly life. '*Lord when saw we thee an hungred, and fed thee? or thirsty, and gave thee drink? when saw we thee a stranger, and took thee in?*' They did not know that they had already made such eternal decisions with regard to Christ in their almost unheeded acts of love towards the outcasts of humanity. Nor were those on the left hand conscious that they had condemned themselves by their opposite behaviour.

Let us realise that this life is critical—the *whole* of life. The critical moment in our lives may occur when we are sitting in church listening to His Word. It is a serious matter that we meet the living Christ under such circumstances as one out of whose mouth proceeds 'a sharp twoedged sword'.[1] It is an equally serious matter that He also moves about the scenes of ordinary human life, that His voice is 'as the sound of many waters',[2] widely broadcast for many to hear its diffused echo and thus to be brought to judgment. 'Watch therefore, for ye know neither the day nor the hour wherein the Son of man cometh.'[3] At any moment of our life we may be as those who stand before the judge. We are confronted by Him not only in the hour when we find ourselves in the House of God listening to the Word of God but also in that hour when we find ourselves faced by our duty towards the least of Christ's brethren! Today Christ is 'sifting out the hearts of men before His judgment seat'.

But though this process of judgment is going on all the while, the verdict is not announced or revealed till the final day, and

[1] Rev. 1.16   [2] Rev. 1.15   [3] Matt. 25.13

at present there is no separation of those who are acquitted from those who are condemned. Here the sheep and the goats mingle in apparently happy fellowship. Here there seems to be no clear-cut dividing line. Though this decisive process of judgment is going on so surely, the results are not seen. Do not wolves enter into the fold of the Church? Jesus teaches here what He taught in the parable of the tares and the wheat. 'Both grow together until the harvest.'[1] 'Then shall two be in the field; the one shall be taken, and the other left. Two women shall be grinding at the mill; the one shall be taken, and the other left.'[2] On the great day the gulf between these two is revealed. *'Then shall the King say unto them on his right hand, Come. . . . Then shall he say also unto them on the left hand, Depart from me.' 'Depart from me!' 'Come!'* These verdicts will put an infinite distance between those who perhaps have grown and worked together in the scenes of this life.

CHRIST AS THE ONE WHO BINDS FOR EVER

'And these shall go away into everlasting punishment: but the righteous into life eternal.'

The gulf between the justified and the rejected is revealed as one which separates for ever; one over which it is impossible to cross. There is no hurried last minute passing over from one company into another, no last moment pleading, no suggestion that another chance is possible. The challenge of Jesus Christ has forced these men each into a decision that stands good, and binds for all eternity. Whenever men hear the Word of God they are forced into such a decision. To the Church which confesses its faith before the world, and proclaims the testimony concerning Christ entrusted to it, Jesus gave the promise, 'Whatsoever thou shalt bind on earth shall be bound in heaven: and whatsoever thou shalt loose on earth shall be loosed in heaven.'[3] The words of Jesus in this parable seem plainly to teach that when we are confronted by Him in whatever form He comes to challenge us, we decide our destiny for ever. May it be for each of us, through the grace of God, an Eternity of blessedness!

The glorious reward given to those who find themselves among the redeemed is a reward of pure grace. *'Come, ye blessed*

[1] Matt. 13.30   [2] Matt. 24.40-41   [3] Matt. 16.19

of my Father, inherit the kingdom prepared for you from the foundation of the world.' There is an idea prevalent that men create their own heaven—that heaven is a state of mind which a man can acquire here and now in this earth, and that the riches that a man's life will display beyond are simply the 'character' he has developed for himself in this life. There is no such suggestion in the teaching of Christ. 'Heaven' in this parable is something that Christ gives, that Christ has prepared for us, something we have yet to inherit. Anything that we experience now of His blessing is merely a seal set to a promise of infinite wealth hereafter.

Such, then, are the claims of Christ for Himself in this parable. What are we to make of them? What are we to think of One who speaks as if all other men are lost creatures and He alone can point the way, as if all other men are in bondage and He is the one free man who has come into this world to ransom and rescue all others from their bondage; and who claims that on the day of Judgment He will sit on the Judgment Seat and all other men will come to His feet for sentence? Either He is utterly false and we must wholly repudiate Him, or we must believe and tremble, and, believing, rejoice. People sometimes say, 'I admire Him but I cannot believe.' But if you do not believe, how can you admire? Here in Jesus we have a man apparently helpless, chained by His captors and standing before the civil magistrate, and He speaks as in this parable! He was asked by the chief priest for a straight answer about Himself. 'Art thou the Christ, the Son of the Blessed?' Jesus said, 'I am: and ye shall see the Son of man sitting on the right hand of power, and coming in the clouds of heaven.'[1] What are we to make of such an answer if it is not completely true? Either we must reject Him totally, or His claims are true and He is the Son of God.

[1] Mark 14.61-62

THE ROYAL WEDDING FEAST

And Jesus answered and spake unto them again by parables, and said, The kingdom of heaven is like unto a certain king, which made a marriage for his son, and sent forth his servants to call them that were bidden to the wedding: and they would not come. Again, he sent forth other servants, saying, Tell them which are bidden, Behold, I have prepared my dinner: my oxen and my fatlings are killed, and all things are ready: come unto the marriage. But they made light of it, and went their ways, one to his farm, another to his merchandise: and the remnant took his servants, and entreated them spitefully, and slew them. But when the king heard thereof, he was wroth: and he sent forth his armies, and destroyed those murderers, and burned up their city. Then saith he to his servants, The wedding is ready, but they which were bidden were not worthy. Go ye therefore into the highways, and as many as ye shall find, bid to the marriage. So those servants went out into the highways, and gathered together all as many as they found, both bad and good: and the wedding was furnished with guests. And when the king came in to see the guests, he saw there a man which had not on a wedding garment: and he saith unto him, Friend, how camest thou in hither not having a wedding garment? And he was speechless. Then said the king to the servants, Bind him hand and foot, and take him away, and cast him into outer darkness; there shall be weeping and gnashing of teeth. For many are called, but few are chosen.
MATTHEW 22.1-14

The people who were plotting to kill Jesus actually formed His audience as He spoke this parable. They had proved their resolute hatred of Him and all that He stood for, and their determination not to enter His Kingdom. But in the face of all this, Jesus in this parable utters yet another appeal to His enemies to think again. He did not curse them, nor did He suggest to them that He could well do without them. Instead, during those last terrible days of His life, days filled with wrangling and conflict with these hardened men at Jerusalem, He spoke words that conveyed a gracious invitation to His enemies to enter the Kingdom of God and partake freely of the great gifts He was still ready to shower upon them.

THE FULLNESS OF GOD'S MERCY

'*The kingdom of heaven is like unto a certain king, which made a marriage for his son, and sent forth his servants to call them that were bidden to the wedding.*' Jesus, in seeking to describe His Kingdom, bids men think of the greatest occasion on earth for sumptuous feasting, real hilarious joy and true pleasure—the occasion of a wedding. To emphasise the greatness of the scale upon which all this is freely given, He makes the bridegroom a king's son. The dinner is prepared, the oxen and fatlings are killed, all things are ready for the rejoicing, and all the people have to do is come to the marriage.

God acts like this in bringing His Kingdom near to men. He is like a gracious royal master who has a passion for hospitality and an infinite wealth to share. He loves to have glad fellowship with His children, and He devises all manner of ways of having that fellowship. He is ready to humble Himself to extol what He has prepared in order to bring men in to share it. And what God gives is like that which was given at this wedding, something rich, full, free, abundant, satisfying.

In the parable many of the men invited with such cordiality by the king were his enemies. Such is the way God treats His enemies. He invites them graciously to His feast! When we see Jesus standing before these narrow-minded, hateful men with their wicked intent, speaking these words of loving invitation, we know that God is far greater than is suggested even by Jesus' description of this bountiful host. God is like Christ Himself, Christ who on the Cross cried, 'Father, forgive them; for they know not what they do.'[1] Here He pleads lovingly and graciously with men who are determined to crucify Him; He pleads in the name of God His Father, and He offers them, not punishment, not a second place, but privileges and riches untold, if they will but turn and that day accept His mercy. Such is the bountiful mercy of God. And it is all given with so little ado, the bounty of this feast. There is no preparation needed, nor period of probation. 'Come now, without delay' is the invitation, and when men come they are immediately taken into the feast. Both 'bad and good' were brought in. Whatever men's pasts or their qualifications, it does not matter, as long as they accept the invitation.

[1] Luke 23.34

THE OTHER SIDE OF MERCY

Though he is so gracious and kind, the one who prepares this feast is also a king. The wedding is that of a prince. The invitation, therefore, brings its challenge with it. It is a test of loyalty, for a king's invitation cannot be neglected or despised without the danger of incurring the wrath of the gracious host. To refuse it is to refuse to acknowledge him as king and lord. There is a command behind this gracious gesture on the part of the ruler—the command of a king whose laws men must obey, whose grace and kindness men must honour if they would dwell in his land. It is for this reason that there is a sudden and startling change of attitude on the part of the king when he hears that his kindness has been despised by many. Towards those who despised this invitation the gracious, patient lord burned with anger when he heard that his gesture of friendship had been refused. '*He was wroth: and he sent forth his armies, and destroyed those murderers, and burned up their city.*'

Men are in danger of the wrath of God precisely at that moment when they are offered His mercy. The Jews were in dire danger at that moment when Jesus stood before them offering the mercy of God. They were then in far more danger than they would have been had alien armies been surrounding their cities and they desperately defending them, for they were in danger of rejecting the mercy of God. This was the sin for which their land was later ravaged, their capital city razed to the ground and their temple burned. Are we not then in danger when, in the quietness of the House of God, we sit and listen to the Word of God read and preached? 'Take heed therefore how ye hear,'[1] said Jesus. Are we not, we too, in danger when we sit at the Lord's Table where the mercy of God is so freely and with such gentleness and grace offered to us? 'He that eateth and drinketh unworthily,' says Paul, 'eateth and drinketh damnation to himself.'[2] When we are faced by God's mercy, we are also faced by the dread possibility of His judgment. The mercy of God and the judgment of God are different sides of the same thing, for there is only one God. It is not outside of Christ that God is wrathful but in the gentle and loving Jesus Christ. The New Testament speaks of the 'wrath of the Lamb'.[3] God judges us with fearful judgments

[1] Luke 8.18   [2] 1 Cor. 11.29   [3] Rev. 6.16

according to our attitude to Him, and our attitude to Him is clearly revealed at the moment when we are confronted by His mercy.

In this parable, then, we are taught that it is their attitude towards the mercy of God that alone can bring judgment upon men. We are taught that the wrath of God is nothing else but the other side of His love, and that if God is angry it is because He has first been merciful. If God cuts a man off from His fellowship it is because that man has first of all, with deliberate hatred, cut the love of God out of his life.

'THEY MADE LIGHT OF IT'

Some reacted with violence when the invitation to the feast was taken to them. They maltreated the messengers, and killed some of them. It was easy to do that, for the invitation was one of genuine goodwill and therefore the messengers had been sent out without means of self-defence or show of force. But the majority showed that they despised the invitation by making light of it. '*They made light of it, and went their ways, one to his farm, another to his merchandise.*' They claimed that business, the ordinary routine of daily life, was more important than what this invitation offered. They did not actively do anything to spoil the feast, nor offer harm to the messengers, nor seek to prevent others from going. They were just too busy to bother with the affair. Other matters seemed more pressing. There were the wives, and the children, and the farms to attend to. They wanted an excuse because they did not think the feast was important.

Is this not our common attitude? We are busy, and after all the things of Christ are not, we imagine, so important as the pressing needs of life. Perhaps tomorrow we shall attend to the invitation. Many a man today, if he could get his financial position straightened out, and get himself on his feet in business, would be regularly at church instead of working seven days a week. He has good intentions, but he is waiting to get on his feet. Many a young couple, if they could find themselves settled in a house of their own instead of in the temporary abode in which they are forced to live, would throw themselves into the work of the Church, but other things must be settled first. The matter of the business, the matter of the house—they are much

THE ROYAL WEDDING FEAST

more important than this invitation to the apparently more distant matter of the wedding of the king's son.

Jesus teaches here that it is as evil a thing to make light of the mercy of God as it is to do violence to it. He names together those who made light of it and those who maltreated or murdered the messengers, and He shows that the king's anger and retribution visit both types with the same severity. While Jesus spoke there were those around Him who were plotting with anger to do violence against Him and maltreat Him. But there were others who were making light of Him. They were too busy to respond to Him. They were not actively implicated in the plot of the Cross, but merely passed by on the other side and let the whole shameful thing go on, not even allowing the case to divert them from their way to business. Jesus warns such men that they are in as much danger as if they were plotting His death. 'Between Christ mocked, and Christ crucified,' says Dora Greenwell, 'there is but a short step.' Between Christ taken lightly and Christ wholly rejected, there is no difference.

But there were some who accepted and then made light of the feast once they were inside. Let us turn from the scene of the judgment which visited those who would not come and take a look within the king's palace. It is full. Even though the chosen ones rejected the invitation, every place is taken and the guests are enjoying the fellowship and the feasting. After the first refusals the servants had gone to the highways and byways, and soon the wedding was furnished with guests. 'God will gather plenty of people to enjoy His grace and goodness even if you reject it,' Jesus says plainly to these Jews at Jerusalem. This prophecy was actually fulfilled, for the Jews rejected Jesus. Yet the Gospel was taken to the Gentiles and men came in from every nation, men good and bad—a great mixture. God does not need anybody. If one man rejects Him, He can always get somebody else to fulfil His purpose. Men sometimes express concern for the future of Christianity but we need not worry about that; God is perfectly capable of looking after that apart from ourselves. What we should rather be concerned about is the future of our own land. Jesus is standing at the door of the Church in our western civilisation, as He stood at the door of the church of Ephesus, and He is warning us that unless we repent our candlestick will be removed from its place. If the

Church of today in the West rejects Him, then there are plenty of others pressing in to this wedding feast. All over the earth men are eagerly accepting the grace of Christ. In the mission fields of the Churches many are hungry and eager to take in all that we can give them of Jesus Christ, whereas around us in our highly civilised communities many are still wondering whether it is worth while trying the thing out or whether they are not too busy for it. The feast in the parable went off as planned, even though so many had refused. No one is necessary. Let us not imagine for a moment that we are needed in any way to further the Kingdom of God. The Kingdom is a feast prepared by God, and if He cannot have one guest, He will have another, that His house may be full.

And as we look over this full company of guests we see that there are some who are inside the feast but are making light of it. We can believe this. We know, to our shame, that some can come even to the Lord's Table in a spirit of lightheartedness. It is strange that some escape the sin of despising the invitation and then proceed to despise the feast once they are inside.

Jesus gives us one example. '*The king came in to see the guests.*' The king had arranged this feast for fellowship. God does not gather His children merely for the purpose of amusing them in a vague way, but, having gathered them, He comes to be amongst them. It is His desire for fellowship. '*He saw there a man which had not on a wedding garment.*' It is possible that garments were provided, for it was sometimes the custom in the east, when a man gave a feast, to do this. But here was a man who was going to show them that he did not need to stand on ceremony in this place. He was there in his own clothes.

'*Friend, how camest thou in hither not having a wedding garment?*' asked the king. '*And he was speechless. Then said the king to the servants, Bind him hand and foot, and take him away, and cast him into outer darkness; there shall be weeping and gnashing of teeth.*' It is difficult to say definitely whom this man represents. Perhaps he is there to remind us of a danger in which we Christians often are in the midst of our activity in the Church. We sometimes attempt to stand upon our own righteousness in the presence of God. 'Put off . . . the old man,' says Paul, 'and put on the new man, which after God is created in righteousness.'[1]

[1] Eph. 4.22-24

We are meant to trust in Christ alone, and to clothe ourselves in His righteousness before God. His life and His Cross are the life and the sacrifice we must trust in. His character must be the adornment of our lives, and we must throw aside our trust in our own works and all the garments of our own righteousness. We must forget all about our so-called 'character'. We must cast away all distinctions that make us different from others, and put on Christ alone. But we are unwilling to take up this attitude. We want to come before God adorned in what we vainly imagine are the shining garments of our own goodness. What other meaning can it have when we take up such an attitude, than that we have fallen from the grace of God and that we are despising the feast that He has provided?

APPENDIX

THE PARABLE AND THE PREACHER[1]

In his endeavour to expound the parables of Jesus, the preacher who turns for help to the work of modern New Testament scholars will not be disappointed. Certainly the present writer has put himself very much in their debt. At the same time there are rules and definitions by which some modern scholars restrict the understanding of the parables in a way that is often baffling to the preacher. As the parables, however, are peculiarly the domain of the preacher, it would appear that these elements require further discussion and clarification if he is to get full benefit from recent research and do justice to the kerygmatic setting in which we have received the parables.

I

An attempt should be made as consistently as possible to interpret the parables Christologically.[2]

When Jesus spoke in parables He sought to reveal to His hearers the significance of His own presence in their midst, and the urgency of the critical situation into which His coming has thrown this world. In doing this, He revealed to His contemporaries in the same parables the meaning of whatever attitude they took up in the midst of the situation of crisis which so urgently called for their decision. The key to the interpretation of many of the parables is in our hands when we regard them as challenges thrown out by Jesus to those who stood before Him to make a judgment about Himself, to be definite in their attitude and response to His ministry, and to take comfort or

---

[1] Reprinted from *The Scottish Journal of Theology*, Vol. 2, No. 1, 1948
[2] This is much emphasised in recent works on the New Testament. Hoskyns and Davey speak of the 'Christological penetration of the parables'. 'The parables ... are shot through with the same Christological significance as the miracle narratives' (*Riddle of the New Testament*, p. 134). 'The parables represent the interpretation which our Lord offered of His own ministry' (C. H. Dodd, *The Parables of the Kingdom*, p. 197). 'They take us into the brunt of His warfare' (A. T. Cadoux, *The Parables of Jesus*, p. 59). 'They are parallel in revelational significance to the acts and works of Jesus' (W. Manson, *Jesus the Messiah*, p. 48).

warning according to whether they yielded to His appeal or hardened their hearts against Him.

The parables cannot be properly understood unless they are given such a Christological significance. To regard them merely as stories illustrating either general moral truths, or laws of the spiritual life, or even the truths and doctrines of the Christian faith, is to miss their vital significance.[1] Jesus spoke in parables because His purpose was to say what could not be said in the way of plain direct speech. The Gospel is news of an event that is a 'mystery', the nature of which it is beyond the power of human reason to comprehend. Indeed, the more the believing human mind understands this mystery, the more it is clear that it is a mystery that baffles understanding. The mystery is so deep and many-sided that it cannot be described in plain language or explained in clear logical propositions easily grasped by the minds of men. It is indeed so many-sided that men must be introduced into it by being led first into a world of stories, and by being made familiar with a world of pictorial analogies drawn from life. A man with this imaginative background of stories illustrating now one aspect and now another of the manifold wisdom of God is in a position in which the mystery can lay hold of his mind with power and reality, for it cannot be grasped even in one of its partial aspects unless at the same time there is a realisation of its total significance. The parable thus seems to be, humanly speaking, the most suitable type of expression by which at the time Jesus could expound the mystery of the event which was being enacted before the eyes of His contemporaries, without being hopelessly misunderstood by the minds of men so slow to see the significance of anything new, so quick to interpret any new phenomenon in terms which their naturally logical and materialistic minds could already master.

[1] 'Was all this wealth of loving observation and imaginative rendering of nature and common life used merely to adorn moral generalities?' (C. H. Dodd, ibid., p. 25). This does not, however, warrant our regarding as not genuine the interpretations attached to the parables in the Gospels which at times seem on the surface to have little more than mere moral significance. Dibelius, for example, rejects as out of place the saying at the end of the parable of the publican and the Pharisee: 'For every one that exalteth himself shall be abased, and he that humbleth himself shall be exalted' (Luke 18.14), saying: 'Thereby the parable receives a commonplace ethical meaning which is far removed from its wording' (*From Tradition to Gospel*, English translation, p. 253). But this disputed phrase cannot be understood on an ethical plane and is obviously full of eschatological significance, the emphasis on which is entirely in place alongside the doctrine of justification by faith taught in the parable.

The manner in which Jesus introduces men into the mystery hidden in the parables is similar to the manner in which He seeks to act upon men in the Sacrament, and the relation between the 'mystery' which is to be known through the parable and the story itself is similar to the relation between the sign and the thing signified in the Sacrament.[1] The object of the expositor must therefore be similar to the object of the minister presiding at the celebration of the Sacrament. As at the celebration of the Lord's Supper he seeks to make the participants live again in the midst of the events of the last days of our Lord, in faith that the living Christ will manifest Himself, so in expounding the parables he must seek as skilfully as he can to draw his hearers into the centre of this world of story, in order that, as they dwell there, the living Christ may reveal to a mind thus prepared the truth about Himself, and Himself who is the Truth.

Since the purpose of the parabolic teaching of Jesus is to introduce men into this mystery, it is almost impossible for the significance of the parables to be systematically and fully expounded in plain straightforward speech without the uninitiated hearer becoming irritated by tantalising contradictions and paradoxes. Such apparent contradictions and paradoxes could be hidden, and the parables thereby made 'simple', only by the preacher making a very partial selection of passages according to a systematic principle alien to the Gospel which would result in an exposition robbing the parables of much of their hidden wealth of meaning.

II

Allowance should be made for a consciously forward-looking or prophetic element in the parables.

There is a tendency among some scholars to assume that Jesus in uttering the parables had no other conscious intention than to refer to the events of His own ministry in the flesh which

---

[1] Cf. the following passage from Professor T. W. Manson: 'The true parable . . . is not an illustration to help one through a theological discussion; it is rather a mode of religious experience It belongs to the same order of things as altar and sacrifice, prayer, the prophetic vision, and the like. It is a *datum* for theology. not a by-product. It is a way in which religious faith is attained and, so far as it can be, transmitted from one person to another. It is not a crutch for limping intellects but a spur to religious insight: its object is not to provide simple theological instruction, but to produce living religious faith' (*The Teaching of Jesus*, p. 73).

are covered in the Gospel narratives. This can give rise even to an explicit denial of any prophetic element in the parables.[1] Professor C. H. Dodd, for example, with a skill which we cannot but admire, and a result which we must acknowledge as throwing fresh light on the text, expounds passages which have been traditionally interpreted as referring to the history of the Church as if they, indeed, have no other reference than to the immediate situation in Palestine during the earthly life of Jesus. He sums up the conviction which dictates this procedure in these words: 'It is in this context that the parables of the Kingdom of God must be placed. They use all the resources of dramatic illustration to help men to see that in the events before their eyes— in the miracles of Jesus, His appeal to men and its results, the blessedness that comes to those who follow Him, in the tragic conflict of the Cross and the tribulation of the disciples, in the fateful choice before the Jewish people and the disasters that threaten—God is confronting them in His Kingdom, Power and Glory. The world has become the scene of a divine drama in which eternal issues are laid bare. It is the hour of decision. It is realised eschatology.'[2]

But the parables make obvious reference to much more than the outward events which took place immediately before the eyes of His contemporaries in the life and death of Jesus. They have a forward look. They prophesy future things. They predict not only an immediate crisis for those who were dealing with Jesus of Nazareth in the flesh, but also a historical process which is to follow His historical life and is to be equally decisive for generations to come. They teach that the period of eschatological tension will be lengthened out and will be followed by a second series of universally decisive events which will complete the revelation already given in the historic life of Jesus. There is no need to cast doubt on the authenticity of those passages in the parables which seem to allow for such a pause in the midst of the eschatological events of the end of the world as will allow for the rise and history of the organisation of the Church as we have known it. It is true that the whole

[1] 'The themes are no longer prophetic but messianic. They declare the divine event to be now taking place and the destiny of men to be dependent upon the acceptance or rejection of this event' (Hoskyns and Davey, *Riddle of the New Testament*, p. 133).
[2] *The Parables of the Kingdom*, p. 197

atmosphere into which we are introduced in the parables is heavy with the expectancy of an immediate world-shaking crisis. The parables proclaim to us that in the history of Jesus the drama of the end of the world has opened. The beginning of the end has been made. But in the historical circumstances of the incarnation, death and resurrection of Jesus only the first act of that drama has been unfolded. There are other acts to follow, and the course of the whole drama is foreshadowed in prophecy by Jesus in the parables.

The significance of the parables, therefore, cannot be fully understood by giving them the circumscribed reference in the mind of Jesus which the doctrine of realised eschatology seems to dictate. The full eschatological tension under which the original hearers of the parables lived has not yet been released. The parables were originally designed to refer to our present situation no less than to the situation of the Jew of the first generation A.D. The events and processes described in the parables are taking place before our eyes in as challenging and concrete a manner as before the eyes of the contemporaries of Jesus. The ministry of the Word and Sacrament is producing in the world the same critical situation as the historic ministry of Jesus in Palestine in His day. The whole sphere of world history is today being disturbed by Jesus Christ, and men and nations are being judged by their reaction to Him in the same way as the Jewish nation was disturbed and judged by its reaction to Him in the days of His flesh. There is a direct and conscious prophecy of all this in the parabolic teaching of Jesus.

It must be admitted that Dr C. H. Dodd allows for the reinterpretation of the parables in terms of the situation in which the Church finds itself at varied times. 'Their teaching,' he writes, 'may be fruitfully applied and re-applied to all sorts of new situations which were never contemplated at the time when they were spoken.' But this means that no reference from the parables to our modern situation can have any authority other than resides in our own imagination. Reading the parables as they stand, it seems obvious that the outline of the Church and the form and nature of its ministry were contemplated by Jesus and deliberately foreshadowed in His parabolic teaching. We must not allow our criticism of the New Testament, and our decision as to what can be accepted as genuinely coming from the mouth of Jesus, to be dictated by a very one-sided Christology which does not leave room for some measure of consciousness in the mind of our Lord covering the nature of future historical developments in the sphere of history affected by His Word.

III

The exposition should not be limited by any restricted definition of the word 'parable'.

A parable is often defined as a simile, which may be lengthened out into a similitude or a story, in which some event or situation or process is described in terms which hold the imagination and stimulate the mind into forming a judgment upon the situation thus depicted. In making this judgment, the hearer is at the same time forced by the skill of the narrator of the parable, possibly in some concluding home-thrust, to see that he himself is in an analogous situation in some other field of experience, and that through the parable he has really made a judgment about his own situation which, thus made, must now affect his conduct. The parabolic form is thus designed to force the hearer into a desired decision. The illustration often given as typical of the true parable form is the story told by Nathan to David about the man who owned the one ewe lamb stolen so cruelly by the powerful rich man. David on hearing this story formed his judgment in indignation against the rich man, whereupon Nathan said, 'Thou art the man!' and David could not escape the relevance of his judgment on the story to his own situation.

The parable is thus, in its descriptive aspect, true to life as men know it in the world, and built round one fairly simple main theme. Indeed, it must be such if it is to lead to a convincing judgment on the situation described. Any large measure of unlikelihood or fantasy about the story, or any overloading with detail which might distract attention from the one point on which judgment is to be made, would have the effect of destroying the true parabolic form according to this definition.

It will be seen that the parable as thus defined is a form of discourse quite distinct from another form of literary expression which we call the 'allegory'. An allegory is also often shaped in the form of a story, but the story in an allegory can be highly imaginative and untrue to life because the story must be shaped in every detail according to the hidden meaning which the narrator is seeking to convey. Each feature, detail and character in the story stands for some significant feature in the field of experience in which it is desired to teach the lesson, and the action is made to move not according to real life but according to the trend of the didactic purpose. Whereas a parable is normally designed to compel decision, an allegory is designed rather to describe and instruct, though in certain spheres such instruction is bound to lead to decision. And whereas one parable is designed mainly to enforce one lesson, one allegory may teach varied lessons, the more lessons taught the more ingenious being the work of the author.

As an example of allegory we may take any typical excerpt from *The Pilgrim's Progress*, such as the incident in which Giant Despair meets Christian and Hopeful in By-Path Meadow, and locks them up in Doubting Castle, where, after lying some days in a stinking dungeon, Christian suddenly remembers that in his bosom he has a key called Promise which is able to unlock any door in their prison and bring them deliverance from Despair.

With these definitions and examples before us, we have to decide whether, in interpreting the parables of Jesus, we have to treat them strictly as parables according to the definition above outlined, or whether they can at any point be made the subject of allegorical interpretation.

There are those who, following the lead given by Adolf Jülicher in his important work on the parables at the end of last century, go the length of asserting that there was originally almost no allegorical material in the parables of Jesus. 'Jülicher showed not that the allegorical interpretation is in this and that case overdone or fanciful, but that the parables in general do not admit of this method at all,' writes Dr C. H. Dodd,[1] for whom the parables of Jesus are all strictly parables according to the definition indicated above, and must be interpreted as such.

Such a theory leads to the application of a most severe critical treatment to many of the parables, with devastating results. For those who hold this view are compelled to say that

[1] *The Parables of the Kingdom*, p. 13

many of the details of the parables as they have been handed down to us were not originally spoken by Jesus and must be cut out if we are to get at the true meaning He wished originally to convey. Any details which tend to make the parables to the least extent complicated in structure, or which carry by themselves an obvious metaphorical significance, are treated with suspicion and often branded as spurious. And any action on the part of the characters in the parables unlikely to be true to life likewise warrants the same treatment.[1] Those holding such a theory are also compelled to say that the allegorical interpretations which are attached to the parables of the Sower and the Tares in the Gospels were not originally spoken by Jesus and are additions made to the text by the evangelists, who misunderstood the nature of a true parable.

This theory under discussion, moreover, also gives rise to an extremely restricted method of interpretation which seems bound to result in a type of exposition which (in words applied to some earlier expositors who deserved them less) 'would leave the parables bare trunks, stripped of all their foliage and branches, of everything which makes for beauty and ornament'.[2] It is not, strictly speaking, allowable on this theory to dwell on the significance of the far country or of any of the miseries of the prodigal as detailed in the story in Luke's Gospel. It is not allowable to speculate as to what Jesus might have meant by such details as the 'talents', or 'exchangers', or 'lamps', or 'wedding garments'.[3] All that is legitimate is

---

[1] Dr A. T. Cadoux, for example (*The Parables of Jesus*, p. 66 ff), approves of the rejection of a large part of the parable of the Pounds because the action of the returning king is not true to life, and the conclusion of the episode distracts attention from the main thread of the story; likewise of the conclusion of the parable of the Ten Virgins because (quoting Dr McNeile) 'an earthly bridegroom would hardly act or speak thus'. [2] Trench, *Notes on the Parables*, p. 35

[3] 'The typical parable, whether it be a simple metaphor, or a more elaborate similitude, or a full length story, presents one single point of comparison. The details are not meant to have independent significance' (C. H. Dodd, ibid., p. 18). Even in short parables, where one of the main details seems to cry out for an obvious allegorical or twofold interpretation, there is a strange unwillingness to allow for such. Thus, in discussing the parable of the Barren Fig Tree, Dr T. W. Manson sets aside any attempt to elaborate the interpretation by saying: 'It is meant to teach one lesson only, the need for timely repentance; and there is no profit in turning it into an allegory' (*Mission and Message of Jesus*, p. 566), but Jesus' action in cursing the fig tree invites such an allegorical interpretation, which can undoubtedly be applied with much profit. In the parable of the Salt, Jülicher (see A. T. Cadoux, ibid., p. 52) insists that the only point of comparison which should be dwelt upon is the contrast between the value and worthlessness of the respective types of salt. But if Jesus had no intention that His hearers' minds should not also

that we should find out the one point in the story about which judgment is called for, and in order to give this one point its proper emphasis, suppress any inclination to attach meaning to the rich details which have exercised such a fatal and regrettable fascination upon so many generations of expositors.

The present writer does not feel that the type of criticism dictated by the theory under discussion is justified, or that the type of exposition to which it gives rise can indicate the best routes for the traveller to take who would explore the heart of the mystery and beauty and wealth hidden in the world of parables of Jesus. The theory seems to merit the utterance of another parable calling for judgment on the folly of a man who tied up his legs tightly with rope and then sat impoverished and hungry because he could not walk.

It must be recognised, however, that a clear recognition of the distinction above drawn between 'parable' and 'allegory' is helpful to the expositor, for there is no doubt that the key to the meaning of a large number of the parables of Jesus is found most readily when they are approached on the assumption that they are, in the main, parabolic in form and intention. But we must not be restricted in our interpretation by any rigid definition of form. Nothing seems more obvious than that the parabolic teaching of Jesus was originally shot through with passages and references which warrant allegorical interpretations. Jesus 'made frequent use of metaphor,' writes D. W. H. Moulton, 'and if He expanded comparison into parable is it unwarrantable to assume that accordingly, metaphor might be so extended as to become virtually an allegory?'[1] The form Jesus used when He spoke 'in parables' is well described by Dr Martin Dibelius as being of a 'narrative class, hovering between parable and allegory'.[2]

---

dwell on the taste and preservative power of salt and bring these qualities into the comparison, would He not have chosen quite a different simile with which to enforce His one lesson without ambiguity? It is obvious that this insistence on 'one point only' breaks down when we consider a parable like that of the Prodigal Son (see M. Dibelius, *From Tradition to Gospel*, p. 255). 'So long as the story of the parable is not unnaturally shaped into similarity with the features of the field to which it is applied, so long as points of similarity grow naturally from the story, they may be multiplied with advantage' (A. T. Cadoux, ibid., p. 51).

[1] In article on 'Parable', Hasting's *Dictionary of Christ and the Gospels*

[2] *From Tradition to Gospel*, p. 256. See also Hoskyns and Davey, *Riddle of the New Testament*, for a similar judgment. 'Nice as is the distinction between allegory and

IV

While keeping in mind what has already been said, the preacher, in his exposition of the parables, should also be ruled by certain other fairly obvious considerations.

(1) The context in which the parable is placed in the gospel will often give an indication of the meaning it is meant to convey. It has been pointed out already that the parables are, where possible, to be interpreted in the light of the critical situation in which they were uttered. In many cases, of course, we have no indication of the conditions under which the parable had its origin. In such cases it is sometimes profitable to imagine some possible context in the life of our Lord to which the parable might belong.

In some cases there are sayings attached to the parable, either by the deliberate intention of Jesus, or by the evangelist in sorting out the evangelical material before him. These sayings often give more help in understanding the meaning of the parable than is commonly acknowledged amongst critics. It is not necessary to suppose that the sayings referred to teach the main lesson which the parable is designed to enforce. The main lesson may be so obvious to the awakened mind that it does not require any extra enforcement, and the attached saying may be there to teach some subsidiary lesson that might be less obvious.

(2) The doctrine which we read into the parables, since they belong to the more obscure parts of Scripture, must be in conformity with the teaching of those parts of Scripture that are more clear in expression.

It may be helpful, in our thinking about this matter of the interpretation of the parables, to make use of the once familiar distinction between the 'clear' and the 'obscure' parts of Scripture. Augustine describes in the following passage our method of procedure in the interpretation of the Bible: 'Among the things that are plainly laid down in Scripture are

---

similitude, it normally exists only in theory. In practice most allegories contain simile and most similitudes are tinged with metaphor.... If interpretation is to avoid becoming completely arbitrary and prejudiced, it must attempt to explain the existence of both these elements in the material as it stands' (p. 129). Dr A. T. Cadoux is less willing to concede this point. 'Sometimes ... there is a persistence in metaphor that borders on allegory but never quite reaches it' (loc. cit., p. 58). Surely a 'persistence in metaphor' is precisely an allegory?

THE PARABLE AND THE PREACHER 213

to be found all matters that concern faith and the manner of life—hope, to wit, and love, of which I have spoken in a previous book. After this, when we have made ourselves to a certain extent familiar with the language of Scripture, we may proceed to open up and investigate the obscure passages, and in doing so draw examples from the plainer expressions to throw light upon the more obscure.'[1] Augustine would no doubt have regarded the parables as coming under the category of passages 'obscured by metaphorical expressions', and his advice on the approach to their interpretation is very sound. It is necessary, in interpreting the parables, to read some meaning into them. We will not otherwise find a key to their teaching. The meaning we read into the parables must be dictated by the doctrine taught by the rest of Scripture. It will thus be seen that, though the parables may be used, in a sacramental manner, by the living Spirit of Christ to lead men to faith in Him, they nevertheless cannot be used with much benefit to prove Christian doctrine. They may be used, however, to illustrate or confirm doctrines otherwise reached. Certain dull and difficult theological treatises could be greatly lightened and illuminated by illustrations from the parables.

Moreover, the parables may be used to test theology. One of the most searching tests we can apply to any theology is to see whether it can take the parables and, by interpreting them consistently with its main positions, fill their whole content with meaning. No theology that does not find itself at home in the world of the parables is worth much consideration. 'It is good evidence,' wrote Trench, 'that we have discovered the right meaning of a parable, if it leaves none of the main circumstances unexplained. . . . If we have the right key in our hand, not merely some of the words, but all, will have their corresponding parts; the key too will turn without grating or over-

[1] *On Christian Doctrine* II, IX (Marcus Dods' translation). Augustine in the same treatise makes a most illuminating suggestion as to why there are such metaphorical passages in the Scripture. 'It is pleasanter to have knowledge communicated through figures, and what is attended with difficulty in the seeking gives greater pleasure in the finding. For those who seek but do not find suffer hunger. Those, again, who do not seek at all because they have what they require just beside them, grow languid from satiety. . . . Accordingly the Holy Spirit has, with admirable wisdom and care for our welfare, so arranged the Holy Scriptures as by the plainer passages to satisfy our hunger, and by the more obscure to stimulate our appetite. For almost nothing is dug out of those obscure passages which may not be found set forth in the plainest language elsewhere' (II, VI).

much forcing.'[1] It is equally good evidence that we have the right theology if it can give us without such forcing the key that allows us widespread access into the world of the parables.

(3) It must also be kept in mind that each parable, even with its admixture of allegorical material, has a homiletic as well as an artistic unity. This can be of assistance in the interpretation. Jesus was not diffuse when He discoursed, and any interpretation of the parable which results in an exposition where the thought is not orderly and closely connected is probably wrong. The expositor must resist the temptation to give meaning to details that cannot be closely related to the central theme. Chrysostom, in his exposition of the parable of the Tares, points out that Jesus did not in His explanation tell the disciples who the 'servants' were, this being but a detail not to be interpreted since it is 'brought in . . . for the sake of some order and to make up the picture',[2] and he adds the warning, 'the parables must not be explained throughout word for word, since many absurdities will follow'.

Though there is but one closely connected message in each parable, however, this does not mean that there are not many points in this one message. If the expositor, in following out the main drift of the argument, can by the way suggest for various details a meaning that does not side-track the argument or withdraw the hearers' attention from the main lesson to be taught, then he is at liberty to do so. 'It must be allowed,' says Tholuck, 'that a similitude is perfect in proportion as it is on all sides rich in applications; and hence, in treating the parables of Christ, the expositor must proceed on the assumption that there is import in every single point, and only desist from seeking it when either it does not result without forcing, or when we can clearly see that this or that circumstance was merely added for the sake of giving intuitiveness to the narrative. We should not assume anything to be non-essential, except when by holding it fast as essential, the unity of the whole is marred and troubled.'[3]

[1] *Notes on the Parables*, p. 40

[2] *Homilies on St Matthew*, 47. Calvin agrees with this judgment. 'Comparisons must not be too closely or too exactly carried out so as to apply at all points' (Commentary on *Harm. Ev.* on Matt. 18.2). Adam Clarke admits, in his attempt at a Christological interpretation of one of the parables, that 'this parable cannot go on all fours in the Christian cause as anyone may see' (*Comm. on Matt.* 21.33 ff).

[3] Quoted by Trench, loc. cit., p. 37. Chrysostom would not allow quite so much

THE PARABLE AND THE PREACHER 215

It follows from this that we should never attempt to decide the meaning of any allegorical detail in a parable in abstraction from the whole parable. In deciding what any feature might stand for, we must first of all take into account its relation to other details and to the whole parable.[1] Dr W. J. Moulton, in interpreting the parable of the Fig Tree,[2] points out that all the dwellers in Palestine knew that the bursting buds and tender shoots of the fig tree gave unmistakable indication that the summer was at hand. So Jesus teaches in this parable that with equal certainty the nearness of the *Parousia* may be inferred from the signs that precede its coming. Then Dr Moulton adds a sentence that could be applied in many cases as a most helpful principle of interpretation. 'There is here no thought of the resemblance of details, as, for example, between the Summer and the *Parousia*. . . . The likeness is one of relationships and not of details.'[3] The analogies which we are mainly to look for in the parables are dynamic analogies of relationships between features, analogies of movement and action. As one feature of the parable is related to another, so God is related to the sinner or to the saved; or so the Kingdom of God is related to this world. In following out such a rule, the element of allegory, though by no means excluded from the interpretation, will nevertheless be kept in its due place.

(4) It is natural to expect that some of the metaphors used in the parables will be similar to the metaphors used in the Old Testament. Jesus was speaking to an audience who were familiar with the meaning which certain terms such

---

freedom to interpret details. 'Neither is it right to enquire curiously into all things in the parables word by word, but when we have learned the object for which it was composed, to reap this, and not to busy one's self about anything further' (*Homily on St. Matthew*, 64). Since it seems on the surface that by this rule he would be wholeheartedly on the side of Dr C. H. Dodd, it may be pointed out that Chrysostom frequently approves of allegorical interpretations, for example, by the virgins' lamps is signified the purity of holiness, and by the oil, humanity, almsgiving, succour to the needy. Even Calvin, the most restrained of the older commentators where allegory is concerned, though he will not allow any speculation on such minute details as, for example, the oil in the lamps of the virgins, which, he holds, has nothing to do with the design of the parable, nevertheless goes so far as to place an allegorical interpretation on the winepress and the tower in the parable of the Wicked Husbandmen (though it is significant that he refuses to interpret the meaning of the hedge).

[1] For example, to decide what 'leaven' means in the parable by reference to its Old Testament usage, and not to its relations within the parable, is to miss the point.
[2] Mark 13.28
[3] See article in Hasting's *Dictionary of Christ and the Gospels* on 'Parable'

as 'light', 'vineyard', 'harvest', had in the Old Testament Scriptures; and it is likely that Jesus in choosing figures which already had such currency would give the chosen terms similar significance to that which is given to them in the Old Testament.[1]

(5) In interpreting the parables we must recognise that they have an elasticity that enables them to fit the manifold and developing situation of the Church in every generation. It may be quite legitimate, for example, in the same exposition to give to one detail two different interpretations. For instance, in the parable of the Sower it is obvious that the sower stands for Jesus Himself, but it is equally true that the sower stands for the preacher of the Word, and it would be very foolish to say that one interpretation excludes the other. 'What more liberal and more fruitful provision could God have made in regard to the Sacred Scriptures,' asks Augustine, 'than that the same words might be understood in several senses?'; and his further remarks on this subject are again well worth quoting at length: 'If a man searching the Scriptures endeavours to get at the intention of the author through whom the Holy Spirit spake, whether he succeeds in this endeavour or whether he draws a different meaning from the words, but one that is not opposed to sound doctrine, he is free from blame so long as he is supported by the testimony of some other passage of Scripture. For the author perhaps saw that this very meaning lay in the words which we are trying to interpret; and assuredly the Holy Spirit, who through him spake these words, foresaw that this interpretation would occur to the reader, nay made provision that it should occur to him, seeing that it too is founded on truth.'[2]

---

[1] Yet even here we cannot make a rigid rule. Leaven in the Old Testament is used to designate evil, and Jesus uses it in this sense in Luke 13.2. But in the parable it is obviously used with quite another meaning. 'The same word does not always signify the same thing,' says Augustine, pointing out that a lion stands for Christ (Rev. 5.5) and for the Devil (1 Pet. 5.8), that the word 'serpent' can be used in a good sense (Matt. 10.6) and in a bad sense (2 Cor. 11.3), likewise the term 'bread' (cf. John 6.51 and Prov. 9.17) (*On Christian Doctrine*, 3.25).

[2] *On Christian Doctrine*, 2.27. The grave dangers of allowing such wide scope for interpretation will no doubt occur to the reader. 'There is no parable or detail of parable that has not received many and conflicting interpretations. The Judge of Luke 18.2, for example, according to some stands for God, and according to others for the Devil' (Moulton). But that there are so many foolish interpretations is no reason for unduly restricting the wise. This rule must be taken in conjunction with all the other considerations that have already been laid down.

V

It is necessary now to speak about the interpretation of the difficult passage in Mark 4, verses 11 and 12. 'And when he was alone, they that were about him with the twelve asked of him the parable. And he said unto them, Unto you it is given to know the mystery of the kingdom of God: but unto them that are without, all these things are done in parables: that seeing they may see, and not perceive; and hearing they may hear, and not understand; lest at any time they should be converted, and their sins should be forgiven them.'

'Every real parable,' writes Professor T. W. Manson, 'is significant in two ways. It has its own meaning as a story, and a further meaning—and this is the important thing—by application to persons and events or both together. It is possible for a hearer to follow and appreciate the former meaning without having the slightest inkling of the latter.'[1] This is true. Men, hearing the parables, can take from them a great variety of moral lessons (and even at the same time some very 'spiritual' lessons too!), and they may go away satisfied with the lessons learned, but they may at the same time have missed completely all that the parable had to say about the Kingdom of God. The lessons they learned, however spiritual, have not risen above the natural level of man's life. They have 'seen', yet they have not 'perceived'; they have 'heard', yet have not 'understood'.

When we ask why it is so difficult to rise from such a natural level of thought and deduction and perception in the world of the parables to the level of the Mystery of the Kingdom of God, the only reason we can give is that there is no direct relation between the earthly analogy and the thing it is intended to point to, any more than exists between the sign and the thing signified in the Sacrament, or indeed between the two natures in the God-man. If we start first with the human analogy and try on a basis of supposed natural continuity to work upwards to the spiritual counterpart, we are undertaking a labour that is in vain.[2] Unless a man is first inside the Kingdom of God, he

---
[1] *The Teaching of Jesus*, p. 65
[2] Professor C. H. Dodd asserts that there is a natural relation here rather than the sacramental relation. 'There is a reason for this realism in the parables of Jesus,' he writes. 'It arises from the conviction that there is no mere analogy

218   THE PARABLE AND THE PREACHER

cannot see the true relevance of the analogies in the parables. The parables can be understood only from above downwards, not from underneath upwards. 'Except a man be born from above he cannot see the Kingdom of God.' This saying of Jesus applies with much relevance to the problem of the interpretation and understanding of the parables. Just as there can be no true knowledge of God from outside the redeeming life of God, so there can be no understanding of the Kingdom of God from outside that Kingdom, and thus no understanding of the parables to 'those that are without'.[1] This is why, in the words of Matthew Henry, 'a parable like the pillar of cloud and fire, turns a dark side towards Egyptians which confounds them, but a light side towards Israelites which comforts them, and so answers a double intention'.[2] The parables thus test men, and it is the hearer himself who by his attitude to the parable reveals whether he is within or outside the Kingdom of God. It must never be forgotten, however, that the main purpose with which Jesus spoke His parables was that those who are meek and lowly in heart might find rest for their souls, and that if they have the effect of offending men and dividing men, it is, like all the judgments of God, their 'strange work'.

but an inward affinity, between the natural order and the Spiritual order' (*The Parables of the Kingdom*, p. 22). It is not surprising that Dr Dodd, holding such a view, rejects as not genuine the passage under discussion from Mark 4 (though he also gives linguistic reasons for this rejection). If such a natural affinity existed between the two realms, then it would indeed be a very easy matter to get at the heart of the 'Mystery', and fewer books on the parables would be necessary. It is interesting that here Professor Dodd is in wholehearted agreement with Trench, who also speaks of a harmony between the two realms 'unconsciously felt by all men', of the type and the thing typified as 'belonging to one another by an inward necessity', and as 'linked together by the law of a secret affinity' (*Notes on the Parables*, pp. 13-14). But Trench at least qualifies his assertion by the word 'secret', and he goes on to suggest that it is solely because of the redeeming purpose of God that the realm of nature and society has been made to foreshadow the realm of the Kingdom of God. Professor Dodd has no such qualifications to his statement of this doctrine.

[1] 'The hiding of the meaning of the parables is the same as the hiding of divine truth from the wise and prudent and the revealing of it to babes. The parables declare "things hidden from the foundation of the world".... But it is always "he that hath ears to hear, let him hear".' (A. G. Hebert, *The Authority of the Old Testament*, p. 231.)

[2] *Commentary on Matt.* 13.13 f. Trench ascribes this saying to Thomas Fuller but Matthew Henry makes no such acknowledgment.

www.ingramcontent.com/pod-product-compliance
Lightning Source LLC
Chambersburg PA
CBHW070314230426
43663CB00011B/2124